MINNESOTA
1918

MINNESOTA
1918

When FLU, FIRE, *and* WAR
Ravaged the State

CURT BROWN

MINNESOTA
HISTORICAL
SOCIETY PRESS

www.mnhspress.org

The Minnesota Historical Society Press is a member
of the Association of American University Presses.

Manufactured in USA

10 9 8 7 6 5

♾ The paper used in this publication meets the minimum
requirements of the American National Standard for Information
Sciences— Permanence for Printed Library Materials, ANSI Z39.48-
1984.

International Standard Book Number
ISBN: 978-1-68134-147-7 (paper)
ISBN: 978-1-68134-081-4 (ebook)

Library of Congress Cataloging-in-Publication Data
available upon request

This and other Minnesota Historical Society Press books
are available from popular e-book vendors.

The letter said it all, we're shipping out
I know they got it wrong without a doubt
The war ain't over there, it's here with me
The battle of the bloody century
What is going on here? What becomes the lot of us?

Milk Carton Kids, "High Hopes"

*

Oh, passers-by, can ye see and hear
The changes that have been wrought
In the age-long span of a single year
While the mighty fight was fought?

Amy Robbins Ware, Red Cross canteen worker
from Robbinsdale, Minnesota, from her war diary,
Echoes of France, *written in 1918 along the Western Front*

*

The pitiful tragedies and thrilling escapes reported were so numerous
that any attempt of a detailed description of them would fill a volume.

Duluth meteorologist Herbert Richardson, writing in April 1919

*

I had thought that the devastation wrought by the retreating Germans
was of such calibre that I would never see anything to exceed it. This
burnt-over area is so completely extinguished of all semblance of
human occupation that the deliberately destroyed territory deserted
by the Germans was almost a Paradise in comparison.

Unnamed soldier, wounded in World War I, returning home after
forest fires consumed northeastern Minnesota; quoted in the "Report of the
Adjutant General of the State of Minnesota," December 31, 1918

*

The work of rescue . . . was practically completed. Just as orders were
in preparation to withdraw the military, an epidemic of 'Spanish' Influenza
assailed the survivors of the fire horrors. . . . Their physical condition
weakened by exposure and excitement, these survivors of fire horrors were
ready victims for the influenza germ.

Minnesota Adjutant General Walter F. Rhinow's report, December 31, 1918

*

The influenza was raging. . . . The winter was coming on. Our boys were
in the war—500 of them. So this fire struck us at the worst possible time.

Anna Dickie Olesen, testifying to Congress in 1930 for a bill
to reimburse 1918 fire victims

Minnesota, 1918

MINNESOTA
1918

Chuck Eckman in front of the Soderberg family root cellar, eleven miles west of Moose Lake, where sixteen people suffocated to death during the forest fires of October 12, 1918. *Photo by Curt Brown*

Moose Lake; Automba

IT'S JUST BEFORE FALL. Russet and mustard flecks dot the still-green trees. Chuck Eckman, spry at eighty, tromps ahead of me through a farm field between Moose Lake and Kettle River in a swampy, sparsely populated stretch of northeastern Minnesota.

Chuck and his wife, Shirley, live on North Birch Lane, and we've walked about a quarter mile north up the dirt road and across a mowed hayfield, heading toward an overgrown copse of birch trees. That's where we find the hidden root cellar—a six-foot-high igloo of sorts built with mossy stones. It's not the Wizard of Oz–style storm cellar I expected, not a hole dug next to a house. It's a squat rock structure in a clump of trees in a remote farm field.

Wearing sneakers, faded blue jeans, a checkered woolen shirt, camouflage cap, and ash-gray mustache, Chuck leans casually at the cellar's pitch-dark opening. The doorway is about four feet high, reaching his armpit. "You can go on in if you want," he says.

So I punch the flashlight app on my mobile phone, illuminating the inky blackness, and step into the void. In the darkness, two rusted hooks hang from the cellar's ceiling. That's where the Soderbergs hung their smoked meat a century ago. Their sacks of potatoes are long gone from the dirt floor now scattered with stones. It's damp, chilly, and clammy.

"They thought the fire would blow over the top of them, see," Chuck says. "But it sucked right in."

On October 12, 1918, this root cellar morphed into a death chamber. Sons of Swedish immigrants, Charley and Axel Soderberg had spent that summer worrying and fretting about their brother, David, who was fighting in the Great War trenches and forests of France.

But the horrors over here proved deadlier than the trench warfare over there. By the time David came home, nearly all his family members were dead—including a dozen nieces and nephews, ranging from a newborn to sixteen-year-old Hilma Soderberg. They'd fled to this cellar to escape the heat and flames of a massive forest fire swallowing up the surrounding countryside. They were discovered the next morning in this tomb of stone. Potato sacks had been strung up in the cellar's doorway—a final, failed attempt to save themselves.

As I deactivate the flashlight on my phone, the darkness of the cellar brings me back to perhaps the darkest days in Minnesota history.

The First World War, with its mustard gas and muddy trenches, entered its final month in Europe. More than 118,000 Minnesotans served in the war; 1,432 were killed in action. Another 2,326 soldiers from the state died from disease, as troop deployments spread more than military personnel from hometowns and family farms to military bases and, ultimately, the battlefields in Europe.

A lethal strain of influenza flooded the globe in repeated waves—a pandemic killing 50 million people worldwide and roughly 12,000 in Minnesota. The flu's virulence was especially wrenching in Minnesota that October in 1918.

After the driest summer in forty-eight years, conditions were bone dry up north, where the great white pine, tamarack, and yellow birch forests were already reeling after decades of having their timber sawed, axed, and processed at countless sawmills punctuating the region. Add to that gusty winds, train sparks, and lumber piles, and you have the recipe for a wicked inferno. Dozens of small brush fires swirled together on October 12, 1918, growing into the state's deadliest fire ever.

More than 450 people were killed in a sprawling burn zone that spanned 1,500 square miles in seven northeastern Minnesota counties. Three dozen communities were torched—several burned to the ground, including the lumber towns of Cloquet and Moose Lake.

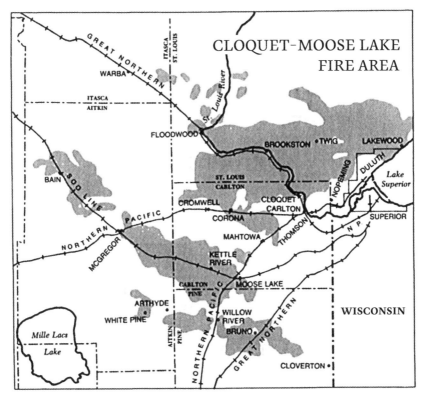

A map showing the area of northwestern Minnesota ravaged by the 1918 fires. *From Francis Carroll and Franklin Raiter's* The Fires of Autumn: The Cloquet– Moose Lake Disaster of 1918, *courtesy of the Minnesota Historical Society Press*

While entire families were found burned in wells and cellars and along charred roadways, another 2,100 were injured among 52,000 people affected. These were mostly immigrant families from Finland, Poland, and Sweden, eking out livelihoods cutting timber and farming the hardscrabble terrain.

Four thousand homes were destroyed, rendering thousands of people homeless and crammed into refugee housing—where the flu easily pounced to jack up the death toll. The final cost of property damage from the fires reached $25 million, roughly equivalent to $400 million in 2018 dollars.

As we walk back to his home, Chuck mentions his aunt, Agnes Eckman Peterson. His wife, Shirley, digs out a book detailing what happened to Peterson on October 12, 1918.

While her husband, Albin Peterson, was off helping to fight the blaze, Agnes, thirty-three and pregnant, dashed over to the home of her neighbor, Knute Gaustad, when the fire approached. Her body was found a couple days later in a well, covered with charred wood debris, along with the bodies of five members of the Gaustad family. They'd climbed in the well in an attempt to save themselves. "Just the skull was recognizable," the *Superior (Wisconsin) Telegram* reported. "The buckle of her dress she was wearing at the time was identified as hers."

The rest of Chuck's family fared better—showing how happenstance, luck, and fate combined to write the stories of survival in 1918 Minnesota.

Chuck's grandparents, Charles and Ida, piled into a Model T automobile with his uncles, Fred and Godfrey, after a straw stack caught fire and ignited their barn. As they drove through dark smoke, the car ended up in a ditch. Ida was thrown from the vehicle, bruising her right side. Her husband climbed from the car and stepped on the road, only to get smashed by another fleeing car, his right leg busted below the knee. A neighbor named Ole Swanson picked them up in his car, but he veered into the ditch a quarter mile down the road east toward Moose Lake. The car was soon engulfed in flames.

The family all survived the night in a nearby oat field. They made it the three miles to Moose Lake the next day, rode a train to Superior, Wisconsin, for medical treatment, and eventually returned to find, much to their surprise, their home one of the few still standing between Moose Lake and Kettle River.

Chuck's father, Harry, had been sucked into the war effort. But when a tent spike pierced his hand at a training base in El Paso, Texas, it proved a lucky break. He wouldn't be shipped to France. And he wasn't back home when the fire exploded.

Without those twists of fate, Chuck might never have enjoyed his eighty years. He might not be living on his grandparents' old farmstead, next to his twin brother, Jim, on this warm mid-September afternoon, nearly a century after that devastating year in Minnesota.

*

Fifteen miles northwest of that dark, rectangular entrance into the Soderbergs' stone root cellar, on a remote parcel of land near the tiny town of Automba, I find Dan Reed. He's sixty-eight, dressed in sweatpants and a T-shirt, sitting at his computer at a bedroom desk covered with old photographs, plat maps, books, and letters. "Automba really started howling along as a lumber town around 1914 or 1915, and everything was wide open at the time of the fire, with sixty train cars a day rolling out of the railroad siding," he says.

Right around the start of April every spring, beginning in the last few years of the nineteenth century, the annual log drive was the social highlight for the settlers and loggers camped along the Dead Moose River and other streams slicing through the region. Families would bring picnic baskets to designated curves of the river and listen for the sound of dynamite to the west—signaling the log drive was under way. Sixteen-foot cuts of white pine, yellow birch, and hard maple—chopped through the frigid winter and skidded over ice to the rivers—would come careening down the twisting tributaries along with splintering ice chunks in a chaotic surge.

"You kept hearing it coming closer and closer," Reed says, retelling the memories an old woman shared with him years ago. "I asked what it was like when the logs came and she said the whole ground shook, that the air vibrated and you couldn't talk to anyone around you because of the BOOM BOOM of logs and ice pounding. She said it was kind of like standing next to a freight train on the railroad track, the same kind of feeling that you're totally consumed by that mass of steel going by. Well, this was the log drive."

Back then, Automba boasted a thousand people—lumberjacks, timber cruisers, Finnish farmers. "Today? We have maybe eight or nine people," Reed says with a shrug.

One of Dan's grandfathers was an Apostolic Lutheran minister in 1918. "Very strict and conservative," he says. His other grandfather, a Finnish immigrant named Nick Koivisto, "was a Bolshevik socialist supporter of farming co-ops and labor unions to the end of his days.

"They were very good friends, but there were some subjects they never went to," Dan says, unleashing a high-pitched laugh that starts in his ample belly.

Dan leans back in his chair and explains that "Finns are storytellers." Finland's national epic poem of heroes and creation, he says, is called the *Kalevala*. It's also the name of the township of three hundred people near his home on Reed Lane, a dirt road he built himself to access his land.

"*Kalevala* means 'land of the heroes,'" Reed says, explaining that the Finnish language wasn't written down until the 1800s. It didn't need to be. Every community had *kalle*, Reed says. The word translates to "call," but Reed explains that *kalle* were the storytellers who would pass down the ancient oral traditions and tales such as the *Kalevala*. "Often there would be two *kalle*, sitting across from each other, sometimes holding hands," he says. "And they would alternate in telling poems in iambic pentameter, repeating the image from the last line."

He offers up an example from the *Kalevala*: "As a lark I strayed afar, as a wayward bird I wandered." After another warm chuckle, Reed talks of his own wanderings. As a youth, he spent time as a church relief worker, building schools and hospitals in southern Sudan. Sickened from the heat, he returned home and, in 1968, began recording interviews with 1918 fire survivors on the fiftieth anniversary of the disaster. He joined forces with a banker and auctioneer thirty years his senior, Edwin Manni, the son of a Finnish immigrant farmer who came to Minnesota in 1889.

In the late 1960s, Reed would tag along with Manni, visiting neighbors and recording their stories. Everyone knew Edwin and would seek his advice on financial matters. They trusted him with their money—and their memories. As Edwin's younger sidekick, Dan Reed earned their trust as well.

Some of the stories appeared in a special edition of the *Moose Lake Star Gazette* on the fire's fiftieth anniversary. Others were typed up and published, single spaced, in now hard-to-find booklets filled with first-person accounts of where people were when the fires started and how they survived.

"These are the stories I heard from the old-timers in the saunas," Reed says, with another laugh. He is a modern-day *kalle*, just like Edwin Manni from the generation before him. "Now, it's time for me to pass these stories down to you," he tells me as we drive around the area in his mint-green Chevrolet Blazer, once a government forestry truck in Michigan. He stops the car but keeps the engine running as he points to a slight depression in a remote farmyard where a dried-out well has been pretty much filled in. "This is Jokimaki country," Dan says, pronouncing the Finnish name YOKE-ee-mah-key.

Census records show that Erik Jokimaki, or Erkki in the old country, emigrated from Finland to Kalevala Township near Automba in the 1880s. He died at seventy-six and was buried at Kettle River's West Branch Cemetery around the first of December 1917—spared from the heartbreak that would sweep across his farm less than a year later.

By 1918, seventeen-year-old Aina Jokimaki, Erik's granddaughter, was one of many grandchildren of the original immigrant settlers in the area. More than fifty years later, Aina was a grandmother herself in her seventies. And like many of the region's Finns, she and her husband were close friends with Ida and Edwin Manni. "On many a pleasant Saturday evening," Manni wrote, he and his wife and Aina and her husband "enjoyed their hospitality, Sauna, coffee, goodies, and 'just visiting.'" Over the hot coffee and hotter steam in the sauna, Aina shared her 1918 memories, which Edwin and his younger story-telling partner, Dan Reed, typed up in their 1978 collection of local history.

October 12, 1918, Aina recalled decades later, "was a nice warm sunny day with a brisk southerly wind." William Jokimaki, Aina's dad and Erik's son, was hustling to hammer up an addition on their two-room house before winter set in. His crew of neighbors put down their tools that afternoon to go fight the fires near the Automba railroad tracks. Aina, the oldest of seven siblings, helped her mother milk the cows and put them out to pasture. "But very soon, they were back at the barn bellowing," Aina told Manni, "almost as if they sensed an approaching disaster." About 4:00 PM, the wind suddenly shifted to the northwest and the men returned and announced that the flames were out of control and heading their way.

Just west of the Jokimaki farmstead, where the Jankala brothers had opened a sawmill, "about a million feet of lumber," Aina said, lined both sides of the road as the fire approached. "One board took off in the air like a flaming arrow and landed on a haystack about a half-mile away and the hay exploded into flames." The fire was spreading so fast, she said, "no human could possibly run and hope to escape." Not that they didn't try. They all headed southeast down an old logging road toward a low, swampy area. The cows and horses followed them. Her father removed the animals' harnesses to help them flee. In the end, only one would survive.

Everyone carried something, "hoping to salvage anything of some value," Aina said. She was given a drawer full of important papers. They found the drawer later. All the papers had been "blown away

Aina Jokimaki, hands bandaged from burns. *Courtesy of the Carlton County Historical Society*

by the fierce winds," Aina recalled. Only her uncle's leather pouch remained in the drawer.

She told Manni in 1975, fifty-seven years later, "it seems to me now, after all these years, like a horrible nightmare." Except she was remembering, not dreaming. "It just seemed like in a few minutes, the terrifying inferno was over and above and all around us."

Separated from the others in the smoky darkness, Aina found herself alone and lost. The ground was covered with burning logs and hot coals. The air was stifling. "Running and jumping over these burning logs, I was desperately seeking my way home," Aina said. "Imagine yourself, a terrified young girl in shock. . . ." She was wearing stockings and high-top boots. Her clothes, somehow, didn't catch fire, but "my feet actually baked inside my shoes and stockings." She was too shocked to feel pain, but her feet would be forever scarred "to my dying day."

As she ran for home, trying to avoid the heat from the flaming sawmill, she noticed Solomon Jackson, one of the men who had been helping her father build the addition. He was sprawled on the roadside, "suffering excruciating pain from the burns"; he would die a few days later.

Dehydrated and parched with thirst, Aina stumbled upon her father, with burns on his hands, hip, and face—but alive. They sought safety by the west branch of the Kettle River. As temperatures plummeted, Aina and her father left the river "to see if we were the only people left on the face of the earth."

They found her uncle, Arthur Jokimaki, who had moved into her grandfather's house. Somehow, the house was still standing. She followed the glow of lanterns held by the men gathering out front.

That's where Edna Reed, Dan's grandmother and Aina's cousin, helped remove her burnt boot. She had taken off the other one by the river. Removing the second one, she quickly realized, "was a terrible mistake, since it exposed the burned flesh." She was in "terrible pain and suffered fiercely." Near what would become State Highway 73, someone with a car drove them to Moose Lake. From there, a train took them to St. Mary's Hospital in Duluth. Aina would stay there for ten weeks, recovering from her burns.

Aina's thirty-nine-year-old mother, Suoma, and her six siblings, all younger than sixteen—Fred, George, Ida, Annie, Edward, and Elma—

had all perished in the fire, along with six-year-old cousin Walfred Jokimaki. Her uncle Waino Himango, whose leather pouch survived, would join those who died in coming days from smoke inhalation and the deadly flu virus. Of all the people fleeing the Jokimaki farm on October 12, 1918, only Aina, her father, and a badly burned man named Oscar Salmi survived. Aina said Salmi "was a cripple for the rest of his lifetime," which would span until 1962.

Dan Reed, behind the steering wheel of his idling green Blazer, points out where the Jankala brothers' sawmill once stood on the forty-acre parcel west of the Jokimaki land. "They had spent a couple days looking for the Jankala brothers, two of their helpers from the sawmill, and their cook," Reed says. "They didn't know if they'd turned to ashes and blown away." That's when the Jankalas' white horse appeared by the old well. A guy named John Peura, who like Aina was seventeen when the fires erupted, once told Dan Reed how the Jankalas' horse "came up just like it knew something and stood right by the well."

They'd already checked that well, which was covered with charred fence boards wrapped in wires. Now they used a stick to clear the boards and stir the water. "And a head popped up," Dan says, re-creating what happened nearly a century earlier. "The bottom guy had put his foot in the well bucket and the rest followed," he says. When the rope burned, they all drowned.

Dan's grandfather, Matt Reed, volunteered to be lowered down, and they used ropes to retrieve the bodies of Hjalmer and William Jankala; their cook, Aina Rajala; and two sawmill workers, Emil Korpi and Hugo Luusua, who was only fifteen.

"That terrible holocaust and horrendous night is rapidly becoming history, because with the passage of time, survivors are rapidly disappearing," Aina Jokimaki told Edwin Manni in 1975. "But for those of us still remaining, time cannot erase the trials and tribulations we suffered, yet somehow survived."

Her feet still scared with burns, Aina died fewer than four years after she lamented the "rapidly disappearing" number of her fellow survivors. She was seventy-seven and was buried in the Eagle Lake Cemetery in Carlton County in 1979. But not before she shared her story of October 12, 1918, with Edwin Manni and Dan Reed—the modern-day Finnish storytellers near Jokimaki country in Kalevala Township.

*

This book's goal is to illuminate those human stories, like Aina's, behind the grim numbers. I want to honor those who died in Minnesota in 1918 and share the tales of those who survived and upon whose resilient shoulders a sixty-year-old state was carried from its brink of despair.

Diaries, letters, and newspaper clippings from the time, along with essays, interviews, and memoirs written in ensuing decades, form a mosaic of both tragic grief and unflagging human spirit. I've stitched together these snippets to give readers a sense of both the horror and the hope that sprang from Minnesota in 1918.

In October 1918, Iris Canfield Betz returned with the remains of her husband, Albert Betz, to the Sauk Centre railroad depot (shown here circa 1900). Betz was a victim of the devastating flu epidemic. *Courtesy of Minnesota Historical Society Collections*

CHAPTER 1

Sauk Centre

SPEWING BLACK SMOKE and screeching to a stop, a train pulled into Sauk Centre's blond stone Great Northern Railway depot. It was the last Friday evening of October 1918, in the middle of Minnesota.

Among those stepping off the train were a just-widowed music teacher named Iris Betz and her in-laws from St. Paul. Herman and Lena Betz had emigrated three decades earlier from Westphalia, a northwestern German region on what had become the war-torn Belgian border. They were accompanying the casket carrying the remains of Albert E. Betz, a thirty-year-old soldier wannabe who had entered the military earlier that month—training to fight amid the trenches and mustard gas of the first world war. His enemies? The children of his parents' onetime neighbors.

Tall with blue eyes and black hair, Albert had been working as a St. Paul carpenter when he registered to join the military on June 5, 1917. Still single, he would marry the Sauk Centre teacher a week later. He told military authorities about some blurred vision in his left eye, but that wouldn't be enough to keep him out of the Great War. Despite his German heritage, he was ready to display his patriotism. But Albert Betz made it only as far as Jefferson Barracks, an army base south of St. Louis, Missouri.

His killer: a virulent strain of influenza that was gobbling up the lives of a startling chunk of the globe's healthy young people, spreading through troop transports from a US military base in Kansas to dozens of army camps across the nation. The deadly virus came in three waves. By the autumn of 1918, it simultaneously crossed into the civilian population and fanned out to the battlefields of Europe and beyond. By the time it was done, the pandemic had claimed an estimated fifty million lives worldwide, from Eskimos in Alaska to rural villagers in India.

The outbreak was popularly known as the Spanish influenza, but that was a misnomer. Although myriad theories of the strain's origins exist, most experts pinpoint its start to a Kansas farmer who contracted the virus from a pig before infecting other soldiers upon arriving at the nearby Fort Riley military base. From there, it moved with soldiers being transported across the country and the world. But British and US media were under tight control to limit morale-damaging news that might hurt the war effort. So when the disease starting killing thousands of people in Spain, which wasn't at war and had no such censuring in place, the headlines reverberated and the lethal strain became widely known as the Spanish influenza.

Considered the deadliest epidemic in world history, the 1918 flu would kill four times as many people in one year as died in four years of the Black Death bubonic plague in 1347-51. The 1918 flu would claim more US lives in the twentieth century than combat deaths in both world wars and the conflicts in Korea, Vietnam, and Iraq's Desert Storm—combined.

In the United States alone, then a nation of 103 million, 28 percent of all Americans were infected, and 675,000 deaths were attributed to the 1918 influenza. That's ten times the US combat death toll from World War I battlefields. The death rate of 2.5 percent compared to rates of 0.1 percent in previous epidemics. And people between ages fifteen and thirty-four were twenty times more likely to die from the 1918 flu than earlier strains. With today's US population of roughly 320 million being three times that of 1918 numbers, it would be like two million Americans wiped out in a matter of months.

Albert Betz was just one of them.

"He was inducted into military service about two weeks before his death," the Sauk Centre *Herald* reported, "and he had not been assigned to any particular branch of the service." The newspaper's four-paragraph story on October 17, 1918, detailed how Iris, his wife of only sixteen months, upon receiving word of his illness jumped on a train bound for St. Louis to be by his side. By the time she switched train cars in the Twin Cities, another wire arrived in Sauk Centre. Albert was dead.

Despite his short stint, the newspaper predicted his burial at Sauk Centre's Odd Fellows Cemetery would "no doubt be under military auspices." The newspaper concluded its story about Betz's death and upcoming military funeral with one caveat: "If the Home Guards are released from their fire fighting duties in the northern part of the state. . . ."

The same Tuesday the flu killed Albert Betz—October 15—crews tirelessly shoveled a massive pit 150 miles northeast of Sauk Centre in the smoldering town of Moose Lake. A series of massive forest fires, kindled by train sparks and licked by seventy-mile-per-hour winds, engulfed northeastern Minnesota's timber country the previous Saturday.

In what still ranks as the state's deadliest natural disaster ever, 453 people died from the fires of October 12, 1918. Charred bodies were discovered in root cellars and wells and along dirt roads crisscrossing seven counties. Dozens of towns caught fire—along with 4,089 houses, 6,366 barns, 41 schools, and 4,295 farm animals. The towns of Cloquet, Moose Lake, Kettle River, Automba, and Lawler all burned to the ground. Roughly 13,000 families were left homeless as fierce winds fanned more than fifty small fires into a massive blaze that burned 1,500 square miles over a total expanse of 8,400 square miles.

It could have been worse. Only a handful of deaths accompanied the fire's ravaging of Cloquet. Twenty miles east, the burgeoning port city of Duluth, home to nearly 100,000 inhabitants in 1918, watched the fire surround it. Townships to the north burned, including the Woodland neighborhood and the Lakeside area down to the Lester River. But Duluth itself was largely spared. "Red, flaming annihilation threatened Duluth last night and this morning," the *Duluth News Tribune* reported on October 13. "Appalling in loss of human life, it is believed that the dead when the final figures are known will be in the hundreds."

Within days, it was time to bury those dead in places such as Moose Lake. "Nearly 100 people worked all yesterday afternoon in the dig-

GERMANY BOWS TO WILSON'S MANDATE

SECTION ONE

The Duluth Sunday News Tribune.

VOLUME 50, NO. 155.　　　　DULUTH, MINN., SUNDAY MORNING, OCTOBER 13, 1918.　　　　42 PAGES　　　FIVE CENTS.

HUNDREDS PERISH IN FLAMES

NAUEN WIRELESS PURPORTS TO GIVE ANSWER TO NOTE

Evacuation of Invaded Territory Accepted As Necessary to an Armistice; Mixed Commission to Make Arrangements; Chancellor Speaks for Government, People.

WASHINGTON, Oct. 12—A wireless dispatch sent out from Nauen, the German wireless station, picked up and forwarded to official diplomatic sources here to-night, purports to give the text of Germany's answer to President Wilson's inquiry to Chancellor Maximilian on Germany's peace proposal. On its face it seem a complete acceptance of President Wilson's terms.

The text of the note as received here says Germany accepts President Wilson's terms as laid down; accepts evacuation of invaded-territory as a necessary preliminary to an armistice and asks for a mixed commission to make the arrangements; declares that the chancellor speaks "in the name of the German government and of the German people," and that its only object in entering into discussions is to agree on the practical details for carrying out the terms President Wilson has laid down.

GERMANY'S REPLY

"In replying to the questions of the President of the United States of America the German government hereby declares:

"The German government has accepted the terms laid down by President Wilson in his address of January the eighth; and in his subsequent addresses on the foundation of a permanent peace of justice. Consequently, its object in entering into discussions would be only to agree upon practical details of the application of these terms.

"The German government believes that the governments of the powers associated with the government of the United States also take the position taken by President Wilson in his address. The German government in accordance with the Austro-Hungarian government, for the purpose of bringing about an armistice, declares itself ready to comply with the proposition of the President in regard to evacuation.

"The German government suggests that the President many occasion the meeting of a mixed commission for making the necessary arrangements concerning the evacuation. The present German government, which has undertaken the responsibility for this step expresses conviction that it is borne by the will of the great majority of the reichstag. The chancellor, supported in all of his actions by the will of this majority, speaks in the name of the German government and the German people.
"SOLF,
"State Secretary of the Foreign Office."
"Berlin, Oct. 12, 1918."

FIRE TAKES HORRIBLE TOLL IN DULUTH AND MINNESOTA TOWNS; ENTIRE FAMILIES ARE DESTROYED

HUNDREDS MISSING; CITIES AND TOWNS DESTROYED BY BLAZE

Scores Believed to Be Dead, Millions of Dollars Loss in Property as Gale-Fanned Forest Fires Continue to Sweep Over Northern Minnesota—Duluth Is Damaged.

HUNDREDS of people are missing, cities and towns have been burned and the fate of people in a large area of northeastern Minnesota is unknown as the result of raging, gale-fanned forest fires which covered everything before them last night.

The loss of life cannot be computed until reports begin to trickle in from towns where communications were cut by the fires last night. The property loss outside of Duluth will run into the millions.

22 Children Believed Dead At Rice Lake

TWENTY-TWO children lying on the Rice Lake road may be dead as a result of last night's fire. Their parents came to the Rice Lake road, six miles from Duluth.

Tornado of Flame Sweeps Across Northeastern Corner of State, Laying Farms, Cities Waste; Hundred Settlers Reported Dead; Urban Dwellers Burned; Duluth Cares for Injured

RED, flaming annihilation threatened Duluth last night and this morning. Appalling in loss of human life, it is believed that the dead when the final figures are known will be in the hundreds.

The missing from outlying farms and hamlets are reported by the score.

Hundreds of the burned and injured are being cared for at the Armory, and hospitals are filled to overflowing.

Cloquet, Munger, Brookston and a dozen villages are in ashes.

In Duluth the property loss is tremendous. The loss of life in the suburbs is believed to be great.

A large part of Woodland is destroyed. Lester Park flamed all night long and this morning was still endangered. An estimate at this time of the homes destroyed is impossible. Northland Country club is a charred heap of ruins. St. James orphanage was in flames. Scores of homes were burned. Farm buildings for miles have been wiped out and the families either reported missing or injured.

ARMS OF DULUTH OPEN TO VICTIMS; FIRST AID GIVEN

Armory Thronged With Patients Cared For by Red Cross Women—Heroic Rescues.

REFUGEE COACHES TO DIRECT WORK

The front page of the *Duluth Sunday News Tribune* following the great fires of October 1918. *Courtesy of the Duluth News Tribune*

Home Guard troops and volunteers used teams of horses and scooping

ging of one huge grave," the Duluth *Herald* reported on October 15, "which will be the resting place for a large number of victims. The grave is 300 feet long by six feet wide." It was a trench not unlike those dotted with soldiers on the Western Front in France. Minnesota Home Guard troops and volunteers used teams of horses and scooping equipment from nearby mines to dig the massive grave. With a somber Governor Joseph A. A. Burnquist looking on, dozens of unidentified blackened bodies were lowered into Moose Lake's mass grave in mid-October 1918.

Reflecting on the devastation that had been wrought on the region during this trying time for thousands of Minnesota families, the *Duluth News Tribune* wrote a few days after the fire: "Suppose a battle-scarred veteran were to come to Duluth today and take a trip into the country. At Moose Lake, Cloquet and north of Lester Park he would be reminded of Belgium. He would see large trench graves filled with 50 to 100 bodies laid to rest in them just as his comrades who were buried in the same way. . . . Farm after farm, village after

Minnesota home guardsmen and other volunteers helped dig a mass grave at Moose Lake to accommodate the unidentifiable burned bodies from the October 12 fire. *Courtesy of Minnesota Historical Society Collections*

village and city after city is wiped out. For miles around he sees nothing but ruins."

Some newspaper stories that month counted ninety-nine bodies going in the Moose Lake grave. One witness told his daughter there were 121 bodies buried there. Duluth meteorologist Herbert Richardson said "87 charred bodies (many unidentified) were interred there in one large trench grave." Other estimates put the number closer to 200. Separate private burials punctuated the burnt countryside—with flu-wary officials ordering victims to be laid to rest immediately. The makeshift morgues needed the room.

"The road to the cemetery was crowded with Guardsmen, soldiers and families, each waiting for their turn," Tillie Odberg would recall fifty years later. Her mother, Augusta, died a day after the fire from injuries suffered at a place that became known as Dead Man's Curve. Drivers in fleeing Model Ts and other first-generation automobiles misgauged their speed at the curve, resulting in a massive pileup of flipped cars that was then overcome with flames.

Augusta Odberg was among the dozens of refugees walking down the road toward Moose Lake through the smoky darkness after the car she hoped would be her getaway crashed. She jumped into a roadside ditch with her husband, Albin, to evade oncoming headlights. But another car ran into the ditch and crushed both of Augusta's legs. "By superhuman effort," Tillie said, "Dad finally managed to get the car off mother's broken legs."

Her clothes igniting as they scurried to find shelter, Augusta pleaded with her husband to leave her and save himself for the sake of their two daughters. She died on the kitchen floor of a farmhouse crowded with burn victims the next day, Sunday, at one o'clock in the afternoon. "Death mercifully ended her suffering," said Tillie, who would attend nine graveside services in the following few days, including her mother's and that of a twelve-year-old classmate named Dora May Ikens, who also died at Dead Man's Curve.

Tillie, only fourteen at the time, was just one member of more than ten thousand surviving families who registered for help. Among them were Ojibwe from the nearby Fond du Lac Indian Reservation and the Finns, Poles, and Swedes who had been harvesting the farm fields and stripping the forests of timber in this corner of northeastern Minnesota.

Those refugees were crammed into tight quarters in the few farm-steads, schools, and churches that remained standing, as well as emergency housing in Duluth and its twin port city of Superior, Wisconsin. Those crowded conditions and the survivors' weakened state combined to intensify the influenza's rapid spread. Hundreds of new cases sprang up, and more than one hundred deaths from flu and pneumonia were reported "immediately after the fire," according to the 1921 report of the Minnesota Forest Fires Relief Commission.

*

Paint with numbers and the canvas turns unimaginably dark: nearly 1,500 Minnesota soldiers dying in combat in the World War I trenches of France; 453 fire victims; more than 10,000 deaths in the state linked to the 1918 influenza scourge. And to make matters worse, 1918 was the peak year in Minnesota for deaths from all forms of tuberculosis, with consumption piling on another 2,543 deaths. All told, that's nearly 15,000 Minnesota deaths in a year when the state population was roughly 2.39 million.

Albert Betz was just one of them.

In the October 24, 1918, edition of the Sauk Centre *Herald*, the Betzes—widow Iris and Albert's parents, Herman and Lena—penned a joint letter of thanks to all the friends, neighbors, and home guardsmen who had greeted their train and helped the family "bear the burden of death of our beloved Albert." A uniformed contingent of the Sauk Centre Home Guard had made it back home from the fires or had somehow eluded that ghastly duty. They took Albert Betz's remains to the Odd Fellows graveyard, along with family and friends. "Mr. Betz had only lived in Sauk Centre a short time," his adopted hometown newspaper said. "He was an industrious young man of good habits."

Born December 29, 1887, amid the rolling farms of southern Minnesota near Waseca, Betz was laboring in the farm fields around White Oak, Iowa, as a twenty-two-year-old, according to 1910 census rolls. He drifted up to St. Paul and called himself a self-employed carpenter when he signed up for the military on June 5, 1917. A week later, he married Iris Canfield in a home in St. Paul. Photographs show Iris in her wire-rim glasses, her long brown hair woven into buns below a large, wide-brimmed hat. After their wedding, the couple traveled from St. Paul to Sauk Centre—likely aboard the same train that would return his remains a year later. "During his short residence here he made many friends who extend sincere sympathy to his heart-broken wife," the *Herald* said.

Betz was one of 118,506 Minnesotans who signed up to fight the Germans in the Great War. His parents were among the nearly one-in-four Minnesotans in 1918 who were born in Europe—roughly 20 percent of those were natives of Germany, then the enemy. Germans were the single largest ethnic group in Minnesota at the time.

In all, 3,758 Minnesotans died during the fight against the kaiser in World War I. But most of them didn't fall on the trench-carved battlefields of France. Some 62 percent of those deaths, including Betz's, were the result of not combat but disease: 2,326 Minnesota soldiers wracked with fever, blood dripping from their noses, skin turning purple from lack of oxygen, violently coughing from influenza and the pneumonia hanging to its coattails before finally succumbing.

A century later, Betz is just another forgotten victim of that awful month for Minnesotans—October 1918. A memorial near the state capitol is dedicated to 57,413 who served overseas in World War I. Betz is not among them. He's one of more than 61,000 who never made it to Europe with the American Expeditionary Forces.

David Thompson, a modern-day military chaplain from Rosemount, Minnesota, argues that a death like the one Betz suffered on his way to war is no different than a soldier sacrificing his life on the front. Indeed, more US soldiers died from the flu during World War I than in combat—most of these deaths occurring in a ten-week span starting in mid-September 1918. But a discrepancy lurks in the way we remember those who left worrying families behind to answer the call of war, whether they fell on battlefields or coughing in military hospital beds at home. "The only difference between the death of a soldier to combat, rather than disease, was honor and respect," Thompson says. "Dead was dead . . . and the pain and grief was excruciating for these families."

Thompson insists Betz's death "was not socially honored, supported, nor publicly mourned by our culture." He points out that many of the veterans killed by the influenza epidemic were buried without military honors. "This story was never included on our memorials or rarely in our mainline history books for close to one hundred years in America," Thompson said. "And it surfaces only now, at the World War I centennial."

At least the Sauk Centre Home Guard accompanied Betz's body

from the depot to the grave. Now a hundred years later, we remember Albert E. Betz and the roughly fifteen thousand Minnesotans who died in 1918 when the Great War, the influenza pandemic, and the forest fires tore a gash in the fabric of Minnesota.

While it's worthwhile to honor individuals otherwise swallowed up in the numbness of the massive death toll, the history of 1918 Minnesota is more than a lengthy series of obituaries. It's a tale of resilience, a story populated with bighearted Minnesotans who stepped up to the three-pronged swirl of calamity—war, disease, and fire—to stitch the tear back together and help a state rebound from the dark month of October 1918.

Two such stories of the quick and heroic response appeared on the front page of the Sauk Centre *Herald* on October 17, 1918, in the same edition that reported Betz's death on page eight. Zipping immediately to fire-scorched Aitkin County were forty members of the Sauk Centre Home Guard, part of the state-run militia that filled the void left when the National Guard fell under federal wartime control. They arrived in the 4:00 AM darkness on Tuesday the fifteenth and began recovering bodies, digging graves, and dousing any remaining hot spots. "It is uncertain, of course, when the boys will be back home," the newspaper said. "This is the first time when the people of the city have had an opportunity to discover that an organization like the Guard is a real benefit to the community."

At the Sauk Centre Commercial Club, meanwhile, the city's branch of the Red Cross met that Wednesday and voted unanimously to "take immediate steps for contributing relief to the needy ones" up north. Treasurer L. L. Kells reported the group had $2,500 in its war-fund kitty, so the committee voted to take $500 of that money and put it in a civilian relief fund "for the fire sufferers in northern part of the state."

The Young Ladies' Society at the Congregational church spearheaded a clothing drive, asking people to donate what they could to the Red Cross sewing room at the junior high school. They assured everyone the clothing drive for the fire victims would not "retard or hinder" the sewing projects already under way for the army. "Sauk Centre folks have been mighty fortunate through a period of years," the newspaper reminded its readers. "Other sections have been devastated by fire, pestilence or cyclones, while we have escaped."

New recruits from Windom, Minnesota, 1917. *Courtesy of Minnesota Historical Society Collections*

In a prelude to the historic carnage that would befall Minnesota in the autumn of 1918, a tornado tore through the town of Tyler on the Minnesota–South Dakota border, killing three dozen people and injuring 225, on August 21, 1918. Fewer than two months later, the Sauk Centre *Herald* injected a dose of Minnesota guilt from its perch smack-dab between the destruction of Tyler's tornado 150 miles to its southwest and Moose Lake's fires 150 miles to its northeast: "The least the people of this community can do to show their appreciation is to come to the immediate and substantial relief of her neighbors, and no doubt they will."

Back on page eight of that newspaper, next to the four paragraphs about Albert Betz's death, editors ran a story of the massive military sign-up under way. Citing official figures from Washington, as of mid-September 1918, 553,717 Minnesota men had registered for military service, including 286,243 men aged eighteen to twenty-one and thirty-one to forty-six who signed up on September 12 when registration was widened to include more age groups. Nearly 13 million men signed up nationally.

There was also a story assuring everyone that it was "quite apparent that the Spanish Influenza has reached its peak and the War Department is getting the disease under control with stringent regulations in force to prevent the spread." Morale-lifting propaganda? Likely. A few paragraphs down, the story reported that seventy inmates had contracted the flu at the state-run women's jail known as the Home School for Girls in Sauk Centre. The newspaper attributed two girls' deaths there to "other causes."

Iris Betz, the thirty-six-year-old widow with the big hat and small glasses, lived right around the corner from the Sauk Centre home for troubled girls.

Sisters Dora and Florence Thortvedt both kept diaries that reveal the many worries of Minnesotans during the turbulent year of 1918. *Photos courtesy of the Historical and Cultural Society of Clay County*

CHAPTER 2

Buffalo River Near Moorhead

THE INK FROM DORA THORTVEDT'S PEN showed the worry she felt about the Great War raging in France. Her diary, written in flowing cursive penmanship in 1918 when she was twenty-seven, resonated with the double-barreled fretting playing out in homes across Minnesota as the war wound down. "Most of the young boys are in France," she wrote. "How many of them will come back is hard to tell. Even if we have peace now, this terrible flu epidemic is awful." On one page, there's a big blotch of ink—a sign that she was paralyzed for a second, letting the ink stain grow. It came as she described how gnawing fear turned into palpable grief.

The fourth of ten Thortvedt children, Dora grew up on a farm along the Buffalo River in northwestern Minnesota, just ten miles east of where the Red River carves the border with North Dakota. Their friends and neighbors from three miles up the road, the Studliens, had settled along the Buffalo River with other Norwegian émigrés back in the 1870s when the railroad extended to what would become the sugar beet fields surrounding Glyndon, Minnesota.

Now Dora's older brother, Goodwin, was fighting in France with his pal and neighbor, Eugene Studlien. On a snowy night, Dora wrote, "we had finished supper and were sitting round the table, saying

2222

how long it was since everybody had heard from the boys." Just
then, the bell rang and her mother, Ingeborg Thortvedt, answered
to find her neighbor Edwin Studlien, bearing grim news. His twenty-
three-year-old son, Eugene, had been killed in action in France on
October 4, 1918.

"It's just so awful," Dora wrote, "as if it should have been a brother
of ours. I just can't realize it." Then the black stain of ink interrupted
her writing briefly before she wrote on: "It will be still worse when we
wake up and find it's no dream. Goodwin's comrade."

She recalled the dances, when Eugene was always "jolly . . . pleasant
and full of fun. . . . It just seems unjust that he and so many others just
in their prime, that they should be deprived of their young lives. . . .
Our good times are past."

She feared Goodwin, too, might be dead. "But I hope to God that
he's alright and that we see him soon." She would soon learn that
her brother was wounded in the right arm in a trench near Eugene
Studlien when his friend was killed. "To think," Dora wrote, "they
were together until the last."

One night soon after getting the news, tears pooled in Dora's eyes
when the national anthem came up on the family's big-horned Vic-
trola record player. "That march was playing while Goodwin and
Eugene went this spring to Camp Lewis," to train for war in Washington state. "It was the last time we saw Eugene."

Dora's sister Florence was ten years younger and also kept a diary
as a seventeen-year-old in 1918. Florence had enrolled at Moorhead
State Normal School, today known as Minnesota State University
Moorhead. She would promptly drop out and attend telegrapher
school with her sister Eva. But at the end of that first week of October
1918, Florence and all Moorhead college students were sent home, she
explained in her diary, "for the sake of the horrible pestilent disease
called the Enfluenza [sic]."

Florence was back home on the Buffalo River farm when she was
jolted with both relief and grief. Her brother, Goodwin, had been
wounded in the arm. But their dear friend, Eugene, was dead: "I must
confess that I was glad [Goodwin] was wounded so he could stay away
from the terrible front, for at least a couple of months and probably by
then the war might be over."

Her optimistic prediction was spot-on. The war would end in a few weeks with the armistice of November 11, 1918—now Veterans Day—but not before the bodies of eight million soldiers and sailors had been ground down on European battlefields nicknamed "the sausage factory."

The Great War started in 1914, but President Woodrow Wilson was hesitant to have US soldiers join England and France in their clash with the Germans. When a German submarine torpedoed the British RMS *Lusitania* on her way from New York to Liverpool in 1915—killing nearly 1,200 of the 1,900 passengers, including 128 Americans—Wilson still stayed out of war. He opted instead for diplomatic channels to limit submarine warfare.

When Wilson ran for reelection in 1916 on a "He Kept Us Out of War" slogan, Minnesotans were unimpressed. The Republican challenger, Supreme Court justice Charles Hughes, beat Wilson in Minnesota by 392 votes—a margin of one-tenth of one percent. Wilson became the first Democrat to win back-to-back presidential terms since Andrew Jackson in 1832. He would also be the last Democrat to win the White House without winning Minnesota. In the end, he captured the popular vote nationally, 49 percent to 46 percent, carrying the Electoral College tally by a whisper of 23 votes, 277–254.

Wilson had cautioned, "If you elect my opponent, you elect a war." Pressure to get involved built, though, as Germans refused to restrict submarine warfare. Then the so-called Zimmermann Telegram surfaced in January 1917. British spies intercepted a message from German foreign minister Arthur Zimmermann lobbying Mexico to join its side, encouraging them to attack the southwestern United States, with German support, and win back parts of Texas, New Mexico, and Arizona. The telegram was shown to US officials in February and then released to the public in early March. "The insidious nature of the . . . revelation stunned and angered a nation that prior to this had regarded the European conflict with little more than passing interest," according to James Carl Nelson, who has authored several books on World War I. When Wilson finally delivered his war message to Congress on April 2, 1917, he went all in, saying, "It isn't an army we must shape and train for war, it is a nation."

Liberty bonds to finance the war were sold in every hamlet across the country. Suspicions were cast on those slow to chip in. The new Sedition Act made it unlawful, with punishments of up to twenty

President Woodrow Wilson, Edith Bolling Galt Wilson, Mary Louise Burnquist, and Governor Joseph A. A. Burnquist, circa 1918. *Courtesy of Minnesota Historical Society Collections*

years in jail, to "utter, print, write or publish" anything disloyal to the US government. With the Russian Revolution toppling the tsars in 1917 and the Industrial Workers of the World organizing labor unions across the United States, paranoia ran deep. Germans represented the largest ethnic slice of Minnesota's immigrant pie, and many of their neighbors feared they would side with the kaiser.

New Ulm, a southern Minnesota frontier town during the 1862 war with the Dakota, became the vortex of anti-German sentiment more than a half century later. After all, the town had been settled by Germans and boasted a large statue known as Hermann the German, his sword thrust skyward.

When New Ulm leaders called a meeting in the summer of 1917 to discuss the constitutionality of the draft, a new, zealous state agency jumped in. The Minnesota Commission of Public Safety had been granted sweeping powers to, among other duties, sniff out disloyalty in labor unions and the populist farmers' group the Nonpartisan League. At the commission's urging, Governor Burnquist had New Ulm's mayor and city attorney thrown out of office for their alleged sedition in organizing the draft debate.

In Wabasha, schoolteacher Irene Bremer had her license suspended after making what some felt were pro-German statements. The commission ordered her to prove her loyalty before she could teach again. Unlike some states that outlawed using the German language in education, Minnesota's new commission urged school districts to insist that English would be the exclusive educational tongue. Many parochial and public schools in Minnesota were teaching in German at the time the war broke out.

In downtown St. Paul, a statue called *Germania* was removed from the company headquarters of Germania Life Insurance—which quickly rebranded itself the Guardian Life Insurance Company of America.

At times, the anti-German mood grew nasty and violent. A farmer named John Meints, whose mother was German, was kidnapped on August 19, 1918, near Luverne in the southwestern corner of the state, suspected of disloyalty. A group of men drove him to the South Dakota line and whipped, tarred, and feathered him. Return to Minnesota, they warned, and you'll be hanged.

Back up along the Buffalo River near Moorhead, Florence Thort-vedt was writing in her diary about the battles both over there and over here. A neighbor six years her senior, Eugene Studlien, was dead, one of 1,432 Minnesotans killed in action during the twenty months of US combat in World War I. He had just turned twenty-three years old.

Florence was wracked with memories of her friend who died four thousand miles from home—"Over There," the ubiquitous phrase composer George M. Cohan coined with his 1917 rallying cry of a song. "He met his fate across the waters, in a new country," Florence wrote. "He sacrificed his precious life for the sake of Democracy. . . . I'm sure he was brave and cheerful to the very end." On one page of the lined journal Florence scratched out the word "cold" and inserted "heartless," just before "and unsympathetic, a cold gray grave among the sands of the other graves."

Her diary promptly turned to the plague at home. "It was some time before we could persuade Papa to let us go back to school," Flor-ence wrote, "because everyone seems to be having this enfluenza." She said two people, on average, were dying in the Moorhead area every day. She rattled off the names of seven neighbors killed by the flu, including the Reverend Anderson's wife. "I'm sure I could name more if I tried," Florence went on, promptly recalling another death. "Oh, yes, also Lawson Clark. . . . It's awful," she wrote. "They have been picked off the face of the earth."

Public gathering spots were shuttered, including schools, churches, and movie theaters. Nurses and doctors were dropping along with their patients. Bodies were piling up at morgues and hospitals. Coffins were buried as fast as they could be hammered together.

Florence's brother, Goodwin, survived his arm injury and would be back on the farm in a few months. He eventually inherited the land from his father, Levi Thortvedt, and worked that soil until his death in 1962. He outlived his friend Eugene by nearly forty-five years.

They are just two examples of the randomness underpinning the calamities of 1918—when many in the trenches, like Eugene Studlien, died next to soldiers like Goodwin, who survived. The killer flu zapped healthy twenty-somethings but barely affected older people, who apparently had built up immunities from exposure to similar flu strains years earlier.

Yet nowhere was the randomness of life or death more pronounced in 1918 than in the bogs and majestic white pine forests of northeastern Minnesota, where a long, hot, dry summer and early autumn had left conditions crackling like kindling amid the piles of lumber stacked in and around the sawmills of Cloquet and dozens of nearby lumber towns, including Moose Lake, Kettle River, and Automba.

The fires of 1918 devastated an already suffering forestland. *Courtesy of Minnesota Historical Society Collections*

CHAPTER 3

Automba; Moose Lake; Cloquet

LEONARD AND LUTRA KRIGSHOLM, teenage siblings, were milking the cows that Saturday in mid-October as the skies grew smoky. Their father, Finnish lumberjack and farmer Arvid Krigsholm, was their mother Jennie's second husband. Her first, Tomi Paulus, had stepped into an old-fashioned deer trap one morning after a heavy snow and tripped the string rigged to the trigger, which fired a deadly shot. Jennie met Arvid not long after burying Tomi. She later moved to Arvid's farm four miles east of the tiny village of Automba.

When she first arrived in Automba in 1889, Jennie lugged supplies, on foot, down deer trails from Moose Lake. Eventually, Arvid purchased a trotting horse and a carriage and Charles Hekkala opened a general store in Automba. By 1918, the Krigsholms had nine children living on the farm. Leonard was third-oldest; Lutra sixth in line. For Lutra and her older sister, Edna, Saturday meant scrubbing the house from top to bottom.

"That summer was an extremely dry one," Lutra, then fifteen, recalled decades later. "The danger of fire became so great that my folks decided to pull the hay stacks out of the woods." Arvid and the boys moved the hay they'd piled in small forest clearings closer to their fields and filled tubs at the well to keep the hay wet. They were prepared but not panicking. Four of Lutra's brothers had gone to help douse some brush fires burning at a neighboring reverend's place.

Even when they ran back to the farm, screaming that the fire was growing and Automba was doomed, Lutra and Leonard kept their cool. "Thinking the fire wasn't coming as fast as it really was," she said, "we decided to get the cows milked before we would start worrying about the fire." Their mother, meanwhile, took the $300 she'd saved in her new stuffed mattress and tucked the cash in a medicine bag.

By October 1918, northern Minnesota was completely parched. Records show it was the driest summer since 1870, with only six inches of rain through September, compared to more than twenty-five inches of moisture in most years. Making matters worse, the forest floor was littered with considerable "slash"—the branches and logging detritus left behind by lumberjacks. Timber companies were required to get rid of such slash, typically with controlled burns, but those burns had been delayed and postponed because of the unusually dry conditions.

Between noon and 2:00 PM on October 12, the humidity nosedived sharply from 31 percent to 21 percent. Longtime Duluth meteorologist Herbert Richardson had never recorded such low humidity. Forty percent was considered normal. A relative humidity of 30 percent is considered dry. It was as if a huge dry sponge were sucking up whatever moisture the forest could offer.

"For days that extremely dry, warm and windy October, there had been the smell of smoke in the air," Evelyn Lyngen, then ten years old, recalled in a letter decades later. That acrid smell didn't prompt much anxiety. Fires were so common up north, "we didn't pay too much attention," Cloquet's Tena MacMillian Smith would later recall. "We had those every year." The fires came in cycles. The Hinckley fire of 1894 killed more than 400 people. The Baudette fire torched more than 300,000 acres in Lake of the Woods County in far northern Minnesota in 1910, claiming 27 lives.

Eight Octobers later, no one was too jittery until the winds picked up that Saturday afternoon. It was a Columbus Day holiday weekend. People were hanging their laundry to dry, milking cows, and visiting friends and relatives under hazy skies growing increasingly smoky.

Looking back, court documents and oral histories confirm the spark that started the deadly fires of October 12, 1918, might have been lit two days earlier. About 4:30 PM on October 10, a passenger train heading from Duluth to Hibbing stopped at Milepost 62 along the Great Northern Railway tracks four miles northwest of the tiny village of Brookston. Called O'Brien's Spur, the stop fifteen miles northwest of Cloquet along the St. Louis River featured a so-called siding where ten thousand cords of pulpwood, cordwood, railroad ties, fence posts, and telephone poles were stored until they could be sent over the rails to a buyer.

As the train pulled away, a couple of farmers, Steve Koskela and John Sundstrom, noticed rising smoke. They walked over to the western edge of the siding and discovered a fire covering about twenty feet, igniting the tall, dry grass near the piles of wood. They ran home to fetch pails and recruit neighbors to help.

Crews spent much of Friday the eleventh trying to contain the fire. But before noon the next day, flames surrounded all the wood piled at O'Brien's Spur. By 2:00 PM, the fire roared into Brookston, a village of five hundred residents. When houses began bursting into flames, about two hundred people crammed onto a Great Northern freight train heading southwest toward Cloquet.

When the sooty passengers climbed off the train in Cloquet at 5:00 PM, their panicked faces told the story: the winds had stirred the fires. This wasn't just another smoky day in Cloquet. The lumber city, and all its seven thousand residents and its million board feet of lumber, was in jeopardy.

Brookston, where the fire started at Milepost 62, is roughly forty-five miles north of Automba, where the Krigsholm barn was about to become engulfed in flames.

This was not one fire. Richardson said that swirling winds connected fifty to seventy-five small fires into a growing inferno that would span more than eight thousand square miles—completely burning nearly a quarter of that affected area.

Years later, experts compared the conditions up north in October 1918 to a weapon about to be fired. All the raw timber, cut and stacked lumber, and bone-dry slash was like the rifle shell, according to the authors of a 1969 US Forest Service research paper, "Climatic Conditions Preceding Historically Great Fires in the North Central Region." Unique climatic conditions—historic dryness, powerful wind gusts, and plummeting humidity—loaded the shell into the rifle chamber.

Smaller fires across the region burning in bogs and along railroad lines were likened to the hammer being pulled back. Taken together, researchers Donald Haines and Rodney Sando wrote, "The trigger is pulled and the bullet is on its way."

Their metaphor lacks one key ingredient: railroads. They were like the person toting the rifle. "Railroads in many cases are the most prolific source of fires," the chief US forester, Henry Solon Graves, warned in 1911. While the relief train with the Brookston refugees chugging into Cloquet would be the first of many heroic train rides saving countless lives, railroads were also determined to be the culprit behind the fires of 1918.

Four months before the fires torched thirty-six towns and killed more than 450 people in northern Minnesota, a federal forester in Denver told a regional supervisor for the US Railroad Administration—the federal agency that had taken over control of the nation's rails as a wartime measure—that "more fires are started by railroad locomotives than any other causes." A subsequent study by Minnesota's state forester showed that 55 percent of all forest fires could trace their origins to locomotives and the sparks and embers they spewed from their smokestacks.

Those locomotives burned coal, drafting heat from their fireboxes to attain full speed. This process often sucked small chunks of burning coal out of the firebox and up into the smokestack. To combat these tiny, flying pieces of coal that could ignite grass and lumber along railbeds, the government came up with a two-pronged solution.

So-called spark arresters—screens made of wire mesh or perforated metal—were used to cap smokestacks and trap the fiery chunks while allowing smoke to escape. High heat often warped the screens, however, which irked train conductors because it slowed the drag and delayed their runs. They often removed the spark arresters or widened the holes, enabling larger bits of hot coal to sneak out. Hot coal often dropped from firebox ashpans, as well, and section crews commonly burned trash and old ties along the tracks.

Minnesota rules added human inspectors to the spark-arresting machinery, requiring railroad companies to send patrols out during fire season to report, monitor, and extinguish trackside blazes. But the manpower needed to inspect and patrol railroad fires had dwindled with so many men signing up to fight in the Great War in Europe.

A train near Moose Lake destroyed by the fires of 1918, which were caused by a train. *Courtesy of Minnesota Historical Society Collections*

Back at the Krigsholm spread near Automba, "the fire swept upon our farm much sooner than we had expected," Lutra said. Leonard, her eighteen-year-old brother, had only milked a single cow. He left the pail in the middle of the barn as conditions worsened. "We pushed the cows out of the barn, let the horses loose and opened the doors so the pigs and chickens could try to save their lives," Lutra said.

Her older brother August took the younger kids and ran to the Bjorklunds, neighbors across a swamp that was swallowed by flames minutes later. With sparks raining down, Lutra, Leonard, and their father "started emptying the well onto the barn roof." When the well ran dry, leaving them with no more water, the barn roof ignited. "I remember Leonard becoming so frustrated that he threw the pail of milk on the barn roof, exclaiming: 'Well, you can have that, too!'"

39

Cloquet in ruins after the fire. *Courtesy of Minnesota Historical Society Collections*

CHAPTER 4

Cloquet; Moose Lake

EVEN AS THE FIRES IN NORTHEASTERN MINNESOTA intensified, the thoughts of many in their path remained four thousand miles away in the Argonne Forest of France.

Fire was the furthest thing from the mind of twenty-six-year-old Pearl Drew, at least early that Saturday, October 12, 1918. With her thoughts on her husband, Herbert, who was fighting the Germans in the French forests, she performed some necessary household chores. After all, seasons were changing: it was time to juggle her war worries with her preparations for the inevitable arrival of another northern Minnesota winter.

"That means warm clothes must be hunted up, aired, cleaned and mended," she wrote in a 1936 essay. She pulled out a new fox-fur muff. She'd saved up for months to purchase it. Then she hung her winter wear on the clothesline behind her home in Cloquet. "The wind grew to such a gale that we had to take it all down again or it would have been ripped to shreds," she wrote. "An unusual wind carrying dirt, sawdust, leaves and sticks! . . . There was a queer glow in the sky."

Old-timers shrugged it off, saying it was just another fire up the line. But Cloquet's forest ranger told Pearl if the wind changed direction, there would be trouble. "Be ready to leave town in a moment's notice," he told her. "You never can tell where a forest fire will go."

Heeding his advice, Pearl Drew knew what she needed to do next. "I went home and wrote a cheerful 'don't worry' letter to my husband, who was fighting in the Argonne and had enough worries and fears."

The Argonne Offensive was part of a three-pronged attack on the Germans during the final months of World War I. British and French forces were taking on the enemy in Flanders and Cambrai while American fighters, under General John Pershing, took on the Germans in the Argonne Forest starting September 26, 1918. It was a smashing success, with Herbert Drew and his fellow soldiers penetrating two miles into enemy territory. After a brief hiatus for reinforcements, the battle restarted on October 4. Within thirteen days, they had won a ten-mile incursion, and the Great War was within a month of ending. But not before 117,000 American, 70,000 French, and 100,000 German soldiers died in the fight in the Argonne Forest.

*

Back in the timber and farm country four miles west of Moose Lake, ten-year-old Evelyn Lyngen had two reasons to think about faraway battlefields as the sky turned purplish red on October 12. Her twenty-two-year-old brother, Victor, had been drafted and was scheduled to leave for military training the next week. Their twenty-four-year-old brother, Melvin, was already fighting in France.

Harsh smoke and ominous sights interrupted any daydreams Evelyn had about her brothers' fates. "We could see bursts of flame and smoke emerge over the horizon," she recalled in a letter written nearly sixty years later. "The wind velocity had intensified and our eyes burned from the dense smoke that permeated the air." Soon, "pieces of burning timber came hurtling through the air, crashing to the ground and setting small fires in the tinder dry grass dangerously close to our farm buildings." Her Norwegian parents hollered for Evelyn and her sister to pump and fill any bucket they could find. It didn't help. "Tongues of fire enveloped our house and we ran."

But first, her mother, Ingborg, dashed up the stairs, grabbed her favorite shawl and heirlooms from Norway, and tossed them out a window. Evelyn's thirteen-year-old brother, Selmer, whom everyone called by the more American nickname of Sam, made a crazed sprint into the burning home, too. "Sam had the presence of mind to run back into the house and save a picture of my brother Melvin, who was serving with the Army on the battlefields of France," Evelyn, a longtime Kettle River schoolteacher, remembered in a letter she wrote from Nebraska in 1977, when she was in her late sixties.

It's safe to assume some of the six siblings of the swarming Soderberg family were thinking, too, of their brother David serving in the sausage factory battlefield overseas. Like many families in northern Minnesota in 1918, the Soderbergs had one foot in each of two worlds. Their immigrant parents made the trek from the Hammer parish in Sweden, John Soderberg at the age of forty-three and his wife, Johanna, thirty. Three of their boys and a daughter were born in Sweden and three more boys and a daughter started out on Minnesota soil.

Tragedy was nothing new for such immigrant families. On the sea passage to New York in May 1881, ten-month-old Hanna Soderberg grew sick and died a few days before the ship docked on American shores. Johanna Soderberg, her grief-struck mother, bristled at the thought of burying her precious baby at sea. They wrapped Hanna in blankets and carried her off the ship with her three brothers, pretending she was alive until a proper burial could be conducted in America.

The Soderbergs settled in Minnesota, four miles west of Moose Lake, surrounded by fellow Swedes as well as Finns and Poles. Johanna was a strict Swedish mother, a church regular on Sundays, and a midwife who traveled long distances to help pregnant women deliver babies. She was constantly squabbling with her brother over the position of a fence separating their farmsteads on Soderberg Road. As her boys grew up and started dancing, gambling, and drinking, Johanna made her disproval known—once writing biblical verses on their playing cards.

Her life continued to be etched with heartbreak. John, her husband of eighteen years, had died in 1892 at age fifty-four. Their youngest son, Titus, fell from a tree to his death in 1897 at age seven. After fifteen years raising her six kids alone, Johanna died from cancer in 1907 at age fifty-six. By the time of the 1918 fires, the Soderberg family consisted of six surviving siblings—one of whom, thirty-two-year-old David, was off fighting the Germans in France.

By the time David returned to Moose Lake a few months later, all five of his siblings and ten of his nieces and nephews would be dead—victims of the fire. "He was the only one left," Don Wold wrote in his 1989 book, *The Other West Side Story*, a local history about the west side of Moose Lake Township in Carlton County.

Brothers John and Joseph Soderberg had taken a horse and wagon, piled in their sister, Emma, and her three children and other neighbors, and headed toward Moose Lake when flames consumed them. The wagon was found in the road with the charred horse's carcass nearby. Emma was clutching a baby in her arms when the fires overcame the wagon.

Charley and Axel Soderberg had taken shelter in their root cellar—a structure made of logs with an earthen roof—along with their wives and ten children spanning in age from newborn to sixteen: Hilma, Chester, George, Arnold, Alice, Virginia, Florence, Clifford, Hulda, and one listed in court records only as "infant." All of them were discovered the next morning, suffocated in the cellar. "Their bodies were badly charred," the *Superior (Wisconsin) Telegram* reported on October 18, 1918, "some being identified only by the buttons and other paraphernalia that the fire was unable to destroy. The only surviving member of the family, David Soderberg, is in France with the American Expeditionary Forces," the paper noted.

The war "over there" proved far less tragic for the Soderberg family than the dry autumn of 1918 in the bog and white pine country near Moose Lake. While the newspaper reported charred bodies, a young eyewitness had a different account, insisting that the victims in the cellar showed few signs of burning to death. Only five years old, she would be haunted by memories of the Soderberg root cellar for the next eighty years.

"I was there when we discovered them, suffocated in their root cellar," Esther Honkala Luoma would recall in a 1991 newspaper interview, when she was seventy-seven. "You can imagine the sight that greeted our eyes when the door was opened. Fourteen people, most of them members of the Soderberg family, all of them friends of ours, the children classmates of mine. They were all lying there, as if asleep, all perished from a lack of oxygen. Other than slightly bloated faces, there was no evidence of burns on their bodies." She would remember, for seven decades, the potato sacks hanging inside the door of the cellar. "Obviously they had made a valiant, if futile, attempt to save their lives."

Like so many in the area, Esther Honkala's parents had been born in Finland. Esther's mother, Amanda Nevala, worked in her family's dry goods store when she married Joel Honkala on a cold January day in 1904. A few years later, they immigrated to America and found their way to the Finnish community that settled near Automba. Brown Road, an east-west track south of town, was an unofficial boundary: Finns settled north of the road and Poles lived south.

Esther's family had just sat down for lunch in their farmhouse outside of Brookston on Saturday, October 12, 1918, when the air began to smell of smoke. "There were no fire departments in those days," Esther recalled. When neighbors came to ask her father to help douse the fire at School No. 89, he refused. He had to save his farm.

Joel Honkala filled buckets from the windmill-pumped well as Amanda and the kids carried belongings to their root cellar. Five-year-old Esther carried the bread loaf her mother had baked that morning—and a pink dress with black velvet cuffs. Her eleven-year-old sister, Elma, asked her to hold the dress before their mother loaded them into a buggy. Joel insisted on staying behind to fight the fire at the farm.

With the wind gusty, hot and thick with smoke, the Honkalas' horse lost its bearings only a quarter mile down the road. It barreled into the ditch, the buggy's wheels mired in mud. Esther passed out briefly from the smoke. "When I woke up, everyone else was gone except my younger sister, who was laying face down under the buggy seat." She yelled her sister Helen's name. "She didn't answer when I called." Afraid to stay in the buggy, and still clinging to the pink dress, Esther stepped over the backboard.

Her father, meanwhile, had somehow suppressed the fire back at the farmstead. But the outbuildings burned. He shrugged and headed down the road, searching for his wife and four kids. He soon found Amanda with nine-year-old Alfred and eleven-year-old Elma. He asked: Where are the younger girls?

Amanda told her husband she had left them, dead, in the buggy stuck in the mud. Joel refused to believe his daughters were gone and insisted on going to find them. His wife pleaded with him not to go, certain he would be the next victim.

"The smoke and wind were so strong, but he got through to us," Esther said. Her father yanked her up and shouted: "Where's Helen?" The youngest sister, two weeks shy of turning three, was twisted in the carriage, which was starting to smoke. "He got to her just in time," Esther said. "The buggy had begun to smolder."

Home guardsmen took the girls to the hospital fifty miles away in Grand Rapids the next day, along with their mother, Amanda, who suffered burns on her face. That proved to be the least of her problems. Within a month, the former dry goods clerk from Finland and immigrant mother of four would contract influenza and die. She would join more than one hundred other fire survivors who made it through the smoke and flames only to catch the deadly virus.

CHAPTER 5

Minneapolis

A DEAFENING CHORUS of thirty wailing children, "standing in their cribs screaming their hearts out," greeted Pearl McIver at 9:00 PM on the top-floor pediatric ward of the University of Minnesota Hospital. It was the fall of 1918 and her first overnight shift as a student nurse. The kids ranged in age from two to ten. "All were desperately sick," McIver recalled, forty years later.

Many of the children had been brought to the hospital in paddy wagons. Police bundled and loaded them up after finding their parents dead or dying from the influenza outbreak that arrived in the state that September. It was first delivered by a sick soldier, returning from Camp Sheridan north of Chicago to his small southern Minnesota farm town of Wells (population: about 1,800).

Within forty-eight hours, Wells had two hundred residents sick with the flu; seven came down with pneumonia and one man died. By October 12, when the fires erupted up north, 2,538 cases were reported across the state. Minneapolis added up another 1,538 cases. St. Paul reported 210 sick with the flu at Fort Snelling, and other military posts counted 1,000 sick soldiers. By the end of the outbreak, 75,000 Minnesotans would contract the disease.

Minneapolis banned all public gatherings as of midnight October 12. Long lines queued up that evening at the city's vaudeville and motion picture theaters, where weary citizens looked for one last dose of entertainment as darkness fell.

More than twenty nurses quickly took sick at the University of Minnesota Hospital. The staff was already stretched thin by the Great War gobbling up all the medical personnel it could find and shipping those doctors and nurses overseas. "The medical fraternity is severely taxed," a Minneapolis *Tribune* editorial fretted on October 3, 1918. "So many physicians and surgeons have gone to Europe or to training that those at home have more than they can attend to comfortably and to good advantage."

The hospital banned visitors. Only flu patients were admitted for eight weeks that autumn before the hospital halted accepting any new patients. On the maternity ward, four patients a night were moved to the hallway when their lungs filled with liquid. Screens went up around them as they waited to die so the staff could tend to the more hopeful. The pediatric ward, which typically cared for fifteen sick children, was double-booked. Overflowing with flu-stricken patients, the hospital turned to medical interns and nursing students, like twenty-five-year-old Pearl McIver.

She was born in the west-central Minnesota hamlet of Nora, the youngest of eight. Her mother died when Pearl was four. After attending teacher college in Mayville, North Dakota, she taught for three years in rural schools before enrolling at the University of Minnesota's School of Nursing, the first such program attached to a major university when it began in 1909.

Besides the crying children, McIver was greeted that first night by an exhausted day-shift staff. Following regulations, they wore tight white masks, white gowns, and snug-fitting white caps. Those regulations would prove utterly ineffective in preventing the staff from contracting the deadly virus. Adding to the harrowing experience, the alien appearance of the medical staff freaked out the already traumatized kids. "Imagine the terror of those children," Pearl said. "To find themselves in a strange environment among a bunch of ghosts."

The day-shift staff was reluctant to clock out and leave a junior nursing student alone until 7:00 AM in a pediatric ward with thirty sick children. But Pearl had an idea, which she kept to herself, as she urged the day shifters to go on home. She would be fine alone.

"As soon as the last nurse had left," she recalled, "I pulled off my mask and cap so I would look more like a human being." Then, one by one, she wrapped the babies in their blankets and rocked them in an old, white rocking chair in the pediatric ward. (Years later, she wondered why the chair was there at all because "picking up any child was strictly against pediatric regulations" of the era.) Gradually, the wailing subsided as the children "responded so well to seeing a person who looked ordinary and who gave them a little cuddling," she said. By midnight, all the kids "fell into a relaxed sleep." As each woke up, she forced them to drink fluids—the key to their treatment regimen.

Four nights later, Pearl was again in the midst of what she called her "rocking episode" when someone walked into the ward and startled her. The horrified man, a medical intern, asked, "What on earth are you doing?" Figuring her days as a student nurse were about to end, Pearl shot back, "These children are scared stiff and I'm merely trying to make them feel comfortable and at home."

An awkward pause followed before the young doctor in training asked: "Have you a second rocking chair?" Every night for weeks after that, he arrived at ten o'clock, stripped off his mask, and rocked the sick children alongside the student nurse. Neither he nor Pearl "ever told a soul about our night routine in pediatrics."

*

Not far away from those rocking chairs quieting sick babies at the University of Minnesota Hospital, Dr. John Sundwall had just arrived from the University of Kansas to spearhead the new University Health Service. It operated out of two vacated fraternity houses on University Avenue. The health service started operation the week before school was set to begin in September 1918. There was something else new on campus that fall. Universities across the country agreed to serve as training grounds following just-enacted draft laws—meaning, at Minnesota, another 2,600 trainees were coming to the campus on top of the usual horde of students. "Military officers—from abroad and all parts of our land—were reporting almost daily to conduct drills and offer instruction," Sundwall later wrote. "Nothing could be more favorable for the introduction and spread of this contagion."

Minnesota's first flu cases were reported on September 27. Within days, seven cases of flu were reported in North Branch, a hundred in the town of Wells, twenty-one cases at Fort Snelling, and thirty at the University Hospital, including twenty-one nurses. The new Univer-

Soldiers at the University of Minnesota campus prepare to board streetcars on the way to military training exercises. *Courtesy of Minnesota Historical Society Collections*

sity Health Service was suddenly swamped with the sick. "There were incessant calls for help," Sundwall said. With Student Army Training Corps trainees crammed together with students, the flu cut through the university—killing at least fifty, although formal counts were sketchy.

By December 1918, the war had ended and the Student Army Training Corps was disbanded. But Sundwall could never shed the memories of that harrowing year. There was that first army trainer he encountered in the frat-house-turned-health-center: "I shall never forget the first victim at the University," Sundwall wrote, "a handsome, robust young second lieutenant. In less than a week his body was sent home."

Two other aspects of the 1918 flu pandemic were also "indelibly impressed on my memory," Sundwall wrote. "The one was the characteristic chain of symptoms—sudden onset; fever; extreme prostration; pains in back, head, and extremities; involvement of the respiratory system, and early pneumonia in a large percentage of cases. The other impression was the helplessness of the medical sciences."

*

At age sixty-four, Dr. Henry Bracken must have thought he had seen it all. But as the federally appointed field director of influenza management in Minnesota, Bracken was frustrated beyond belief. He tried recruiting more doctors but told US surgeon general Dr. Rupert Blue: "A number who we have called for have made excuses and have not come at all."

Bracken not only asked Blue to send senior medical students, he asked the army's top surgeon and the dean at the University of Minnesota. After three weeks of begging for more hands on deck, he "still was unable to obtain senior medical students for assistance, because each party insisted that someone else had to authorize it," according to a 2007 public health report on lessons learned from the 1918 flu in the Twin Cities. "In the end, Bracken failed to receive any medical students."

Although he longed for more help, Bracken was among the experts whose reaction to the outbreak, and how to deal with it, evolved as cases mounted. Reluctant at first, Bracken watched Minneapolis health commissioner Dr. H. M. Guilford shut down schools and public gathering places. "If you begin to close, where are you going to stop?" Bracken asked. "When are you going to reopen, and what do you accomplish by opening?"

He originally sided with the approach in St. Paul, which reacted to cases with isolation, in contrast to Minneapolis's more proactive strategy. But eventually, as the death toll climbed, Bracken came around to support shuttering schools, quarantining army bases, and forbidding public gatherings. Still, at nearly every turn, education, military, and political leaders shrugged him off and refused to listen.

The son of a doctor, Bracken was born before the Civil War, in 1854, near Pittsburgh. After his medical training at the University of Michigan and a New York medical school, he headed to Venezuela in 1877 as a surgeon for a mining company. He moved to Scotland for

51

graduate studies and then took a job at a boarding school, Uppingham-by-the-Sea, where typhoid had slipped into the wells, killing three students a few years before he arrived. Within a year, Bracken became a ship's surgeon on a beat-up vessel called the *Moselle*, contracting scarlet fever and malaria on voyages to Central and South America. When he regained his health, Bracken took his ship doctoring to the *Eider*, sailing to Barbados and Martinique and marveling at "the tall, supple, straight" posture of the indigenous West Indies islanders' "bare backs, bare shoulders, bare legs and bare feet."

His wandering ways continued into his thirties, and by 1884, he was working as a mining camp doctor in Sonora, Mexico, until Geronimo-led Apache raids halted mining activities. Finally, after a stop in New York for more post-graduate studies, Bracken arrived in Minnesota. He opened an office in Minneapolis, then landed a therapeutics professorship at the University of Minnesota. In 1895, at age forty-one, he began a long tenure on the state board of health.

A straightforward and energetic force, Bracken helped modernize the state's fledgling public health network, working with local health boards at the township level. "His extreme formality and sincere urge to help the cause led him to forget tact and caution," writes Philip Jordan, a University of Minnesota history professor, in his 1953 book *The People's Health*, a chronicle of Minnesota public health history through 1948. "On occasions—and there were many—he swung with a heavy fist," Jordan says. Bracken's official letters were "apt to ignore suavity and to be couched in blunt statements and heavy sarcasm." That often alienated the men in the field he relied on. "Yet even Bracken's enemies admitted that, while they disliked him thoroughly, they considered him completely frank and honest," according to Jordan.

In the early days of October 1918, Twin Cities newspapers and officials were painting an optimistic picture of the flu epidemic, insisting it was in check. "Spanish influenza does not exist in Minneapolis and never has," Guilford, the Minneapolis health commissioner, said on September 19, before taking a cautionary tone, "but it probably will reach here during the fall."

He was right. Within two weeks, 150 cases were reported in Minneapolis, mostly among soldiers in training and nurses at the University Hospital. By October 7, forty-six civilians had contracted the flu in Minneapolis and seven had died. The *St. Paul Pioneer Press*, on Octo-

Dr. Henry Bracken, medical point man on the Minnesota State Board of Health.
Courtesy of Minnesota Historical Society Collections

ber 2, promised the epidemic was under control, with only a handful of isolated cases.

Recently deputized by the US Public Health Service as the state's influenza point man, Bracken knew better. Within days of the rosy outlook, Minneapolis officials reported a thousand sick people—including 510 cases at Fort Snelling. One of Bracken's fellow state health board members, Dr. Egil Boeckman, was stationed at Camp Grant, south of Rockford, Illinois. More than one in ten of the soldiers there had contracted the flu by early October, and "it spreads like fire," he wrote to Bracken. "Very severe in onset and very prone to complications."

Boeckman studied throat cultures, lung autopsies, and sinus secretions and found pneumonia often set in within six days of the first symptoms. "Very fatal," Boeckman wrote, with the flu virus and the pneumonia that accompanied it killing one-third to one-half of those stricken. And these were healthy young men. Boeckman also reported that country boys were dying more rapidly than those from urban areas.

The army's treatment called for bed rest, aspirin, and quinine—a medicine popular in malaria cases. The patients lucky enough to survive, the army said, should be kept quiet for three days after their fevers broke.

"I want to impress upon the [state health board] that you are dealing with the most serious epidemic of any kind you have ever been up against," Boeckman wrote to Bracken on October 5, 1918.

From across the state, calls came in, swamping Bracken with pleas to send nurses and doctors to their towns. Federal health managers authorized Bracken to hire assistant surgeons at $200 a month with four dollars for daily expenses. The Red Cross jumped in, paying nurses $70 a month and setting up local chapters statewide that prepared and served meals to the sick and sent out volunteer housekeepers and childcare providers. A special state appropriation of $10,000 was earmarked to help the state health board combat the mounting influenza epidemic. Adjusted for inflation, that translates into roughly $175,000 in 2018 dollars.

When Bracken floated the idea of quarantining military camps such as Fort Snelling, he was rebuffed. "It does not appear to this office desirable to attempt to limit the movements of the authorized escorts for the dead, or the casual soldier on leave," Lieutenant Colonel W. P. Chamberlain, a high-ranking member of the army's medical corps, wrote to Bracken on October 7. "Hundreds of thousands of civilians who have been equally exposed to the infection are freely traveling about the country."

Flummoxed, Bracken issued orders requiring that all flu cases must be reported. Patients must be isolated. Attendants must wear face masks. Healthy people must stay out of infected homes. Children in such homes must stay away from school until five days after the last detected symptoms in the family. Public funerals for flu victims would be permitted only if the caskets were closed during memorial services. By mid-October, Minneapolis ambulances would transport only flu victims. Bracken said all public gatherings such as conventions and church and school group meetings should be postponed.

Even elevator use was restricted in St. Paul. Pointing to elevators' cramped space and lack of fresh air, city health officials ordered that buildings with fewer than six floors allow stairway use only. With blowback from building owners, rules were eased at hotels and apartment buildings. After all, forcing ill people to climb stairs or denying easy access to outdoor air was arguably just as bad.

Twin Cities schools stayed open, however, despite federal recommendations to the contrary. "Spanish influenza is primarily an adult disease," one Minneapolis school board member said, citing a doctor's report that stated no kids were among the 156 flu cases he was monitoring. Parents and public health authorities rebelled, and all Minneapolis classes were canceled within a day of the school board's decision to stay open.

Although the University of Minnesota had postponed its opening until October 9, figuring the flu would be under control by then, classes remained in session for much of the month, even as the flu was targeting college-aged people. Saloons, stores, and streetcars also remained open for business.

Meanwhile, the flu spread like the fires up north. On October 24 alone, Duluth reported 18 new cases, Milaca added 82, Bemidji and Mankato tallied 100 apiece. The small town of Dilworth, with a population of fewer than 900 just east of Moorhead, reported 125 new cases.

Of all the things irking the brash Bracken, one thing especially worried him: the railroads. The main mode of transportation in 1918, trains were carrying flu sufferers across the state and the country. That included dead soldiers being shipped home from army bases, such as the late Albert Betz from Sauk Centre. "Bodies were coming back from cantonments to Minnesota and going through Minneapolis and St. Paul in such condition that the train crews were unwilling to handle them," according to state health board correspondence from late October. "In many instances the odors were terrific . . . and some of the bodies were dripping."

Eventually, flu sufferers were allowed to ride the rails only if they wore masks. And sputum cups were issued to collect coughed-up phlegm. Those steps proved too little, and too late, for a little girl about to become an orphan. Her name was Mary McCarthy.

She was six years old, the oldest of four, when she stepped on a train in Seattle in late October 1918—joining what felt like a grand adventure. Her family was moving back to Minnesota. McCarthy remembered sitting with her father in the Pullman car, watching the Montana scenery stream by as the train cut through a pass near Rocky Mountain National Park. "As we look up at the mountains, my father tells me that big boulders sometimes fall off them, hitting the train and killing people," she recalled in a 1946 memoir. "I start to shake and my teeth to chatter with what I think is terror."

Those shakes were the first sign that Mary McCarthy had contracted influenza. The virus had latched onto her family at the upscale and lavish New Washington Hotel, where they stayed the night before boarding the eastbound train in Seattle. It was precisely the kind of scenario that haunted Dr. Henry Bracken down the line. "Waving good-by in the Seattle depot, we had not known that we had carried the flu with us into our drawing rooms along with the presents and the flowers," McCarthy wrote. "But, one after another, we had been struck down as the train proceeded eastward."

Her family's story shows how the flu virus didn't discriminate. Poor people in crowded housing or young soldiers crammed in barracks might be more vulnerable, but rich lives weren't immune.

Mary's grandfather J. H. McCarthy had come from farmer stock in North Dakota to amass a fortune in the grain elevators of Duluth and Minneapolis. Her father, Roy McCarthy, had played football at the University of Minnesota before becoming, according to his daughter's memoir, "a periodical drunkard who had been a family problem

Author Mary McCarthy, who lost her parents to the flu as a child.
World Telegram & Sun staff photo, Library of Congress Prints and Photographs Division

from the time of his late teens." He was studying law at the University of Washington, but his lavish lifestyle, and a serious heart condition traced to lingering football injuries, prompted his parents to insist that Roy relocate his family to Minneapolis.

Their house emptied for the move, the McCarthys checked into the best hotel in town on their last night in Seattle—Roy, his wife Tess, Mary and her three small siblings, plus Mary's aunt Zula and uncle Harry, who'd been "summoned home from Yale to look after" his ne'er-do-well brother. They all checked into the New Washington Hotel on the eve of their train ride to Minnesota. "A very unwise thing, for the first rule in an epidemic is to avoid public places," Mary would write decades later, recalling her father's general ill health even before the flu got him. "Indeed, the whole idea of traveling with a sick man and four small children at the height of an epidemic seems madness."

But Roy's brother, Louis, an aviator, was home in Minnesota on furlough, and visiting a brother trumped any sense of danger. Foolhardy in retrospect, the McCarthys' decision to go ahead with the trip illustrates how people didn't take the flu seriously enough.

But by the time the train screeched to a stop at the five-year-old Minneapolis Great Northern Depot, "one by one, we had been carried off," Mary recalled. "On the platform, there were stretchers, a wheel chair, redcaps, distraught officials, and, beyond them in the crowd, my grandfather's rosy face, cigar, and cane, my grandmother's feathered hat." For a six-year-old girl, the dire scene took on an "imparting air of festivity to this strange and confused picture, making us children certain that our illness was the beginning of a delightful holiday." Even during the previous days on the train, "Mama's lying torpid in the berth" signaled only one thing to an oldest child: "Serious illness, in our minds, had been associated with" child births and new siblings coming home.

Within a week, the "delightful holiday" had been wrenched into something quite different. Mary's mother, Therese Preston McCarthy, whom everyone called Tess or Tessie, died during the first week of November 1918. She was twenty-nine. Mary's father, Roy, died the next day—although no one told the children. "Mama and Daddy, they assured us, had gone to get well in the hospital," Mary said.

Mary was sleeping in a sewing room at her grandparents' home in the Whittier neighborhood of Minneapolis, where she awoke "to an atmosphere of castor oil, rectal thermometers, cross nurses . . . a coming and going of priests and undertakers and coffins." As Mary's fever broke, she realized "everything, including ourselves, was different." The change showed up in little things, like her flannel pajamas, which had grown "thin and shabby" from all the disinfectant used to wash them. "The happy life we had had—the May baskets and valentines, the picnics in the yard, and the elaborate snowman—was a poor preparation, in truth, for the future that now opened up to us."

Instead of the spoiled life she led in her first five years, Mary began to grapple with life as a young orphan at her grandparents' home, with food trays "dumped summarily on our beds and no sugar and cream for our cereal." Medicine was forced down the children "in a gulp because someone could not be bothered to wait for us." She remembered nurses dressing them, "our arms jerked into our sleeves and a comb ripped through our hair . . . our questions unanswered and our requests unheeded." Once insistent, Mary grew passive. "We no longer demanded our due," she said, "and the wish to see our parents insensibly weakened. Soon we ceased to speak of it and thus, without tears or tantrums, we came to know they were dead."

Mary and her siblings were soon sent to live with their great-aunt Margaret and her abusive husband, Myers. The couple had been summoned from Indiana to raise four kids under the age of seven in a house at 2427 Blaisdell Avenue. The grandparents purchased the house in their Minneapolis neighborhood.

On Sundays, the children were taken to the cemetery, where Civil War tombs and fresher doughboy graves punctuated the hillside. Mary's parents were initially buried at Lakewood Cemetery—perhaps Minneapolis's most prestigious graveyard, located between Lakes Calhoun and Harriet. The cemetery, with its rolling hills, stored countless caskets in late 1918 until other cemeteries, swamped with burials, could handle them in the spring.

The remains of Roy and Therese McCarthy were disinterred and moved about three miles east to the Catholic graveyard at St. Mary's Cemetery at Forty-fourth Street and Chicago Avenue. "The two mounds that now were our parents . . . we contemplated them stolidly, waiting for a sensation," Mary wrote. "But these twin grass beds, with their junior executive headstones, elicited nothing whatever." After "interminable staring, we would beg to be allowed to play in some collateral mausoleum, where the dead at least were buried in drawers and offered some stimulus of fancy."

On visits back to her grandparents' home, she remembered the "whispering ladies who sometimes came to call on us, inspired, it seemed, by a pornographic curiosity as to the exact details of our feelings." She'd hear them, in hushed tones, asking her grandmother Elizabeth McCarthy: "So you suppose they remember their parents? Do they say anything?"

"Our grandmother was quite uninterested in arousing an emotion of grief in us. 'She doesn't feel it at all,' I used to hear her confide, of me, to visitors . . . as if I had been a spayed cat that . . . she had 'attended to.'"

A Dakota layered and dyed cotton muslin skirt with tin jingle cones made from tobacco cans. *Courtesy of Minnesota Historical Society Collections*

CHAPTER 6

Fond du Lac Reservation

THE 1918 INFLUENZA SCOURGE killed Native American people living on reservations at four times the pace of people living in large cities, with the death toll for native people who contracted the flu reaching a staggering nine percent. Beginning October 1, 1918, nearly one in four Indians living on reservations, nationwide, came down with the virus.

One of those sufferers was an Ojibwe girl living near Mille Lacs Lake in east-central Minnesota. The Ojibwe people called the shallow, sprawling, sealike body of water Bde Watan, or Spirit Lake. The girl's father became distraught as his daughter grew sicker by the day. He sought a vision to save her life and, awaking from his dream, made a healing dress with jingling metal trim. He asked her to dance, using soft, springlike steps during which her feet never left the ground.

It worked. She grew stronger and continued to perform the special jingle dress dance—which spread from tribe to tribe to become a staple at the powwow celebrations across the continent a century later. Repurposed tin snuff lids were a popular source for the earliest jingles, with copper and other metals added as the ceremonies grew more elaborate.

The jingle dress origin story has been passed down among Ojibwe storytellers for ten decades. Brenda Child, an author and professor of American studies at the University of Minnesota, first heard the story on the Red Lake Reservation, about 150 miles north of Mille Lacs. Some of the oral history suggests the dress and dance originated even farther north, in Ontario. Analyzing old photographs, Child said the jingle dresses emerged just before 1920. With special songs and dances accompanying the jingle dresses, a new Ojibwe tradition sprang and spread from the 1918 flu outbreak, and the healing rituals were believed "to possess a strong therapeutic value," Child writes. Verifying oral history can be tricky, but Child insists it's "plausible that the first jingle dress dancer suffered from the widespread epidemic of Spanish Influenza during the time of World War I." She points to "an extensive body of evidence," including oral histories, photographs, and documents, that trace the jingle dress to the 1918 flu epidemic.

Yet while the virus devastated American Indians across the country, killing two percent of the nation's indigenous population, quite a different tale emerged as the wicked fires of October 12, 1918, roared in a southeastern direction from the train sparks near Brookston at Milepost 62.

Somehow, while hundreds of white immigrants were choking on smoky air and dying from the incomprehensible burns, none of the Ojibwe perished on the Fond du Lac Reservation that stood directly in the fire's path just north of Cloquet. "There was loss of life among the settlers, but the Indians seemed more fortunate or better able to take care of themselves," wrote George W. Cross in his official report six days after the fire. A Native American himself, Cross was the Fond du Lac Agency's superintendent and agent with the US Office of Indian Affairs. "Their keen wits saved them from perishing," according to Cloquet's *Pine Knot* newspaper.

The state forester, William Cox, said the Ojibwe enjoyed centuries of experience living in the area, making them more adept at dealing with woodland living and its periodic forest fires—something their new neighbors from Finland, Sweden, and Poland couldn't bank on. The ancestors of the Ojibwe had moved west from the Atlantic Coast roughly five hundred years earlier, creating thriving communities by the mid-1700s in what would become northern Minnesota a century later. With ample hunting territory, lakes teeming with wild rice and fish, and sugar bush camps tapping sweet syrup from the black and sugar maples, the Ojibwe flourished despite frequent wars with the Dakota people they displaced.

By 1918, Fond du Lac's band of one thousand members had nearly tripled since a census conducted in 1843. The hundred-thousand-acre Fond du Lac Reservation had been carved out along the St. Louis River following an 1854 treaty that saw the Ojibwe (or Chippewa) cede the Arrowhead-shaped corner of northeastern Minnesota in exchange for promises of cash annuities, or government assistance. The deal created three up-north reservations: Grand Portage, Nett Lake, and Fond du Lac.

When Congress passed the Dawes Allotment Act in 1887, reservation land could be parceled off for individual Indians—a practice that flew in the face of native people's communal traditions. Pretty soon, a patchwork quilt appeared, with white settlers buying Ojibwe parcels and then flipping them to lumber barons. "This was particularly true of Fond du Lac's northern border along the St. Louis River, where the railroad had been built, the timber cut, and the land settled by Finnish immigrants," according to the 1990 book *The Fires of Autumn* by Francis Carroll and Franklin Raiter.

Those immigrant settlers lived closer to the rail tracks, improving their chances of jumping on a rescue train to escape the heat and smoke. The Fond du Lac Ojibwe lived farther from the tracks yet found a way to survive—whether that meant jumping in rivers, paddling boats out into deep lakes, or fleeing before the fires got too close.

Grace Sheehy, an Ojibwe woman, faced the fire alone while her husband, Paul, was working the docks thirty miles east in Duluth on October 12. That's not counting their five children, ranging from eleven months to twelve years, raised on their hardscrabble farm on what everyone called the Duff Road about three miles south of the fire's origin in Brookston.

Noticing the growing intensity of the winds and the smoke, Grace walked up the road in the early afternoon to consult with the neighboring Christensens. By then, the wind was knocking trees down. Grace figured she couldn't make it back to the neighbors' farm with the kids, so she put on some old shoes and began shoveling a fire break.

At 3:30 PM, another tribal member, Mike Beargrease, showed up. The neighbors had sent him to help. He picked up the Sheehy's son while Grace wrapped the baby in mosquito netting. They made a dash for the Christensens', but flames leaped across the road. Retreating, they trudged a mile south toward the Twin Lakes by Charlie Cress's farm. From a hilltop near the lake, they looked back over their shoulders to the northwest. The fire was growing, spewing tongues of flame and pinecone sparks.

Just then, they found a boat on the banks of the western Twin Lake, and Beargrease paddled them to the lake's center. They stayed in the boat, watching the fire churn to the east toward Cloquet. At 8:00 PM, Beargrease paddled back to shore—but the grass and shrubs were smoldering. "We couldn't pull the boat up on the shore so we jumped out in the water and I handed him the children," Grace later testified.

By 9:00 PM, they joined several fire refugees at the Cress farm. Grace stayed there until Monday, when she made her way to Cloquet and reunited with her husband.

*

Betty Gurno was five years old when the fire tore through the Fond du Lac Reservation. But she recalled the fury nearly sixty years later. "It was horrid," she told local historian Dan Anderson in 1976. "Fire and me don't see eye to eye. I respect fire."

Her grandfather was a timber cruiser, riding a horse into the forests around Brookston to scout and fetch trees for the lumbermen. Realizing the fire had swelled out of control, he rushed to his daughter's house, hollering for four generations of his family to get in the St. Louis River. "So my mother, grandmother and great-grandmother, we all took blankets and some food and left everything else just as it was," Betty said.

They screamed to neighbors to follow them to the river. Her brothers stood waist-deep in the water, dunking blankets and trading them with the ones beneath which the family huddled. "They'd dry out as fast as they'd put them on," Betty said.

Nearby, a man and his son were splashing cold water on their kinfolk, too, when they heard shouts in the Ojibwe language—up the hill, through the smoke, by an old cemetery. Between the crackling roars of the fire, they could hear voices, screaming, "Come and help us, we're burning." By the time they scrambled up the hill to see who it was, nothing was left. Even the church by the cemetery had burned to the ground. "My grandmother always said that the dead were hollering," Betty said. "They were burning, too."

When the fire erupted on a Saturday, it found many people performing mundane autumn chores. Fond du Lac neighbors Frank

64

Houle and Joseph Petite, for example, were pulling things out of the ground. For Houle, that meant yanking tree stumps. He noticed thick smoke "along about half past three or four o'clock."

Petite, meanwhile had been "pulling [ruta]bagas and carrots and beets all day," he later testified. Just after four o'clock, he passed the church in Indian Village, the largest settlement on the reservation. "The sparks all fell over big as balls, some of them," Petite said. "You can see the fire flying all over us. The fire was right close to us, just a half mile away from us . . . and the wind was so strong that it caught up to us pretty near. . . . You could hear it crackling."

Frank Houle quit pulling tree stumps at his farm northwest of Indian Village sometime in the late afternoon. "Well, I didn't get any alarmed until the fire was on top of me," said Houle, whose wife had grown plenty alarmed. "Somewhere about a quarter to six, or half past five, she told me she wanted to go." He told her to go on to her sister-in-law's farm while he loaded the wagon and hitched his team of horses. As he left with a nephew, big chunks of fire were falling on the horses on the road to Cloquet. He took the family to the Great Northern Railway's water tower, unloaded his furniture by the church, and left his team of horses near the hay barn at Cloquet's Northern Lumber yard on a spit in the river known as Dunlap Island.

He recrossed the river, hopping over log booms, and met his wife on Posey's Island. Petite lost his house, barn, wagon, sleighs, furniture, clothing, feed, two pigs, a coop, and about fifty chickens. But the people survived.

"Fond du Lac Reservation devastated by fire," Cross, the Indian agent, said in a Western Union telegram sent to his bosses in Washington on October 13. "Office records and furniture burned. Loss of life not known. Wire five thousand dollars care First National Bank Duluth." In a longer letter typed on October 18, Cross told the commissioner of Indian Affairs that fifty-seven Indian homes were destroyed but "we have the situation well in hand." He said Fond du Lac tribal members were in hospitals on the reservation and in Duluth and Superior, while the Red Cross "generously aided us."

The government farm and barns had escaped the fire, said Cross. But the office and records all burned. "That leaves us in a very bad condition to do business," he typed. "But we are doing the very best we can giving our attention first to the lives of the Indians, and second to the care of the stock." He purchased flour and groceries for Fond du Lac refugees, along with feed for the surviving farm animals, beds, blankets, mattresses, and other household necessities.

He thanked his bosses for the quick $5,000 he had requested, saying, "It will help a great deal, but will not be sufficient." He asked for another $5,000 (about $90,000 in 2018 dollars). He'd use the money to pay for 50,000 feet of rough lumber and tar paper to construct small, twelve-by-twenty-foot shacks. Cross detailed the loss of livestock and feed as well as historically important Ojibwe crafts—from arrowheads to bows, tomahawks to beadwork. They'd also lost a large number of blankets, which fetched a good price from tourists.

Finally, Cross told his boss the good news: "We are very happy indeed to be able to report that the lives of all the Employees and Indians were saved."

He asked for two new Underwood typewriters for the offices from which he and his wife were working: one in Duluth and one at the Fond du Lac hospital. "I am going back and forth from Duluth to Cloquet every day looking after the care of the Indians," Cross told the brass in DC, adding a little play-by-play to grab their attention. "Tongues of flame would shoot out for a hundred yards and little tongues of fire were everywhere," he wrote. "It seemed the air was full of gas and explosions were occurring all over. . . . It was impossible to do anything other than try to save the lives of the people."

That letter, dated October 18, 1918, was addressed to the commissioner of Indian Affairs, in Washington, DC. Two Minnesotans were also in the nation's capital. One, an Ojibwe woman, was nursing the flu-stricken. The other, a Minneapolis lawyer, was testifying to Congress about possible pro-German disloyalty roiling the wartime patriotic fervor back in Minnesota.

CHAPTER 7

Washington, DC

THE MAWKISH AROMA hinted of rosemary and basil as Lutiant LaVoye rubbed the backs and chests of the sick soldiers with camphorated sweet oil. A nineteen-year-old Ojibwe from Roseau in far-northern Minnesota, Lutiant had been working twelve-hour shifts, 7:00 AM to 7:00 PM, for ten days, as a Red Cross–recruited volunteer nurse at the barracks at Camp Humphreys. The new cantonment, located in Virginia about twenty miles southeast of Washington, DC, was one of countless, hastily hammered-together military bases that sprung up in 1917 and '18 after the United States entered the Great War.

With segregated black troops doing the brunt of the hard labor, swampy and forested land in Fairfax County was cleared and 790 temporary, wood-frame buildings went up in eleven months to house twenty thousand men. By the fall of 1918, four thousand of those soldiers had contracted the flu. More than a third of those cases proved deadly.

"As many as 90 people die every day here with the 'Flu,'" Lutiant wrote in a letter dated October 17, 1918, to a friend named Louise back at her boarding school in Nebraska. "Soldiers, too, are dying by the dozen." She sat down to write the letter in her room at a new brick boardinghouse at 213 Fourteenth Street Southeast in Washington, a mile due east of the capitol. After ten days at Camp Humphreys, "where we volunteered to help nurse sick soldiers with influenza," Lutiant was exhausted. "We had intended on staying much longer than we did," she wrote. "But the work was entirely too hard for us . . . so we came home to rest up a bit." She had already volunteered again to help the Red Cross, hoping to be assigned to Potomac Park in Washington, where the death toll was climbing among three hundred sick soldiers. "I might find myself there before the week is ended," she wrote, intimately recalling details of the "pitiful" October she'd endured.

During her day shifts, Lutiant was assigned three or four patients to care for in various wards. She gave medicine, took temperatures, fixed ice packs, and rubbed ailing soldiers' backs or chests "with camphorated sweet oils." Two of the officers under her care constantly moaned for their wives before they died. After two others died, that meant four soldiers has sucked their last breath as she watched, helplessly, during her first six days at the base. "I was right in the wards alone with them each time," she wrote, "and Oh! the first one that died sure unnerved me—I had to go to the nurses' quarters and cry it out."

She quickly hardened. "The other three were not as bad," she confided, still rattled. "Really, Louise, orderlies carried the dead soldiers out on stretchers at the rate of two every three hours for the first two days [we] were there. It is such a horrible thing."

Brenda Child, the professor and author at the University of Minnesota, unearthed Lutiant's seven-page letter at the National Archives nearly a century after it was written. Calling it "an important historical document of the global epidemic," Child included the entire letter in her 2014 book, *My Grandfather's Knocking Sticks*. "Lutiant spent weeks in the thick of the global pandemic," Child wrote. "She is a terrific writer, blending humor easily with incredibly serious and vivid descriptions of the epidemic's toll on the people who are living, and dying."

Child draws parallels between Lutiant's nursing and the dream-spurred vision of the jingle dress and dance that a sick daughter back near Lake Mille Lacs used to combat the same deadly virus—both examples of the "deep-rooted traditions of healing among Ojibwe women." Child's gumshoe detective research—scouring census logs and school records—breathed new life into an otherwise forgotten character. She learned that Lutiant Ruth Verne LaVoye was born in

1899 on the border of the Red Lake Reservation in Roseau, Minnesota, just south of Canada.

Watching soldiers die from the flu was far from her first exposure to heartache. The oldest of four children, Lutiant was five or six years old when her mother died. Records show an infant baby died five months after their mother. Lutiant's father was a French Canadian laborer, but census rolls refer to her as "Indian," meaning her mother was Ojibwe, the dominant tribe in northern Minnesota. When her mother died, Lutiant went to live with an uncle on the White Earth Indian Reservation in northwestern Minnesota, where she attended white public schools before enrolling for three years at St. Benedict's Academy, a Catholic enclave 160 miles southeast in St. Joseph.

She was then sent to Indian boarding schools in Nebraska and Kansas. Both were part of a network of more than sixty such schools, dating back to 1860, intended to "civilize" indigenous children as part of a "Kill the Indian, Save the Man" assimilation policy. Along the way, Lutiant studied French, Latin, and music, "but never learned to speak the Indian language of my tribe or any other tribe," she wrote in an autobiographical essay kept in her school file. "I have always had a great desire of becoming an efficient stenographer, to live on my own resources, and to be independent."

Lutiant graduated in June 1918 from the Haskell Institute, a notorious boarding school in Lawrence, Kansas, where tiny handcuffs were used to restrain students resisting their forced assimilation. That dark history provided context to the letter, written four months after graduating, to her friend Louise back at Haskell.

In the opening lines, Lutiant wrote: "So everybody has the 'Flu' at Haskell?" She then "wished to goodness Miss Keck and Mrs. McK. would get it and die with it. Really, it would be such a good riddance, and not much lost either!" Boarding school censors took umbrage with those words, prompting a deeply apologetic letter from Lutiant, according to Haskell records reviewed by Child. By then, Lutiant moved on to Washington, where she referred to herself as a "war-worker" at the Interior Department. She was likely doing office work toward her stenography goals.

In addition to her firsthand account of aiding flu patients, Lutiant's October 17 letter gives a glimpse at that dire time in the nation's capital. "All the schools, churches, theaters, dancing halls, etc., closed here," she wrote. She told her friend about her walk to work at the Interior Department, passing the capitol and the War Department. The Washington Monument, the 555-foot-tall obelisk that opened thirty years before, "is within walking distance . . . and we walked there last evening after work," she wrote, saying she had hoped to ride the elevator to "look over the city . . . but the place was closed temporarily, on account of this 'Flu.'"

Portrait of Lutiant LaVoye printed in *The Indian Leader*, publication of the Haskell Institute. *Records of the Bureau of Indian Affairs, 1793–1999; Red Lake Agency: Photographs, 1910–65, National Archives and Records Administration*

She went on to describe the relatively new sight of airplanes flying over the city "at all hours of the day now, and sometimes so low that one can hear the noise of the machine." Add that to the chaos of wartime, with "hundreds of soldiers, sailors, Marines, French 'Blue Devils,' and even the National band of Italy here in Washington." Throw in celebrities— such as opera diva Geraldine Farrar and swashbuckling moving picture star Douglas Fairbanks, both drumming up patriotic fervor and selling a million dollars of war bonds to finance the battles in Europe—and it was an eventful time for a teenager in the nation's capital.

In the middle of her letter to Louise, Lutiant included a possibly far-fetched tidbit: "Two German spies, posing as doctors, were caught giving these influenza germs to the soldiers," she wrote. "They were shot last Saturday morning at sunrise." There's no documented account of such an execution, but there are verified cases of government officials planting stories in newspapers linking the flu outbreak with German spies, delivered by U-boat submarines, launching a chemical attack by unleashing Spanish influenza germs.

In an October 13 letter, published a week later in the *New York Times*, a reader named Alfred M. Brooks from Bloomington, Indiana, suggested calling the spreading influenza "the German plague." He wrote, "Why give it the name of a respectable nation such as Spain?"

theorizing that the "epidemic had not swept from place to place from a given point like epidemics do usually." By "breaking out simultaneously in army bases from the Atlantic to the Pacific," it must have been "of German sowing," the letter writer insisted, "another of the Germans' barbarous methods of warfare. . . . Let every child learn to associate what is accursed with the word German not in the spirit of hate but in the spirit of contempt born of the hateful truth which Germany has proved herself to be."

Even Bayer aspirin, made in the United States under a German-held patent, was suspected to be somehow tainted with the flu. The anti-German paranoia was so widespread the Justice Department deputized two hundred thousand members of a volunteer group called the American Protective League to root out disloyalty—be it among slackers failing to buy enough war bonds or anyone speaking out against the draft or the war effort.

One Minnesotan embodied the over-the-top patriotic loyalty crusade more than any. His name was John Franklin McGee. A stout man with a moon face, bald head, and delicate wire-rimmed glasses, he was Minnesota's precursor counterpart to anti-communist witch-hunting senator Joe McCarthy of Wisconsin a generation later. A close ally of Governor Joseph A. A. Burnquist, who was up for reelection in 1918, McGee was a Minneapolis lawyer whom the governor had appointed to the new Minnesota Commission of Public Safety. The powerful wartime panel was created in the spring of 1917 to bolster the war effort through bond sales—and by stomping out disloyalty. If civil rights of free speech and assembly were jeopardized in the process, McGee had few qualms.

Born in Amboy, Illinois, on the first day of 1861, McGee was fifty-seven years old when he marched into a Senate committee meeting room in Washington to testify in the spring of 1918. He'd come a long way. McGee's father, Hugh, had emigrated from Ireland in 1850 and worked as a railroad mechanic. The younger McGee's formal schooling ended with an Amboy High School degree when he was twenty, but he'd already started studying law in the office of a local attorney. He earned admission to the Illinois bar before he turned twenty-two.

He moved west to become a prosecuting attorney in Devils Lake in the Dakota Territory, honing his skills with criminal cases. He moved to Minneapolis in 1887, still in his mid-twenties, and soon created an

John F. McGee, patriotic zealot and member of the Minnesota Commission of Public Safety. *Courtesy of Minnesota Historical Society Collections*

independent practice with some big-time clients—including the Chicago and Great Western Railroad and several grain elevator companies. Before he turned forty, McGee was appointed a judge in Minnesota's fourth judicial district. Although he was elected to a full six-year term, he left the bench early to practice law again.

Most Irish Americans opposed US intervention in the Great War. After all, the Irish were battling against Great Britain's rule, so siding with the British in war was hard for many Irish to stomach. Not McGee. He displayed no interest in Irish American causes such as Irish independence. He was a rabid supporter of the Allied cause, and by 1918 the immigrant railroad worker's son was hanging out amid the Minneapolis elite as a member of the Minneapolis Club and the city's Civic and Commerce Association. He was also tapped by the governor to administer the state's fuel consumption during wartime—another powerful appointment that prompted one historian to call him "the state's coal czar."

Although McGee would inflame the debate countless times, he blustered some of his most outspoken comments to Congress on Wednesday, April 19, 1918. Testifying before the Senate Committee on Military Affairs, McGee strode to the lectern to champion a bill that would shift the venue of trials for those accused of sedition from civilian to military courts. He clearly thought the regular courts weren't taking traitors seriously enough, and he first set his sights on the nation's legal brass. "The United States Department of Justice in Minnesota has been a ghastly failure," McGee told the senators. He went on to describe the US district attorney in Minnesota like this: "patriotic but he lacks a fighting stomach."

McGee was just warming up. He went on to attack the populist farmers organizing out of the Dakotas under the banner of the Nonpartisan League—which had tapped Congressman Charles Lindbergh, father of the future flier, to challenge Burnquist for the Republican gubernatorial nomination. McGee viewed the Nonpartisan League as radicals trying to topple America's power structure—just like the Bolsheviks had done to the tsar in Russia. "A Non-Partisan League lecturer is a traitor every time," McGee barked to the Senate committee. "Where we made a mistake was in not establishing a firing squad in the first days of the war."

Senators must have looked up or coughed.

"We should now get busy and have that firing squad working overtime," McGee ranted on. "Wait until the long casualty lists begin to come in and the Minnesota woods will not be dense enough to hide the traitors who will meet punishment for their crimes."

McGee promptly zeroed in his attack on Minnesota's newly arrived and growing group of immigrants from Scandinavia and Germany, including those in New Ulm who had been debating the draft and asking whether it was fair to have Minnesota's German-born soldiers fighting their childhood neighbors in the trenches of France. To McGee, anyone questioning the draft was disloyal at best—a spy at worst. "These men who are fighting our soldiers and stabbing them in the back are going to die," he predicted. "The disloyal element in Minnesota is largely among the German-Swedish people. . . . The nation blundered at the start of the war," McGee insisted, "in not dealing severely with these vipers."

The backlash to those comments swept from Washington back to Minnesota—where Burnquist's reelection bid didn't need alienating accusations from his patriotism point man. Burnquist, after all, was a child of Swedish-born parents. In Otter Tail County, a Republican voter complained to Republican senator Knute Nelson that McGee was "doing more to promote the union of the farmer & labor vote" than the Nonpartisan League. One of McGee's fellow Public Safety commissioners, a former governor named John Lind, called his statements to the Senate "bitter and unreasoning." The nation's top lawyer, attorney general Thomas Gregory, wrote in a letter to Lind that McGee, "while in Washington . . . did a great injustice to the people of your state."

Nanny Mattson Jaeger, a leader in the Scandinavian Woman Suffrage Association, complained that McGee had besmirched her group's members. She received assurances from Henry Libby, another of McGee's fellow commissioners and the secretary of the Public Safety panel. Libby told her he was "positive" that McGee would have a good explanation when he returned to Minnesota from Washington. Perhaps he'd been misquoted. Accounts of his testimony included some minor differences, but the essence of his statements about traitors and firing squads was consistently reported.

McGee, returning home, didn't backpedal much. He acknowledged calling Chisago County, northeast of St. Paul, a "Swedish" and Brown

County, with its New Ulm seat, a "German" one. Both regions, McGee insisted, were teeming with disloyalty—adding that reporters took his statements out of context. As for the firing squads, McGee stood by his guns, saying such executioners would have "a most-restraining influence on the disloyal, seditious and traitorous."

In a letter to the Scandinavian suffrage leader, Libby asked her to cut McGee some slack because of his family's sacrifices to the war effort. After all, two of McGee's sons were fighting in France and his daughter was serving as a nurse at the Great War battlefields.

New Ulm city attorney Albert Pfaender. *Courtesy of the Brown County Historical Society*

New Ulm mayor Dr. Louis Fritsche. *Courtesy of the Brown County Historical Society*

CHAPTER 8

New Ulm

THEY WERE TWO OF NEW ULM'S ELITE. And they were squarely in the sights of John McGee since he became Minnesota's "loyalty enforcer" in the weeks after the United States entered the Great War in early April 1917.

Albert Pfaender was the square-jawed and handsome city attorney, a former state legislator and the son of Wilhem Pfaender—one of the German immigrants who founded the city in 1854 along a double-terraced bluff overlooking the Minnesota River. Pfaender's brother-in-law, Dr. Louis Fritsche, was one of the state's first licensed physicians. He'd studied medicine in Germany and married into the Pfaender clan. When the war started, he was New Ulm's popular mayor.

By the time McGee was done with them, both the mayor and the city attorney would be ousted from their elected positions. McGee painted New Ulm and its leaders as a breeding ground of pro-German disloyalty. In May 1917, McGee warned that "in centers of population strongly German . . . drilling is going on preparatory to resisting the draft." He no doubt felt vindicated when Pfaender and Fritsche organized a meeting of ten thousand citizens at New Ulm's Turner Hall in July to lobby for a provision to prevent German American soldiers from fighting directly against Germans. After that, McGee's wording grew more pointed: "You're a traitor and ought to be stood up against a wall and shot," he told Pfaender.

The clash between McGee and New Ulm's top elected officials illustrates just how zealous the state became in the tug-of-war between a justifiable quest for national unity and the trampling of basic freedoms. McGee's close ally, Governor Joseph A. A. Burnquist, described that balancing act, and revealed some inherent contradictions, when he wrote in February 1918: "While the right of free speech must be given the fullest respect and loyal and lawful meetings should be given full protection, everything possible must be done to prevent and punish all seditious utterances." Minnesota historian Carl Chrislock, perhaps the leading expert on McGee and the Minnesota Commission of Public Safety, points out the irony behind the New Ulm imbroglio: "The war to guarantee democracy throughout the world had created an atmosphere that discouraged democratic liberties at home."

To fully appreciate the Constitution-juggling atmosphere that engulfed Minnesota in 1918, it helps to roll back the clock a bit. In the summer of 1914, New Ulm's mayor, Dr. Fritsche, traveled to Germany after presenting a paper on public sanitation and health at an international municipal conference in London. Following a stop in Paris, where he checked out water filtration systems and garbage collection, Fritsche returned to his motherland to visit friends and relatives where he'd earlier studied medicine.

Just then, Europe slipped into war as England, France, Russia, and others took to the battlefield to squelch Kaiser Wilhelm II's land-grabbing, empire-stretching designs on the continent. With aircrafts and poison gas being incorporated into warfare for the first time, the Great War would soon become the planet's bloodiest since a Chinese civil war known as the Taiping Rebellion claimed an estimated twenty million lives fifty years earlier. Fritsche, the good doctor from New Ulm, found himself in the thick of things when World War I began. "Looking up my distant relatives in Saxony," he said, "I found that nine of my second cousins had gone to the front and the tenth one was about to leave."

When the mayor returned to New Ulm a month later, the Second Regiment Band welcomed him home. He spoke to townsfolk a couple of weeks later at Turner Hall, squarely blaming Russia, England, and France for the bloodshed. They were jealous of Germany's growing trade power and were simply out for revenge. "Germany is fighting for its very existence," Fritsche said. "But every citizen of the Empire knows that they are fighting for a just cause and are convinced they will win."

Fritsche's mayoral office was promptly decorated with maps and photographs of Germany and postcards from German soldiers. He and the people of New Ulm—nearly all of whom were either born in Germany or descended from its emigrants—closely followed newspaper accounts of the war. Many of the town's churches and schools continued to use German as the preferred language.

Jumping ahead to the spring of 1917: when President Woodrow Wilson presented his case for war to Congress, he insisted the battle would be waged against Germany's imperial government, not against the German people and its culture. Just as the US Congress was voting to enter the Great War, Minnesota's legislature was in the final days of its 1917 session. During this session, state lawmakers decided to put a state constitutional amendment prohibiting alcohol before the voters on their 1918 ballots. They also passed a child welfare act.

But a bill establishing a Minnesota Commission of Public Safety dominated the session's final days. Although it would be another week before Congress voted to go to war, Minnesota state senator George H. Sullivan introduced a bill on March 31, 1917, calling for the creation of a seven-man commission to ensure public safety during wartime. The panel would include Governor Burnquist, Attorney General Lyndon Smith, and five others, to be appointed by the governor. The bill granted the new panel the "power to do all acts and things non-inconsistent" with the state and federal constitutions to ensure public safety and protect "life and public and private property." This included "all acts and things necessary or proper so that the military, civil and industrial resources of the state may be most efficiently applied toward maintenance of the defense of the state and nation toward the successful prosecution of . . . war."

On April 10—just days after the United States went to war—the Minnesota state senate unanimously approved the bill creating the Commission of Public Safety; the state house of representatives approved it two days later, with just one dissenting vote. Burnquist signed it into law on the sixteenth and appointed the commissioners.

In its lifespan of nearly two years, the commission accomplished

The Minnesota Commission of Public Safety, circa 1918: (left to right) A. C. Weiss, Thomas E. Cashman, Henry W. Libby, Governor Joseph A. A. Burnquist, Clifford L. Hilton, Ambrose Tighe, Charles Hoyt March, John F. McGee. *Courtesy of Minnesota Historical Society Collections*

several practical services—doling out food, controlling wartime prices, and conserving fuel. But determining who was loyal and who wasn't became its defining role to the point of obsession. The state hired nearly six hundred undercover agents to spy on citizens in hotels and saloons, where they craned their necks to hear any whispers of disloyalty. The new panel even issued an edict in June 1917 limiting saloon hours to four a day, with no women allowed and no "dancing or cabaret performances." Although not directly targeting Germans, the measures struck at the crux of the German beer garden culture.

And the heavily German community of New Ulm soon provided the first major battlefield in the war within the war—the skirmish between national unity and personal freedom.

John McGee wasn't a legislator, but he helped shape the safety commission bill as a sort of lobbyist for patriotism. He was particularly pleased with the $2 million appropriation to finance the panel (roughly $36 million in 2018 dollars). And he was proud of the new commission's bite, saying it had teeth that were "eighteen inches long," in correspondence with Knute Nelson, the seventy-four-year-old Republican US senator, former governor, and Civil War veteran who'd been in Congress since the 1880s. "If the governor appoints men who have a backbone," McGee wrote to Nelson, "treason will not be talked on the streets of this city and the street corner orators, who denounce the government, advocate revolution, denounce the army and advise against enlistments, will be looking through the barbed fences of an internment camp on the prairie somewhere."

Governor Burnquist tapped McGee for one of the five appointed slots on the commission, and McGee's strong, vitriolic personality would come to alienate other original appointees. That included John Lind, the former governor, who quit in early 1918 because he couldn't stand McGee. The commission's makeup also drew instant fire from organized labor because no union men were appointed to the group of lawyers and businessmen.

The commission quickly issued a litmus test for loyalty, saying that in wartime it came down to whether "a man is wholeheartedly for the war and subordinates everything else to its successful prosecution." The law enacting the commission gave it the right to "require any person to appear before it or before any agent or officer of such commission for examination."

In New Ulm and its surrounding Brown County, German Americans were torn between their ancestral roots and their adopted homeland. Among the forty-one soldiers from Brown County who died during the war were men named Mecklenburg, Schlumpberger, Frantz, and Goltz, but most of the people in and around New Ulm "refused to regard the war as a holy crusade against the forces of evil," according to Chrislock. "To them it was an unpleasant enterprise of dubious origin" that should be concluded quickly.

With US involvement in the war looming, a group of a thousand people gathered in New Ulm on March 30, 1917. They affirmed their loyalty to the United States but spoke out against joining the war. They wanted a referendum put before voters to determine whether the nation should join the Allies on the battlefields of Europe.

No doubt word of this meeting drifted up to McGee. Behind his tight wire-rimmed glasses, McGee eyed New Ulm from the beginning. And with the overthrow of Tsar Nicholas II of Russia by Bolsheviks later that year, McGee's loyalty crusade turned toward the working classes. As a lawyer for big railroads and a member of the Minneapolis Club, McGee viewed the labor organizing on the Iron Range and in the Twin Cities as a threat to the economic security of the ruling class.

Political upheaval wasn't merely a faraway thing happening in Russia. The streetcars, which seemed to stop on every Twin Cities corner, were torn apart by a transit strike engulfing the Twin City Rapid Transit Company in late 1917.

When streetcar workers asked for a three-penny hourly raise, they were told, "No," by Horace Lowry—the rich son of city elder and transit company founder Thomas Lowry. A union was quickly formed, national organizers flooded in, and Lowry fired union leaders. When a strike began after midnight on October 6, 1917, thousands of picketers swarmed into St. Paul streets, crippling streetcar service. Governor Burnquist sent in five hundred federal soldiers from Fort Snelling, equipped with bayonets and rifles, to break up the strike. McGee's fledgling Public Safety Commission leaped into the chaos. Making demands, unionizing, striking—it wasn't helping morale during this time of war, commissioners argued. "This is not a convenient time for agitation about abstract principles like Unionism or non-Unionism," the commission said in an order.

Further violence erupted on December 2 as more than two thousand union supporters gathered near Wabasha and Seventh Streets in downtown St. Paul. "Cries of scab were heard as the street cars with difficulty made their way through the packed streets," the *Pioneer Press* reported. "Then someone threw a brick through the window of a car on Wabasha Street and the pent up energy of the rioters broke loose." Burnquist again sent in troops—this time, his newly organized state Home Guards. McGee likely encouraged the governor's stern actions. After all, McGee had the governor's ear.

The suppression of dissent had been under way for months by this point. In the summer of 1917, when a newly formed antiwar group, the People's Council of America for Democracy and Peace, chose two large tents in Minneapolis's Minnehaha Park for its first meeting, Burnquist barred it from gathering anywhere in Minnesota because he said it would jeopardize public order.

As a June 5 deadline to register for the draft approached, McGee turned his focus back to New Ulm—specifically the *New Ulm Review*. The liberal-leaning weekly had spoken out against attacks on German culture and wartime stifling of Americans' rights to gather and voice dissent. The *Review* further came out in support of a proposal from congressman Frederick Britten of Illinois to exempt German American draftees from fighting overseas. The weekly said sending German American soldiers to the trenches across from German soldiers would be akin to attacking "the breast that nourished them or their fathers."

On Monday, July 23, 1917, New Ulm conducted a lottery to see who would be tapped to fulfill its quota of 156 draftees. With that lottery fueling the debate over Britten's provision, a huge anti-draft rally was scheduled for Wednesday night, July 25, at New Ulm's Turner Park. Nearly ten thousand people showed up.

Mayor Louis Fritsche, the German-trained town doctor, called the meeting to order and insisted the gathering was not intended "to cause any disaffection of the draft law." Instead, he wanted to send a message to Congress and President Wilson that they shouldn't "force those drafted to fight in Europe against their will." As petitions circulated making that point, Fritsche surrendered the podium to his brother-in-law, former legislator and New Ulm city attorney Albert Pfaender.

Congress, Pfaender told the gathering, has the power to draft men to thwart invasions, but he questioned the constitutionality of a draft to send men overseas to fight. Far from spouting revolutionary ideas or advocating draft dodging, Pfaender urged all men called up to faithfully report for service. "Nothing can be gained by resisting the draft," he told the crowd. "It is the duty of these men to respond promptly when called."

Meanwhile, he said, the petitions should be sent to Washington in hopes of tinkering with the draft law so only volunteers would be sent to fight against Germans. "Have we in this country had any more right than the people in Germany in making this war?" the city attorney asked. "If we have no quarrel with them, if they are our brothers, why then should we be commanded to kill them?" The Constitution, Pfaender insisted, "does not provide, not even permit, men to be taken across the border unless they are willing to go on their own free will and accord."

Another speaker that night, Adolph Ackermann, president of New Ulm's Dr. Martin Luther College, further riled up the crowd by saying, "We don't want to fight for Wall Street, England or France. If they tell us it is a war for humanity, they better create humanity in our own country first." He then brought up the recent killings of black men near St. Louis and poor working conditions across the country.

As word of the meeting spread, New Ulm was cast as a cesspool of pro-German disloyalty. "It will take New Ulm a quarter of a century to live down the infamy with which it has been stamped by these traitors," said St. Paul Democrat Daniel Lawler, a popular Irish candidate for several statewide offices.

The *Princeton (Minnesota) Union* newspaper flashed back five decades and brought up New Ulm's gritty stand against so-called Sioux fighters in two battles during the bloody, six-week US–Dakota War of 1862—when German immigrants withstood Little Crow's advances but much of New Ulm burned. After the massive draft meeting in New Ulm in 1917, Princeton's editor said, "there are those who regret the Sioux did not do a better job fifty-five years ago."

McGee and his three-month-old Public Safety Commission now had a target for its anti-German wrath. It issued a statement that charged New Ulm "ringleaders" with orchestrating a "cunning, but futile effort to observe the letter of the law while outraging its spirit." Fritsche, Pfaender, and others had "excited responsive enthusiasm in their audience" by portraying drafted German Americans as "martyrs dragged to an unjust fate by a tyrannical and cruel government."

Governor Burnquist himself jumped on the pile, calling the New Ulm rally "unpatriotic and un-American" because it painted the draft as "unjust and illegal." The governor said, "The intended effect was to interfere with the plan of the United States government in the raising of its army and in the prosecution of the war."

Burnquist didn't wait for the Public Safety Commission to complete its investigation. He promptly suspended Mayor Fritsche, city attorney Pfaender, and Brown County auditor Louis Vogel. Vogel had merely led a parade, with American flags, to the park before the meeting. He would later be reinstated. "It is an appalling situation when a county auditor . . . encourages and even leads a procession of drafted malcontents," according to a Public Safety Commission statement. "And when the mayor and city attorney of one of the most prosperous cities in the Minnesota valley openly promotes pro-German propaganda." The commission's statement continued, "Pfaender was particularly incendiary . . . perverting the president's declaration that this country had no quarrel with the German people."

After Burnquist slapped the brothers-in-law, Fritsche and Pfaender, with suspension, they submitted their resignations to the New Ulm City Council. On a recommendation from the Public Safety Commission, however, the resignations were not accepted. McGee and his panel wanted their pound of flesh, and this was their moment to flex new jurisdictional muscle. Weeklong hearings followed, with commissioners grilling twenty witnesses. They brought up Fritsche's 1914 trip to Germany and his friendship with German consul Hans von Grunow.

In early December, four months after the draft rally, Burnquist formally canned New Ulm's mayor and city attorney. "Instead of inspiring the drafted men to patriotically do their duties for the cause of God and their country," the governor said, "they were pictured as martyrs. Intoxicated by the success of the meeting, other meetings were organized in neighboring villages."

He got that right. After the July meeting uproar, Pfaender and others kept speaking out at rallies in towns neighboring New Ulm: Nicollet, Henderson, Gaylord, Glencoe, and Gibbon. All the while, the hired spies of the Public Safety Commission tracked the so-called New Ulm ringleaders, even persuading officials in Gibbon to deny a permit for their rally. "I have enough fight in me to show the Commission that we can hold a meeting tonight," Pfaender said. They moved the meeting to a field just outside the city limits and attracted more than five thousand people. Pfaender and others addressed the crowd from atop a hayrack illuminated by a lantern.

Borrowing a page from the New Ulm dissenters' playbook, the Public Safety Commission organized a rally of its own in September 1917. The so-called Dedication Day festivities honored departing draftees in downtown New Ulm. Burnquist served as the keynote speaker, decrying Germany as the blackest force in the world and championing America's cause to democratize Europe and free it from the autocratic rule of the kaiser. Among the speakers that day was a Democratic politician named Julius Coller, a businessman imported from Shakopee. "I am of German blood," Coller said. "Prior to 1917 I yielded to no man in the earnestness of my hope that the German eagles should emerge supreme in the conflict across the sea. But the call of blood, strong

Recruits from Brown County march through New Ulm on their way to Camp Dodge for training, September 21, 1917. *Courtesy of the Brown County Historical Society*

though it may be, sinks into insignificance when there comes the call of my own, native land."

If the people of New Ulm were conflicted over a war pitting their new land against their mother country, if they grew weary of enduring the nationalist zealotry of McGee and his ilk, telegrams kept cutting through the controversies to remind everyone what was at stake.

"We deeply regret to inform you that it is officially reported that corporal Benjamin J. Seifert, aero squadron, died of aeroplane accident, April 2." That telegram, from Adjutant General M. C. Cain to Kate and Christian Seifert, arrived in Milford Township west of New Ulm at the end of the first week of April 1918. Benjamin was their tenth child. He would be the first of forty-one residents of Brown County to die from the Great War. Some of those men died on the battlefield. Many succumbed to the influenza outbreak.

Benjamin Seifert died while repairing a plane at the American aviation camp in Scampton, England. A low-flying plane suddenly dropped over him and one of the wings penetrated his body. Seifert, the pilot of the crashed plane, and another man doing repairs all died instantly.

"So you know at least there was no suffering," wrote a Red Cross spokesman in Washington, W. R. Castle, in a letter to the Seiferts. Castle went on to say that Benjamin's commanding officer told a Red Cross worker that "he thought most highly of Seifert; that he considered him to be one of the best men in the organization and that in the past he had relied upon him in every way. . . . This, I know, you will be glad to hear, because it will show you that your son not only died in the course of duty, but that his excellent performance of duty had enabled him to do such good work that he was respected by his officers." Castle concluded his letter by saying, "The American Red Cross had a beautiful spray of flowers put on each coffin and nothing was omitted that would possibly have been done in the way the family would have wanted it done. As soon as the graves are in order photographs will be taken and sent to us to forward to you."

After the war, in 1920, Kate and Christian Seifert would have Benjamin's body exhumed from the graveyard in England so his remains could be buried at the New Ulm Catholic cemetery. The Seiferts, by then, had been in Brown County for about seventy years. The German family had emigrated from what was Bohemia, now the Czech Republic, in the 1850s. As ethnic Germans living in Bohemia, land was hard to come by. Fields behind houses in their village of Jivany were the only opportunities for farming. The Seiferts came to early Minnesota to avoid conscription in the army and to find sufficient farmland for their large families. If they sought peace, they didn't find it. When the US–Dakota War started in 1862, patriarch Johann Seifert entered in the Cottonwood Company, joining settlers in the second battle to secure New Ulm.

More than five decades later, the family again was confronted by war. Benjamin had just turned twenty-three, in March 1918, a few weeks before his death at the airfield. Born on the Milford Township farm in 1895, he graduated from local public schools and took an auto mechanics class in Minneapolis before landing a job in a garage. He then went to Mankato Commercial College, which led to jobs as a wholesale grocer and as a bank teller. Work sent him to Montana and Valley City, North Dakota, where he kept the books, collected bills, and got drafted. After driving a truck for a few weeks at Fort Dodge, Iowa, he was sent to England and promoted to the aviation service. According to the *New Ulm Review*'s front-page story on April 10, 1918, a letter from Benjamin to his family had arrived two weeks earlier, saying he had arrived safely in England.

"News of the son's death so shortly afterwards came as a thunderbolt from a clear sky and Mr. Seifert and the rest of the family are simply prostrated with grief.

The Seifert family, circa 1914. Benjamin Seifert, who died during World War I, is seated at the far left.
Courtesy of Dr. Ellen Vancura

"He was a cheery young fellow," the newspaper reported, "whose going leaves a dreadful vacancy in the family circle that no one can fill."

CHAPTER 9

Kettle River

THREE FINNISH WOMEN lived together in the little town of Kettle River when the fires swept through northeastern Minnesota's Carlton County in 1918.

Hanna Leppa was a dressmaker, widowed at thirty-six. Her daughter, Ailie, had just turned sixteen and was five months into her job as an operator at the Kettle River Telephone Exchange, known as "Central." The phone company installed a switchboard right in their home. To earn a few more dollars on top of what came in from the dresses and the call center, the Leppas took in a boarder, nineteen-year-old Lydia Salmi. Lydia's father, John, had been among the original Finnish homesteading farmers who came to the area in the late 1880s and founded the Lutheran church in nearby Kalevala.

By 1918, nearly thirty thousand Finns were living in Minnesota, more than half of whom resided up north. Why? Cheap farmland, logging and mining jobs, and, perhaps, the frigid winters, deep snow, glacial lakes, and rock-strewn fields reminded them of their ancestral, Finnish homeland. Ailie and Lydia were members of the second generation of Finns in the area, most of whom settled north of the east-west Brown Road that divided Carlton County.

Ailie was working the switchboard on October 12, 1918. Since the phone company installed the call-routing machinery, she was considered "on duty" around the clock. There had been fires all through the hot, dry summer—kicked up by the coal-burning engines' sparks along the Soo Line Railroad. But this was different. Ailie could tell by the frequency of the frantic calls. "The telephone lines were swamped with calls from residents, pleading for assistance," she recalled in a 1976 letter. "Soon the entire neighborhood was in panic and confusion."

Around 6:00 PM that Saturday, the sky outside her window gray with smoke and flickering with debris, she answered another call. It was the cashier at the local Farmers State Bank, John Mattson, urging her to come to the bank. Not only could he store possessions in the bank's basement, but he had a man with a truck who could take them the seven miles to Moose Lake.

Lydia, Ailie's friend and housemate, was working as a clerk at Michaelsons' general merchandise store in downtown Kettle River. "The sky was red and it was starting to get real dark," Lydia remembered fifty years later. "No sun."

John Michaelson, her popular merchant boss, began hauling stuff—clothing, valuables, and even some dynamite—to his sister's house a mile away. He figured the big farmhouse, surrounded by fields, would be safer than the bank space Mattson offered. Michaelson's wife had gone to Duluth with her baby for a weekend visit. Michaelson left the store in the hands of Lydia and his son, Ralph, who at fourteen was five years younger than his coworker.

About 4:00 PM, Lydia leaned out the door of the general store. A girl across the street, who worked at Wilson's market, said they were heading to Moose Lake. "She told me people were packing trunks and suitcases and taking them to the bank building basement."

Ralph Michaelson and Lydia put the money from the till and the store's stack of important paperwork into the vault before they decided to shut things down. Ralph wrote a letter to his parents and slid it into the vault. "It was blowing so hard the whole building seemed to sway," Lydia remembered. Lydia said good-bye to Ralph and dashed home to pack her suitcase.

When she got to her boarding room at the Leppa house, Ailie was frantically trying to make phone connections for people searching for family members or thirsting for the latest news on the fires. Lydia and Hanna urged Ailie to give up the switchboard. She had done a phenomenal job all day, fielding the frenzied calls. But now it was time to think of herself, her mother, and her housemate friend. Fueled by adrenaline, the three women hauled out heavy furniture, Hanna's sewing machine, and a new heater. Any men who could have helped had scattered early in the day to fight the fires. "I don't know how we managed," Lydia would later say.

They packed what they could in suitcases, put on heavy winter coats with white cape collars, and scurried to the bank. "There sure was a lot of stuff there—trunks and bags," Lydia said. "We were standing outside, figuring out what to do." That's when John Mattson, the banker, hollered for them to pile into Leonard Lofback's pickup truck. Leonard had been fighting fires all day and would take them to Moose Lake.

Hanna Leppa rode in the front seat. A twenty-two-year-old schoolteacher from Ely, Ida Hiipakka; one of her students, thirteen-year-old Stella Paapanen; and Stella's mom, Ida, crammed in the back seat with Ailie and Lydia. Some other men and boys jumped on the truck's bed. "We were terribly frightened," Ailie said. "The area at that time was covered with virgin timber and we could see the horizon to the south, like a sea of flame, moving very rapidly towards Moose Lake."

Leonard stopped to pick up more people on the way. A Finnish woman name Aho cradled a baby in her arms. Their car had stalled; they pleaded for help. Now with ten people in the truck, Leonard floored it, "in a panic, driving at maximum speed," said Ailie, who wondered why he didn't consider stopping in an open field.

At a sharp turn, known ever since as Dead Man's Curve, the pickup rolled over and landed in a ditch. "We were all blown out," Lydia said. Hanna Leppa's hand was pinned between the overturned truck and the charred brush. Some men helped free her, but the hand was severely burned, leaving her in excruciating pain. Ailie, thrown against a barbed wire fence, heard her mother calling her name, "despite her own suffering." They joined hands then—Hanna, Ailie, and Lydia, their boarder—and started running toward Moose Lake.

"We used the white capes from our coats to shield our faces and body as best as we could from the fierce, hot wind and flames," Ailie said. They dashed through a nightmare. They saw Dora Beach, the fifty-two-year-old hotel owner's wife from Kettle River, on the roadside. She was burned to death. Exhausted, Ailie stopped to rest for a moment on what she thought was a soft log. In horror, she realized the log was actually the charred body of Ralph Michaelson, her teenaged schoolmate who had been working in the store with Lydia. "You can imagine my reaction," she said. "We were surrounded by flames and thought surely we were the only people alive."

They weren't alone, though. Car after car had piled up on Dead Man's Curve—a turn in what is now a straightened portion of Minnesota State Highway 73—a couple miles south of Kettle River, and only four miles west of Moose Lake. "At Dead Man's Curve, and in the region around it, the most disastrous episodes of the great fire took place . . . stories of tragedy and death," wrote Francis Carroll and Franklin Raiter in *The Fires of Autumn*. Unlike today's wide, asphalt-surfaced Highway 73, the road between Kettle River and Moose Lake was a thin ribbon of dirt lined with trees and fields. "It was so narrow, in fact, that when automobiles met they had to drive up on the grass with their right wheels in order to get past each other," according to Carroll and Raiter.

The fire roaring toward Moose Lake veiled the skinny road in thick, black smoke. That darkness "was compounded by the sharp bends in the road," they wrote, causing a massive "pileup of automobiles on Dead Man's Curve." Some vehicles weaved through the dangers of the sharp corner unharmed, but all told, "about 15 or 16 automobiles, most of them overloaded with terrified people, went off the road into the rocks and burning brush," according to *The Fires of Autumn*. Carroll and Raiter tallied the varied accounts and estimated between seventy-five and a hundred people died at Dead Man's Curve—"some pinned under wrecked automobiles, some in the woods, some on the roadside." That included a family's car crashing with a load of children. "They hit the curve, careened off the road into the rocks and burning stumps and overturned," Celia Kowalski recalled nearly sixty years later. "I will never forget the terrible screaming of those poor souls slowly burning to death."

In the chaos, those who survived the multiple rollovers sprinted this way and that. Ailie Leppa said it was "each person for himself." The teacher and pupil who joined Ailie in the back seat of the pickup— Ida Hiipakka and Stella Paapanen—were last seen running into the woods. Their clothes were on fire. They weren't wearing the heavy coats that saved Ailie and Lydia. Stella's body was recovered the next spring. Ida's body wasn't discovered until 1920. The only way they

Burned cars lay in ruins along the roadsides throughout northern Minnesota after the fires. *Courtesy of Minnesota Historical Society Collections*

could identify her? A class ring she wore since graduating from Ely High School.

Ailie, Hanna, and Lydia were luckier. Although they were "exhausted by this time, fighting the wind, heat, and smoke," Ailie said, three men directed them toward a small creek known as Glaspie Brook. "Otherwise we would have walked right into the fiercest flaming forest," Ailie said. They huddled in the brook as the cold night set in. When two men found them, shivering, later that night, they placed some wood planks across the streambed, and all trudged off for what was known as Haikola's Hill. Dozens of others were at the top of the hill, huddled around a small fire, of all things, trying to keep warm. "We were wet and cold," Lydia said. "Ailie and I prayed and sang some songs." The heels on her shoes were gone. Her stockings had burned. Her long hair was a mess from the wind. But her warm coat had saved her.

Eventually, a man with a Ford Model T gave Ailie and Hanna a ride to Moose Lake. The ride featured more gruesome sights. "There were trucks picking up corpses," Lydia said. In her 1976 letter, Ailie recalled one story, singed deep in her memory: "I saw a car along side of the road with eleven women, their clothing and bodies consumed by the flames ... on all of them, their hair blown straight up and not burned. I do not expect anyone to believe this, but it happens to be the truth."

From Moose Lake, Lydia Salmi and the Leppas were placed on a train and taken to a hospital in Superior, Wisconsin. After five months recovering from burns, Ailie went on to attend business college in Superior and wound up working at the bank in Kettle River. As for her possessions, stashed in the bank's basement: all were destroyed. Only the bank's brick outer shell was left standing after the fire flattened Kettle River. Ailie later married Charles Nikkila. While she was escaping the deadly fires of 1918, he was one of the lucky soldiers who survived the vicious battles in the Argonne Forest of France. "Surely," she wrote, "he also had a guardian angel."

Lydia's family had no such protection. Her mother, Olga Salmi, loaded her wagon and hooked it to a team of horses. But the fire engulfed their farm a mile west of Kettle River so fast. Olga and four kids—Helmi (twelve), Walter (ten), John (eight), and Helen (two)—found their escape route to Moose Lake cut off by flames. They tried to retreat to their farm but were overcome by fire. Somehow, Olga's three-year-old son, Eino, had been separated from the rest.

John Salmi, Lydia's father, stayed behind and tried to squelch the flames. Eventually, he jumped into a car owned by some Moose Lake people who had been futilely fighting the fire. He wound up facedown in a watery ditch, his wet clothes saving him—just barely. He was severely burned on his face, hands, and body. In shock, Salmi wandered the charred countryside. He found his son Eino wandering near what was left of the Kettle River bridge. Some men fighting the fires had kept him by the river all night.

John Salmi, the patriarch who had helped settle Kettle River after his 1888 trek from Finland, recovered from his burns but caught pneumonia and died five years later. His case likely was among the countless examples of influenza that led to pneumonia as the official cause of death. He was sixty-one years old.

The storekeepers Lydia Salmi worked for, the Michaelsons, also survived the 1918 fires. They found the letter their son, Ralph, had written and put in the safe. "Mrs. Michaelson sure treasured that note," Lydia said, "because Ralph never saw his folks again."

Postcard view of St. Marys Hospital in Rochester, circa 1916. *Courtesy of Minnesota Historical Society Collections*

CHAPTER 10

Rochester

Where is the best place to go
When you are down and out,
Why to the Contagious Hospital,
And that without a doubt.
When you are sick and suffering,
And don't know what to do,
Especially if you are suffering
From the terrible Spanish Flu.
Hurry, Hurry to the hospital,
Get there right at the start,
And if there isn't any hope at all,
The nurses will do their part . . .

IT SEEMED LIKE AN ODD TIME FOR POETRY. Yet, somehow, with patients pouring in and eighteen of their fellow nurses contracting influenza on the same day—October 7, 1918—the St. Marys Hospital nursing students found a moment to pen some poems for their yearbook. Their singsong rhymes masqueraded the grim reality of death and exhaustion—bed capacity and sputum cups both overflowing.

Another poem from that 1919 yearbook, titled "Toll of the 'Flu,'" began:

Gone! Did you say?
Our noblest and best,
In the dawn of womanhood
She was called to her rest . . .

From October through December of 1918, nearly two hundred influenza patients were admitted to St. Marys Hospital in Rochester. Twenty died, including six nuns from the Sisters of St. Francis, the order that created St. Marys amid the rich, rolling southern Minnesota farmland with Rochester as its hub. Crops weren't the only thing poised to grow in what was then a city of thirteen thousand residents. St. Marys Hospital would soon join the Mayo Properties Association. Eventually, it would become known as the Mayo Clinic, improbably morphing the town into one of the world's leading medical centers.

When the 1918 flu arrived, it came slowly, on the first two days of October. Three patients, all with mild cases, were promptly released. By October 7, twenty patients at St. Marys, including eighteen flu-stricken nurses, were transferred to a new isolation ward in the just-converted Lincoln Hotel. Within a week, patients from other hospitals and boardinghouses squeezed in, eclipsing the forty-patient capacity. Cots were set up in the hallways. "Assigned duties and stations were forgotten, and every doctor, nurse, technician and secretary worked whenever he was needed most at the moment," according to *The Doctors Mayo*, a 1941 book by Helen Clapesattle. Doctors would work the floor until 4:30 PM before driving the countryside and sending the most dire cases to the new ward in the old hotel.

Staffing hospitals was tough enough during the Great War, with doctors and nurses sailing overseas to tend to wounded soldiers in Europe. With the flu outbreak, the nursing staff at St. Marys grew so strained that Sister Mary Ledwidge, the English-born nursing superintendent who was nearing her sixtieth birthday, was forced to clean the sputum-stained sheets in the laundry room after juggling her day-shift duties with two other nurses. Only two additional nurses were still healthy enough to relieve them at night. "And on top of everything else, the sisters were driven nearly to distraction by the constant phone calls from anxious friends and relatives of the patient," Clapesattle wrote.

Only four months earlier, in June 1918, the sisters of St. Francis had opened the remodeled Lincoln Hotel next door to St. Marys Hospital. The old clapboard house had a sorry past and was once considered haunted. The place was owned by the aging Mangner sisters, a pair of spinsters, who turned it into the Lincoln Hotel in 1899. By 1918, the Mangners were ready to give up the inn-keeping and sold the building to the Sisters of St. Francis for $25,000, as part of the property being gobbled up for what would become the Mayo Clinic's sprawling campus. A maternity ward was proposed for the old inn, as well as other uses. In the end, the hotel—with its five-pillared front porch and proximity to St. Marys—was turned into an isolation hospital to care for contagious patients. The timing was ominous.

The flu epidemic was just around the corner. Even eerier, the ward's first patient on June 14, 1918, was a young soldier with the mumps who was transported from Fort Riley in Kansas—the same army base where experts believe the deadly influenza pandemic of 1918 began.

Before, a so-called "pest house"—a one-story frame house in a field along the tracks by the Star Bread Company—served the city's infectious patients. But now Rochester had a new facility to care for its most contagious. The Lincoln Hotel-turned-Isolation Hospital was clearly a fortuitous step up—the latest addition to the fledgling Mayo Clinic. By 1918, the clinic was already ascending to its lofty spot among elite medical facilities, rivaling Johns Hopkins in Maryland in the number of surgeries performed.

Almost as odd as poetry during a pandemic, the clinic was burgeoning in a rather obscure farm town. But in some ways, the Mayo Clinic was a family affair not all that different from farming operations in the area.

William Worrall Mayo, born in 1819 near Manchester, England, emigrated to New York when he was twenty-seven. He worked his way west, taking jobs as a newspaper publisher, pharmacist, tailor, census taker, ferryboat operator, justice of the peace, and veterinarian. He moved to Le Sueur, Minnesota, in the 1850s after completing medical training in Indiana. The Union Army rejected his bid to become a regimental surgeon in 1861. He landed an examining surgeon appointment a couple of years later, evaluating military recruits for the enrollment board in Rochester. Mayo and his wife, Louise, settled there and raised a family.

Mayo would often bring the kids along on his medical runs around the rolling agricultural region. "We came along in medicine like boys on a farm," his son Charlie would later say. Of the Mayos' six children, two died as infants. The eldest, Gertrude, married a Rochester veterinarian. Her sister, Phoebe, died at twenty-eight. That left sons William and Charles, who assisted their dad in his medical practice before it was time for them to go to medical school. Wanting the best for his eventual successors, the elder Mayo sent Will to the University of Michigan and Charlie to Chicago Medical College, later part of Northwestern University, north of Chicago. They returned to Rochester, where everyone called them Dr. Will and Dr. Charlie.

An 1883 tornado galvanized the connection between the Mayos and St. Marys Hospital. The Sisters of St. Francis waited out the August twister in their convent cellar. At the elder Mayo's urging, the nuns cared for forty injured residents in their convent the first night after the tornado. That prompted Mother Mary Alfred Moes, the leader of the order, to begin lobbying the Mayos for a new hospital. At the time, hospitals were still considered places people went to die. And the elder Mayo balked, saying it would cost $40,000 (about $650,000 in 2018 dollars). "If you promise me to take charge of it," Mother Alfred said, "we will set the building before you at once."

By 1889, the sisters had saved up the $40,000 and St. Marys Hospital was set to open October 1. They jumped the gun with a dicey procedure the day before because of a pending emergency. Dr. Charlie, assisted by his brother Will, removed a cancerous tumor from a patient's eye.

After their dad retired in 1892, the brothers Mayo began to attract other leading doctors to Rochester. One of them was a bacteriologist named Dr. Edward Carl Rosenow, whose research in Chicago caught the Mayo brothers' eyes. They offered him a spot on their diagnostic team in 1909, when Rosenow was thirty-three. He declined, saying he preferred to continue his research. Born in Wisconsin in 1875 to a German father and Swiss mother, Rosenow remained in the Mayos' sights, his stature in Chicago growing. In April of 1915, Dr. Will wrote him again with an invitation to join the growing staff at the Mayo Foundation as an experimental biologist. "We have always had it in our minds that someday you might join us, on your own terms, to do what you wanted to do in your own way," Will Mayo wrote.

Dr. Will Mayo, circa 1916. *Courtesy of Minnesota Historical Society Collections*

The pitch worked. Rosenow transferred his laboratory from Chicago to Rochester, and when the influenza virus struck in 1918, he quickly began examining the sputum samples coughed up by the hospital's sick patients. He found a microorganism called streptococci in many cases and conducted extensive tests on guinea pigs until he was able to get the rodents to mirror the symptoms found in the human flu sufferers. He came up with a vaccine to treat the pneumonia that often killed flu patients as a secondary infection. Figuring the three-shot vaccine couldn't hurt, he offered to give the shots over three weeks to residents of Rochester.

Mapping its scientific effectiveness was nearly impossible in the throes of the fast-spreading flu—"a classic example of the kind of catch-as-catch-can effort forced on otherwise careful researchers by raging epidemics," according to Alfred Crosby's 1989 book, *America's Forgotten Pandemic*. Rosenow admitted that any conclusions about his vaccine were premature, but hinted it appeared to be an effective prophylactic against the flu itself and the pneumonia infections that often followed. He published his preliminary findings in the *Journal of the American Medical Association*, showing greatly reduced numbers of flu cases and deaths in those who were given his vaccines compared to groups that didn't get treatment.

When he offered, in his journal article, to furnish his serum at low cost or show bacteriologists how to make it, his Mayo lab was inundated with four hundred telegrams pleading for a supply. One of the secretaries fielding the requests sent some of the vaccine to her hometown doctor, telling her parents to scoot down to his office and take the shots. That doctor casually mentioned to the postmaster that he'd be getting some new flu vaccine. "The news spread through the town with the wind," Clapesattle says in her book on the Mayos, "and the doctor's office was soon jammed with panic-stricken persons who wanted to be treated."

The scene played out in doctors' offices across the state. In the desperate whirlwind, standard scientific protocol went out the window. Doctors failed to keep detailed records. Control groups weren't rigidly tracked, and Rosenow's vaccine sparked loud skepticism. Rosenow's vaccine was "useless," according to John M. Barry, who wrote the authoritative tome *The Great Influenza* in 2004. Another expert, Crosby, said of Rosenow's injections, "if you pump anything, even distilled water, into the arms of a population in the waning days of an epidemic, the statistical results will indicate prophylactic success."

But back in 1918, Rosenow was basking in fame—defending his findings and stirring up a frenzy of hope. "Ninety percent of the deaths from influenza and pneumonia are preventable when a properly prepared vaccine is used," the *Kearney (Nebraska) Hub* newspaper reported in late 1918, quoting Rosenow's address at the annual meeting of the American Public Health Association in Chicago. He told those assembled that 20,000 people had been given the three-shot vaccine, compared with 61,000 people not vaccinated. For each 1,000 cases, nine vaccinated people contracted the flu compared to 220 who never

received the shots. "Highly favorable results have been obtained in prevention of influenza and milder respiratory infections" from the three weekly injections, Rosenow insisted. Respiratory infections were three times greater—and deaths six times more likely—in unvaccinated control groups compared to groups given the vaccine.

His boss, Will Mayo, was cautious about the results and not too worried about the flu in the days before the waves of the deadly virus began to crest. Never mind that US surgeon general Rupert Blue would soon report 350,000 civilians had died between September 1 and December 1, 1918, from influenza and pneumonia. In an October 8 letter to a Minneapolis doctor seeking the vaccine,

Dr. Edward C. Rosenow, 1921. *Courtesy of Minnesota Historical Society Collections*

Dr. Will wrote, "I personally think the epidemic will have to be much worse before I submit myself and my family to any other treatment than three moderate meals a day and eight hours of sleep." He clarified that Rosenow wasn't using any "serum," but instead a vaccine to stave off pneumonia—the secondary infectious killer. "The value of this vaccine is purely theoretical," Will Mayo wrote. "There have been no extensive experiments on either animals or human beings." He reminded people that Rosenow considered his vaccine "purely experimental . . . based on the belief that death in these cases of influenza" comes from pneumonia infections not the influenza germ.

Editors of the *Journal of the American Medical Association* found Rosenow's claims dubious and dangerous, creating a firestorm of doubt among medical experts. "We have a right to ask that the experiments in the field, where so much is at stake, where our hold on the confidence of the general public is involved, and where self deception is peculiarly liable to occur, be planned and carried out with as much precision and critical acumen as possible, so that proper conclusions may be drawn and the whole matter not left fogged with uncertainty," said the *Journal*'s editorial, published in the January 4, 1919, issue.

Editors went on to blast Rosenow's data as "simply too inadequate to permit competent judgment. . . . Positive results are certainly more gratifying to the average investigator than negative; all the more reason, therefore, why he should hold himself a little stiffly and be ever on guard against an uncritical acceptance of a desired fact." They called Rosenow's findings vague. When the Mayo doctors reported the serum's effectiveness in communities with both high and low death rates, *Journal* editors asked: "What were the communities and what was the population, what was the incidence and what was the mortality rate; where and to how many was the vaccine given, and what were actually the results?"

The editors lambasted Rosenow's article, which appeared in the same issue of the *Journal*, for first claiming the vaccine's success at warding off secondary infections that followed the flu and then insisting it worked against the flu directly in studies of patients at the Rochester State Hospital for the Insane. They went on to skewer Rosenow's analysis. When he mentioned that fourteen nurses developed influenza within two days before the first shot while only one got sick after six weeks of treatment, the editors asked "out of how many? . . . at what period in the epidemic? . . . out of how many possibilities?" The editorial concluded, "In other words, unless all the cards are on the table, unless we know so far as possible all the factors that may conceivably influence the results, we cannot have a satisfactory basis for determining whether or not the results of prophylactic inoculation against influenza justify the interpretation they have received in some quarters."

Letters heaping praise on the Mayos and Rosenow offset the stuffy, conservative editorial in the AMA *Journal*. They also show how the Mayos took special precautions to get the vaccine into the hands of the wealthy and powerful—men such as G. W. Bailey, the South Dakota-based assistant general superintendent of the Chicago and North Western Railway.

By early November 1918, 482 of the railroad's employees in Minnesota and the Dakotas were sick with influenza. "This seriously hampered us in carrying on our business," Bailey wrote to the Mayo brothers on December 7. "We made several appeals for the Rosenow serum and were given very prompt and efficient support by you." He insisted the results were "wonderful," and no railroad workers who took the vaccine suffered from "serious results."

More importantly, perhaps, Bailey's three flu-ridden children appeared to benefit from the vaccine. One of the children had just come down with the virus, and two were showing early symptoms. "We gave them the serum," he wrote to the Mayos. "They came out fine." Unable to get nurses or domestic workers to help, Bailey said he and his wife had to tend to the sick children themselves in Huron, South Dakota. "If anyone would have contracted it, we would," he wrote in his thank-you letter to the Mayos. "We took the serum and were not affected at all."

When his local doctor ran out of the second shot of medicine, Bailey wired Rochester and asked for a small supply for his family and some workers. "We received it promptly on the first train," he wrote. Will Mayo wrote back, saying he and Rosenow were grateful for the kind words—especially in light of all the criticism. "We took pains to see to it that the North Western road was supplied first of the railroads," Will Mayo wrote in late 1918, "for we are all North Western people."

Support came from outside the area, too. The regional director of the US Railroad Administration in Washington, R. H. Aishton, wrote to say, "It certainly was mighty nice of you" to furnish the railroad with vaccines. A school official in Foxwarren, Manitoba, thanked the Mayos "for the generous amount of vaccine supplied by you [that] undoubtedly prevented what was already a grave situation from developing into a serious outbreak." A doctor in Denver named Chauncey Tennant wrote in late October to "acknowledge the receipt of the Antigen." He said he had recovered from his own flu attack, but the vaccine arrived too late to help his Harvard-trained assistant, Dr. J. E. Wilson, "who probably contracted it from me." Wilson died "12 hours before the arrival of the serum of a subsequent pneumonia" that took only a few hours to kill him.

Perhaps no correspondence about the vaccine pleased the Mayos and Rosenow more than a letter from Dr. B. C. Wilson, a director of a tuberculosis center and the secretary of the Kentucky State Board of Health. He took to task the "ultra conservative attitude" of the *Journal of the American Medical Association* and the editors who chastised Rosenow. "Our results have been gratifying in that thousands of doses of the vaccine have now been used and the entire population of schools . . . have been successfully inoculated" without any harmful results.

He said the interval between shots needed more study, "but personal interviews with many physicians and reports received daily from every section of the State [of Kentucky] grow more and more encouraging." He urged the Mayos and Rosenow to conduct larger-scale tests and to carefully keep accurate records. The AMA *Journal*'s scathing editorial "is naturally a handicap," Wilson wrote, criticizing the critics who demanded more proof of the vaccine's value. "Scant consideration is given to the accumulated evidence of the harmlessness of the procedure or the potentialities for good." The editorial, Wilson continued, "offers no encouragement in the attempt at immunization . . . no valuable suggestions to prevent the further spread of influenza and pneumonia."

Will Mayo, in his response to Wilson, reacted to the blistering editorial—first insisting his correspondence with the Kentucky health official was private and not for publication. "I am not a sanitarian and such a statement coming from me would not be in good taste," Will Mayo wrote to Wilson in Bowling Green, Kentucky. "There will be sufficient data before long on which to base positive statements and Dr. Rosenow will present his results at such a time." Then Will Mayo explained why they had to loosen up some of the scientific rigor at the height of the epidemic in 1918: "It is idle to expect work to be carried out from a purely experimental standpoint in the midst of a great death dealing epidemic." They couldn't just sit back, he argued, and not use a harmless vaccine "and wait and let people die who might be saved in order to demonstrate the ultimate results." He continued, "The curious feature in connection with those who have belittled the vaccination is the fact that those who have not used it make up the opposition while those who have used it practically unanimously endorse it."

By November 11, 1918, when news of the armistice spread, Dr. Will began sending cables to his scientific friends in Germany and Austria—long the masters of surgery and medicine but now viewed as suspicious. Within a few hours, US government security agents showed up at Mayo's office door, wondering if and why he was attempting to "communicate with the enemy." Flabbergasted, Dr. Will said, "I thought the war was over!"

When the peace stuck, Mayo was ready to jump-start his fledgling clinic. "Now that the War and the influenza are both over," he wrote to a bishop on January 29, 1919, "patients are coming in by the hundreds." The Mayos were able to bolster their staff as soldiers, doctors, and nurses returned from the trenches and field hospitals in France. Plans to expand his hospital to the east, "will materialize," Dr. Will wrote. "We need 150 to 200 beds for medicine, obstetrics, children, and contagious diseases."

He proposed tearing down the old Lincoln Hotel that had become St. Marys Isolation Hospital on Zumbro Street to construct a new, larger facility. "I am rather anxious to get the new hospital under construction," wrote Will. He worried about competition from three hospitals built in downtown Rochester since 1914 "with a total number of beds much greater than at St. Marys." He warned Bishop Patrick Heffron, from the Winona diocese, that it was time to get onboard with the expansion of his family's Mayo Clinic. "If there is delay," Mayo wrote, "another hospital is liable to spring into existence, which I should much regret."

Root cellars such as this one in St. Louis County served as desperate, but ulti-mately ineffective, shelter from the fire. *Courtesy of Minnesota Historical Society Collections*

CHAPTER 11

Kettle River; Split Rock Township

THEY STARTED OFF TOGETHER in southern Poland. Now, Leo Soboleski and John Homicz were climbing into wells on their farms, trying to escape flames—and fate. Intertwined for more than thirty years, their stories would take separate paths on October 12, 1918.

They left Poland for America together as boys. Birth records vary, but Leo was about sixteen and John a few years younger. Their 1888 emigrant trek wasn't about yearning or dreaming. They needed work and found it in the coal mines of Nanticoke, Pennsylvania. In 1825, coal had been discovered in the area tucked between the Susquehanna River and the Blue Ridge Mountains just south of Wilkes-Barre, and by 1878, Nanticoke had become a coal-mining vortex. For a dozen years, Leo and John went into those mines nearly every day and emerged coughing the dust that came with the coal. Finally, a doctor in 1900 told Leo he had two choices: quit his job or die with black lungs.

Leo and John had heard that the government was giving away undeveloped land in the North Country. Their applications for eighty-acre parcels near Kettle River, Minnesota, were approved in 1901, according to family stories passed down orally and then written down in 1998 by Leo's grandson, John Buczynski. "A five-acre farm in Poland was considered big," Buczynski wrote, "but 160 acres! That was immense, almost unheard of back home."

Now in their twenties—muscles taut from mining, lungs clouded with soot—Leo Soboleski and John Homicz boarded a train for Duluth and then switched trains, heading west another twenty miles to Carlton. John wound up on eighty acres in Split Rock Township, about six miles west of Kettle River. Leo went to work nearby improving 160 acres for cultivation. Leo helped construct St. Joseph's Catholic Church in 1902 in Split Rock Township. He then married Elizabeth "Lizzie" Patrick in the new church. The Patricks were Austrian émigrés who had settled in Mankato and then homesteaded near Kettle River.

Both Leo and John planted more than grain seeds. Leo and Lizzie had seven children between 1904 and the 1918 fires. John and his wife, Victoria, outdid them with eight kids of their own in the same span.

The Soboleski clan featured one other member: Shep, the family dog. On Friday, October 11, 1918, Shep gazed westward from the Soboleskis' front porch. Through the pines and hardwoods, the lumber town of Automba sat about a mile away. Shep howled a few times and remained on the porch, staring off to the west, before finally resting his head between his paws. Lizzie Soboleski had never seen the dog act like that. "It's got to mean something," she said, according to Buczynski's unpublished manuscript, located in the Carlton County Historical Society. "He knows something, Mama," replied Leo Jr., her oldest child, then fourteen.

In a scenario similar to that of many farmsteads, Saturdays at the Soboleskis' meant bread baking, floor scrubbing, and family bathing. This Saturday, of course, wouldn't be routine. Nothing had been routine that fall. As conditions grew drier and drier, farmers began to pull from the small forest clearings the loose hay piles they'd collected by hand.

When winds picked up in the late afternoon of October 12, it became hard to even talk over the roar. The western sky began to glow. Word spread that a train near Lawler, eight miles west, had dropped sparks that started a fire. The winds had whipped it into a firestorm, gobbling up everything in its path, including the town of Automba.

Panic began to squeeze the Soboleskis as the sky darkened from the smoke pouring in from the northwest. Soon, the fire glow spanned the horizon. Leo and Leo Jr. began pumping water frantically from the cistern. They tried to wet down the buildings, splashing bucketloads of water on the barn, house, and outbuildings.

A different sound, that of pounding hooves and a clanging wagon, soon broke through the fire's roar. The Jusolas, a Finnish family from two farms over, had piled their belongings and three small children in the wagon. Only the family's father, Leo Jusola, spoke any English. First, he argued that the Soboleskis should hitch up their wagon and head east toward Moose Lake. Then they rethought any attempt to flee. "All of them couldn't outrun this fire," Buczynski wrote. "They had to find shelter, an open clearing, a root cellar, a well—anything."

The Soboleski farm had two wells: one out in the field, shallow and dried out; the other, near the barn, larger and deeper. The two Leos—fathers of the Polish and Finnish families thrown together in crisis—must have peered into the deeper well and seen all the water. Or maybe they judged it too close to the wood of the barn and other outbuildings sure to burst into flame. They chose, instead, the shallow well in the field and made a run for it. "It was the only answer," Buczynski wrote.

Lizzie hollered for the seven Soboleski children to fetch shoes and stockings. The fathers and older sons turned the livestock loose, grabbed some water, a heavy canvas, a hammer, and nails. Buczynski said his mother, Albena Soboleski, then five years old, was the only one who could find her stockings. She had tucked her favorite black ones under the kitchen table minutes earlier.

Lizzie paired off her kids and sent them dashing, hand in hand, across the field toward the well. Stick together, Lizzie urged her children. Leo Jusola and his seven-months-pregnant wife, Jenny, unhitched their horses and sent them scattering for their lives. When Leo and Jenny reached the well in the field, they found a four-foot-square hole, shored up with logs down to the bottom—eleven feet deep in the murky shadows. They tossed a bale of straw in first, then dropped a wooden ladder. The top rung was flush with the top of the well's opening. Lizzie climbed down first, carrying her four-month-old baby, Anton. While the others stood for hours on different rungs of the ladder, Lizzie and little Anton sat on the straw at the well's bottom. The mother had brought three things along with her infant: fresh cream, holy water, and a crucifix. She proceeded to pray as the others squeezed into the well's shaft.

There were fourteen people in all—nine Soboleskis and five Jusolas. They must have shoved and rushed. The barn was burning and flames were starting to lick their way up the farmhouse. As the fathers hammered the canvas to the logs framing the well's opening, Shep appeared through the smoke. Leo screamed for the family dog to run. Sparks were dancing on Shep's fur. The dog's brown eyes locked on Leo's, and then Shep ran straight toward the flames in the farmyard.

As the men crawled under the canvas and into the well, they hung a kerosene railroad lantern up top, believing it would help keep smoke out. The coughs from the parched throats of fourteen people interrupted the crackling pops of the fire raging outside their crowded vertical shaft.

Lizzie's cream, she hoped, would calm the children, eight of them younger than ten years old. But the cream quickly curdled and smelled rancid. Lizzie poured it out on the straw and used sips of her holy water to ease the dryness in the children's mouths. But thirst was the least of their problems. Scorching winds sent sparks through the canvas's small cracks, often falling on the children's heads below. Die 'em out, the men up top shouted, die 'em out. Slapping out the sparks turned into the chore that gave focus to the people clinging to the ladder and the mother and infant sitting at the bottom.

After the fire burned itself out and screamed off in other directions, morning came and—one by one—all fourteen members of the Soboleski and Jusola families emerged from the well.

The Soboleskis found their buildings had been reduced to charred ashes and blackened lumber—the house and barn gone. In a nearby root cellar, the fathers found a pig and potatoes, roasted in the heat. They fetched some water from the other well and quenched their thirst. Once the pig and potatoes took care of their hunger, the families headed down the blackened road.

The clatter of wagon wheels soon signaled that hope was near. Home Guard troops, out searching for survivors, followed the jubilant reunion with word of the disaster that had consumed the countryside. St. Joseph's Catholic Church, built by Leo Soboleski and others sixteen years earlier, had somehow survived, along with a few farmsteads. Everything else was gone.

As the home guardsmen led the survivors to the still-standing Shusta farm for shelter and food, nightmarish scenes popped up. A horse in the road, its eyes glazed, stood smoldering and burned. The guards shot it to end its misery, noting their location so they could return and bury the animal. Cow hooves were found, gruesomely separated from the animal's charred and hoofless carcass at the next farm.

Lizzie and Jenny bathed their children at the Shusta farmhouse, wiping soot and grime from little faces. Leo Soboleski headed out to find what had happened to John Homicz—his fellow Pole, partner in the coal mines, and neighboring farmer near Kettle River.

John, like his friend Leo, had also jumped into a well. The search party of Home Guards and survivors found him the next day in the well six miles west of Kettle River. "No person will ever know just what horrors he went through or what physical pain he suffered," according to a reporter for the *Moose Lake Star Gazette*, who was covering Homicz's probate hearing nearly five months later.

There were no survivors at the Homicz farm on "that fateful day" of October 12, 1918, so no firsthand memories. The reporter's summary, written the following winter, on February 27, 1919, is the best account. And fewer than five months is actually a fairly fresh version of what happened, compared to most of the surviving recollections jotted down generations later.

"The fire swept down upon them in the afternoon and the brave father placed his family, as he thought, in a safe refuge—in the root house," the *Star Gazette* reported. Root cellars, often sod-topped and jutting out of farmyards in a jumble of lumber, stone, and mud, were used to store potatoes and other foodstuff to get these immigrant families through the long northern Minnesota winters.

John Homicz sealed into the cellar his family, including his eight children and their mother, his wife, Victoria, thirty-seven years old, daughter of Polish and German parents Anton and Agneska Karulak. The eight children ranged in age from seventeen-year-old Stanley to not-quite-two Sophia. The Moose Lake reporter identified fourteen-year-old Leonora as "Nellie" and eight-year-old William as "Billy." Stella and John Jr., ages thirteen and eleven, joined their six siblings and their mother before their father closed the root house door. He likely tossed a bucket of water on that door "and then went out and locked horns with the fire demon in a vain attempt to save their buildings," the newspaper story said.

"Hurrying from one place to another where the fire raged most furiously, the father fought and worked desperately." John Homicz's clothes began to catch fire. He suffered burns to his face and limbs, his skin scorched and blistered. After shutting Victoria and the eight kids into the root cellar, John Homicz did what his friend, Leo Soboleski, had done on his own farm. Homicz ran for his well—which sank about a dozen feet down, the bottom third filled with water. "He dropped himself down into the well as a last desperate chance to save his own life. His body was found there a day or two later, and the flesh was so badly burned that the shoes dropped from his feet," the newspaper said. "His clothing was all burned from his body except a part of his shirt."

When searchers opened the root cellar door, they found the family—"every one of them . . . dead," the *Moose Lake Star Gazette* reported. "Nine in one family!" According to Buczynski's 1998 retelling of the Soboleski family history, John Homicz was discovered in chest-high water. "Cramps had set in and he perished shielding his head with one hand."

"The sad sight in the root cellar set all to tears," Buczynski continued. All nine members of Homicz's family—Victoria, Stanley, Nellie, Stella, John Jr., Billy, Bohlak, Valentine, and Sophia—"were positioned in a row, perhaps like they had been instructed to do," Buczynski wrote. "Clothes were burned from some of the bodies of the children and the buttons were left in a row on their chests and stomachs."

The Moose Lake newspaper reporter admitted in his account that "nobody will ever know the details" of what happened in the root house because no one survived. "But imagine them first smelling the smoke seeping through the cracks of the door, later permeating the entire room, then all growing dark and the heat overhead becoming intense, the smoke thicker and thicker.

"We can see the frantic mother trying to keep her flock around her, probably on her knees imploring Providence to spare their lives. We can hear her prayers, and we can hear the wailings of the children as they swarm around and shriek with fear and trembling until their voices become hoarse and their little throats parched and choked with the relentless smoke."

The reporter's imagination trudged on: "We can see them, one by one, fainting away and falling on the floor in the inky blackness of that awful place—until the death dealing vapor around them, locked in each other's arms as long as possible, the last whimper is hushed, the last tear dried—they have passed beyond the reach of worldly suffering."

Red Cross aid arrives in Moose Lake. *Courtesy of Minnesota Historical Society Collections*

Leo Soboleski would live until 1945, when he died in his early sev-enties and was buried in the graveyard behind St. Joseph's Church—the one he'd helped build in 1902. Until his death, he'd tell family members the hardest moment in his life was not standing all night on jittery legs while surviving the 1918 fire on a ladder in his well. No, the "hardest thing he ever had to do," Buczynski said, was bury his best friend, John Homicz, his wife, and eight children in the mass grave in Moose Lake known as Riverside Cemetery.

Shep, the Soboleski family's dog, was found with a neighboring cat under a table on a farm "some distance away," Buczynski said. "Except for burned paws and an insatiable thirst, they seemed confident they were going to be found."

Leo Soboleski hugged the dog and broke into tears when the family was reunited with Shep. Soon, the Red Cross would arrive and help the Soboleskis build a house and secure food, livestock, and medical supplies. Along with the surviving neighbors, "they would get back on their feet," their grandson, John Buczynski, wrote eighty years later. He checked with modern-day scientists to see if the train lantern had indeed sucked away the smoke that might have killed his mother's family and the Jusolas from the neighboring farm. No, they said, it was likely the wet canvas nailed into place that saved the Soboleskis in the well. And one other factor, according to Buczynski: "The Soboleskis were lucky, extremely lucky, that's all."

The Homiczes weren't so fortunate. Their story was tethered to the Soboleskis' since the two teenage boys emigrated from Poland in the 1880s to the mines of Pennsylvania. All that changed October 12, 1918, when one family survived, while the other was "buried . . . there beside many others, who suffered a similar fate on that awful day," the *Moose Lake Star Gazette* reported.

CHAPTER 12

Welcome, Martin County

FRED JOHNSON TRIED TO ENLIST IN THE MILITARY to fight in the Great War. He was rejected for unspecified physical reasons. If that weren't relief enough for Fred's parents, his wife, small child, five brothers, and four sisters, his rejection certainly was good news for Henry Rippe, who owned the grain elevator in the little farm town of Welcome, down near the Iowa border in southern Minnesota. Mid-October was harvest time, and that meant lots of work at the grain elevator that Fred managed for Henry.

Any relief that Fred wouldn't be fighting in the trenches of Europe was short-lived, though. Late on the night of October 11, 1918, Fred Johnson died from influenza in his home on the outskirts of Welcome. His death—at age twenty-six—was the fifth influenza fatality in a week's span in the farm town of about six hundred people. More than seventy were sick.

"I was deeply grieved to hear of his death," said Henry Rippe, sixty-four. "He was a fine young man, hard working and efficient in every way. His reports were always correct to a penny, which rule held true to all of his dealings with us. He was an unusually likable and able man."

Rippe's praise of Johnson's accuracy and amiability appeared in the *Fairmont Daily Sentinel* on October 12—the same Saturday that would find fires burning out of control up north. For the roughly twenty thousand people living near Welcome in Martin County, those fires were a far-off calamity 250 miles away. They had their hands full with the flu. And the disease wasn't the first of the biblical plagues to descend upon Martin County. Forty-five years before influenza invaded the area, Martin County had endured a cloudlike swarm of locusts in 1873.

The county was carved out of southern Brown County in 1857, one year before the Minnesota Territory morphed into a state. No one's quite sure for whom the county was named. It could have been christened after Henry Martin, a Wallingford, Connecticut, bank commissioner who spent two years near Mankato—hunting and fishing in the chain of lakes around Fairmont, the Martin County seat. He returned east within a year of the county's creation. Another Martin—Morgan Lewis Martin—served as a congressional delegate from Green Bay, Wisconsin. On December 23, 1846, he introduced a bill to organize the Minnesota Territory. Before that, Martin County had been part of the Louisiana, Missouri, Michigan, Wisconsin, and Iowa Territories.

Most of the early white settlers were English, including Connecticut lawyer H. F. Shearman, who hunted in Martin County in 1872. In addition to whatever game he killed, Shearman bagged 2,600 acres south of Fairmont for farming. He then published a booklet, promising investors that if they funneled their resources into Martin County, they could make fortunes within ten years through one can't-miss crop: navy beans. Shearman lined up wealthy investors in England, convincing them that they could hire farm laborers, stay across the Atlantic, and skip the brutal Minnesota winters. The investors consisted of recent college graduates and military officers—none of whom knew anything about farming.

More than a thousand acres of navy beans were planted in 1873 around Rolling Green township. That June, a thunderhead-sized swarm of Rocky Mountain locusts came through and ate most of the crops in one day. The Englishmen replanted, only to lose the second attempt to an early killing frost. New investors were brought in, but they lost their shirts because of more locust clouds and bad weather—pulling the Bank of Fairmont into failure with them.

The newspaper in the Martin County seat, the *Fairmont Daily Sentinel*, dates back to those locust days of the 1870s. It could not have been more aptly named, especially in the autumn of 1918. The newspaper literally kept watch on the farm towns around Fairmont as the flu epidemic swarmed through. Clippings from the *Sentinel* reveal how quickly the influenza spread, how deadly it became, and how unpredictably it behaved. On October 19, 1918, the newspaper reported schools were poised to reopen under a headline proclaiming, "Epidemic Is Waning." Two weeks later, on November 4, the schools were closing again because four teachers were ill.

All the while, the bodies were piling up. Two days after elevator manager Fred Johnson's death, another Fred was dead in the little village of Welcome. "An exceedingly bright and popular lad," fourteen-year-old Fred Lintelman became the sixth flu death in Welcome. He died Sunday and was buried Monday. That same Monday, at 12:50 PM, Ernest Schweiger died at age twenty-five in Fraser Township, some six miles northwest of Welcome. He was described as "one of the promising young men of the township, industrious and likeable."

A week later, Dr. George Panzer was dead at thirty-seven. He had registered for the draft in September and was described in his sign-up card as a "short, stout physician" from Truman, Minnesota, in the northern reaches of Martin County. The *Sentinel* said the doctor was "himself stricken" after being "worn out by a three weeks battle against the scourge on behalf of others. . . . Dr. Panzer complained of not feeling well a week ago, but kept on his feet to the last minute attending to the many influenza patients in and around Truman."

The good doctor left behind a wife and two sons, aged six and eight. "He had the epidemic pretty well under control" when he fell ill on October 17. "He rallied Friday and was reported in good shape, but on Saturday became worse and sank steadily until death came this morning." His body was sent to his hometown of Cincinnati, Ohio. Most of the flu dead were buried quickly and locally—including Hilda Klopp, a twenty-seven-year-old, German-born farmwife and mother of five. She died on Monday and was buried two days later in Truman, a day after the town doctor died. "Influenza seems bent upon taking the lives of those in the prime of life, young, strong, and looking ahead to years of usefulness," the *Sentinel* reported on October 15.

The same day, the *Sentinel* also reported that undertakers in Fairmont had received an order from Dr. Henry Bracken, the state health officer up in St. Paul: "From this date onward, funerals for all who have died of influenza or pneumonia following influenza must be strictly private. The order applies to the bodies of returned soldiers as well as those who die in civil life. Caskets must be kept closed."

Bracken went on to explain exactly what he meant by a private burial: "The exclusion of all persons not resident in the tenant with the deceased, from the house or premises where such death occurred, except the embalmer and his necessary assistants and a minister of religion who shall be present only when the embalmer in charge of the case also is present, and who shall be directed by said embalmer as to the precautions to be taken."

*

Painting the flu outbreak in Martin County by numbers shows a relatively small percentage of flu deaths: six of six hundred in Welcome, roughly twenty of twenty thousand countywide. But that one percent belies how everyday life was wrenched that autumn of '18. Churches fell sermon-less for weeks. Early motion-picture theaters and schools were shuttered.

And the *Sentinel* kept watch on everything—except the first names of the women who died. From Mrs. Strobel, the doctor's wife in Welcome, to four women leaving a combined fifteen motherless children in Fairmont, the female flu victims were always listed under their husbands' names.

Tracking down Mrs. Strobel's first name presents a bit of a puzzle. In the 1910 census, William George Strobel was twenty-four, single, managing a magazine shop in Minneapolis, and living as a boarder while he studied at the University of Minnesota. He went on to Rush Medical School in Chicago and St. Luke's Hospital and the Mounds Park Sanatorium in St. Paul.

In 1914, he left his job as resident physician at the school for "retarded" children in Faribault, Minnesota, and moved a hundred miles southwest to hang his shingle in Welcome. By 1920, he was listed on census rolls as a widower, and by 1930, he was remarried to a woman named Alice. Only on Dr. Strobel's World War I draft registration card, filled out three weeks before his first wife's death, do we learn her name. Under the "nearest relative" line, space No. 19, we meet "wife, Jeanette Strobel, Welcome, Martin, Minn." Often called Nettie, she grew up the youngest of six kids in Caledonia, Wisconsin, two hundred miles due east of Welcome near Lake Michigan.

Her death, at twenty-eight, on Sunday, October 6, 1918, was the second in Welcome, coming eight hours after that of Richard Kakeldy, a thirty-one-year-old laborer, who passed at 1 PM that day. These deaths kicked off the *Sentinel's* series of warnings to citizens about the "Spanish influenza spreading rapidly."

"It was said that she was recovering but got up too soon and suffered a fatal relapse," the *Sentinel* said of Jeanette Strobel, calling her "one of Welcome's most prominent women . . . an active figure in every loyalty movement." Jeanette had three young children and "was an ideal mother, wife and counsellor, and her death is a terrible blow not only to the family but all of Welcome."

The two deaths on October 6 prompted the state to send to Welcome six medical corpsmen of the army's Fifth Minnesota infantry. They brought along five hundred gauze masks to Welcome, which, the *Sentinel* said, "appears to be thoroughly impregnated with the [influenza] germs."

The next day, a flu-stricken, pregnant mother gave birth prematurely and her baby died—Martin County's third death. "The disease has spread from farmhouse to farmhouse," with thirteen cases north of Fairmont, the *Sentinel* reported, adding that schools, churches, Sunday schools, and theaters would be closed for a week. The Strand, a popular Fairmont theater, voluntarily closed its doors "as they would not wish to be responsible for any possible spreading of influenza." A screening of the silent movie *The Garden of Allah*, scheduled for Fairmont's Haynic Theater, was also cancelled.

By October 10, thirteen new flu cases had sprouted up in Welcome and "an epidemic [was] raging" in Huntley, twenty-five miles east. Truman, with a dozen more cases, shut its schools and churches. Five Red Cross nurses arrived in the county just as Welcome's lumber store manager, Homer Ellsworth, died at age twenty-nine. "Mr. Ellsworth was one of Welcome's best and most respected business men," the *Sentinel* said, "and his death, coming so closely after two others, has plunged the village into further sorrow." The flu zeroed in on merchants such as Ellsworth, who had frequent contact with people at his lumberyard. Henry Schierkolk, a popular twenty-five-year-old hardware store owner's son, died Friday, October 11, just as grain elevator manager Fred Johnson was reported at "death's door."

Meanwhile, the gauze masks that had been distributed all over the county—and the country—would later be deemed useless in protecting against the influenza. Only preventing exposure slowed the disease. Shuttering schools and churches and theaters proved more important than the millions of gauze masks tied to faces nationwide.

After two weeks of deaths and locked-up public places, Fairmont took a cautious breath of relief on October 15. Schools, movie theaters, and churches would reopen. The epidemic is "quieting down," Fairmont health officer Dr. R. C. Hunt said, while warning that "no relaxation of precaution against the disease" should occur.

Town health leaders "are to be commended for their sensible and vigorous action right at the beginning." When schools reopened, new orders would be in place banning any pupils for five days after suffering from a cold or the flu. Students should stay at home if any family members were ill. Teachers and principals, too, were ordered to stay home if there was sickness in their families. But despite rosy reports of overall improvement, deaths continued to mount—near and far— and the brief respite reported in the *Sentinel* didn't last.

John Ehlers, a "hard-working carpenter," became Fairmont's first flu death on October 22, leaving a wife and three kids. Word trickled in that two schoolteachers who had left the area also fell to fatal flu complications: thirty-year-old Ruth Rademacher in Gary, Indiana, and twenty-seven-year-old Mary Elizabeth (Bird) Cotton, in Columbus, Montana. Harry Wishnick, a Russian-born peddler, joined the dead on November 2 in Fairmont. Two brothers were at his bedside and took his body back to St. Paul for burial at the West Side Hebrew Cemetery. Wishnick was thirty-nine "and earned the respect of all as an honest, industrious and able business man. Few persons were more popular than Harry Wishnick." Fairmont schools and churches were ordered closed again on November 4 when four teachers became ill.

For the Senf family, the worry of 1918 was initially focused on their oldest son, Fred, who was fighting in France. He would live until 1981, when he died at age eighty-six. But his sister, Martha Koeppen, the oldest of the ten Senf kids, died of the flu and pneumonia, leaving her husband, Albert, and their one-year-old daughter. Martha was twenty-six and one of four young mothers who died in Fairmont during the middle of November. "A sad feature of the bereavements being that all of those who died are mothers of families," the *Sentinel* lamented. "In all, fifteen children are left without the tender care which a mother can provide."

Between October 20 and November 18, 1918, more than three hundred new flu cases and fourteen deaths were reported in Martin County. "It can be seen that the hoped for abatement in the epidemic has not yet occurred," the *Sentinel* admitted. All told, the county reported 456 flu cases, including nineteen deaths, and that only counted the cases when a physician was called. But just as the death toll seemed to climb every day, things quickly improved.

"'FLU' CONQUERED," the *Sentinel* headline screamed on November 23, quoting Fairmont's Dr. R. C. Hunt, saying, "I think we can call it over." Cases had dropped by 75 percent. "Fairmont's medical forces have compelled Old Man Influenza to surrender and sign an armistice effective Dec. 1," the newspaper said, just a few weeks after another armistice signing signaled the end of the Great War.

Dr. Hunt's announcement that the flu had run its course "will be hailed with joy by all residents of Fairmont and the county," the *Sentinel* gushed. "While experts state there is little danger of contamination except where victims of the disease are closely approached, there has been a feeling of uneasiness which could not be overcome until an official announcement was made today that the pesky germ has been worsted."

The newspaper said it hoped movie theater operators "will get a cargo of funny films that will last for a month. . . . A movie show will look to Fairmont now like a Yankee soldier boy marching into Brussels looks to a Belgian." Likening the German invasion to the flu's attack might be a forced metaphor, but Martin County was free. The *Sentinel* even found a silver lining in the winter clouds approaching.

"Coming of clear, cold weather is another blow to influenza and respiratory diseases, which thrive much better in the damp and foggy weather of recent date and which continued for so long," the *Sentinel* said.

Arthur Townley, founder of the Nonpartisan League, speaking to a gathering, circa 1915. *Courtesy of Minnesota Historical Society Collections*

CHAPTER 13

St. Paul and the 1918 Campaign

TOWARD THE END of a feisty, two-day political get-together, a thirty-seven-year-old former flax farmer spoke in a quiet but strong voice to a crowd of Minnesota farmers and urban workers estimated near seven thousand. Pausing for dramatic effect, Arthur Townley asked, "Farmers of Minnesota, is there any hatred in your hearts toward organized labor?" The fellows from the country responded with a thundering chorus of "No!"—shaking the auditorium in downtown St. Paul.

Townley, the onetime Socialist and founder of the Nonpartisan League, asked those farmers who pledged allegiance to city workers to rise. Thousands leapt to their feet as the noise grew deafening. Then Townley asked, "Workers of the city, if you likewise pledge your allegiance to the farmers of Minnesota, please stand." Now everyone was standing in the jammed hall, tossing hats in the air. "The impossible in American politics, a farmer-labor alliance, was coming to pass," historian Robert Morlan wrote in his 1955 book, *Political Prairie Fire*. Townley forged his new farmer-labor partnership at the closing rally of the two-day Nonpartisan League convention. It marked the unofficial start of the political campaign season.

Townley's name wasn't on the ballot. But he was the one holding the matchstick that ignited the prairie fire. Minnesota membership in his Nonpartisan League mushroomed from thirty thousand to fifty thousand between the fall of 1917 and the end of 1918. His movement, launched a few years earlier with startling success in North Dakota, called for eliminating the profiteers of agriculture and manufacturing by giving government control over mills, grain elevators, warehouses, stockyards, meatpacking houses, creameries, and paper mills.

The farmers at the convention in St. Paul, who came from forty-eight state senate districts, also hammered out a platform pushing for a tonnage tax on iron ore production up north, a state insurance system, state-run free employment bureaus, pensions for aging workers, and an eight-hour workday—except during agricultural endeavors. The day before Townley capped the rally amid that climactic loud ovation, the convention had endorsed former congressman Charles A. Lindbergh Sr. to challenge governor Joseph A. A. Burnquist in his reelection bid in the Republican primary three months away in June. Townley's Nonpartisan League didn't operate as a third party but rather tried to unseat leaders within the major party primaries.

Born December 30, 1880, near Browns Valley in far-western Minnesota and a graduate of Alexandria High School, Townley headed west in his early twenties to try to make his fortune. He served as an itinerant plasterer's apprentice and tried his hand at large-scale wheat farming in Colorado. By 1904, he was growing flax in Beach, North Dakota, on the border with Montana, established fifteen years earlier. Heralded as "the flax king of the Northwest" by railroad land agents, Townley planted eight thousand acres of flax in 1912—buying machinery on credit to handle his crops. Bad weather cut his anticipated yields, and instead of the expected three dollars a bushel, the flax he was able to harvest fetched less than a dollar per bushel. He was soon $80,000 in debt.

He joined the Socialist Party after realizing "the same crowd that fixed the price of flax owned the Republican Party and the same crowd that controlled the Republican Party controlled the Democratic Party." Townley ended his one-year experiment with the Socialist Party in 1914 because he felt its agenda was too broad. The next year, he launched the Nonpartisan League, which borrowed Socialist demands for state ownership of grain elevators, rural credit facilities, mills, and insurance systems. He appealed to struggling North Dakota farmers because he was one of them. A contemporary said that when

Townley "commences to speak he appears to be about five-foot-ten; when he finishes he seems about ten-foot-five."

In the 1916 North Dakota elections, Townley's new Nonpartisan League lost only one statewide race, for treasurer, but filled 81 of 113 legislative seats and got its candidate, Lynn Frazier, elected as governor. By then, the league had spilled east across the Red River and was holding meetings near East Grand Forks in Polk County, Minnesota. In some townships, 95 percent of farmers signed up as members in 1916.

Bad timing undercut Townley's ascent in Minnesota. Just as his Nonpartisan League was becoming a legitimate force, the nation entered the Great War in the spring of 1917. Wartime meant calls for unity and patriotism, his critics insisted, not radical change. The Nonpartisan League platform trumpeted loyalty to the war effort, and members flew American flags from their automobiles and farm trucks. But Governor Burnquist and John McGee, his loyalty pit boss on the Minnesota Commission of Public Safety, turned the 1918 gubernatorial election into a black-and-white referendum on patriotism.

The manager of the Minnesota branch of the Nonpartisan League actually invited Burnquist to address the 1918 convention, which opened on St. Patrick's Day in St. Paul. The governor not only declined but also wrote a scathing letter that snatched the headlines as the league gathered in the assembly room on the ninth floor of the Pioneer Building. In his letter, Burnquist flashed back to a Nonpartisan League gathering that had taken place six months earlier in the St. Paul Auditorium, which, he argued, underscored the league's un-American ways.

Townley insisted his movement was for and by the "producers"— farmers and wage earners, but not merchants or small-town bankers. He tried to ease the friction between the farmers, who wanted the highest price for their wheat and other commodities, and the wage earners, who cringed when food prices rose. Townley called a three-day Producers and Consumers Conference in September 1917 to float his compromise: farmers would accept a $2.20 a bushel ceiling price for wheat, set by the National Food Administration. In exchange, the government would nationalize food processing and distribution to eliminate profiteering middlemen, while rigidly controlling the prices consumers paid. Townley also called for taxing war profits.

Among the speakers that fall was Robert La Follette, the progressive Wisconsin senator, zealous orator, and outspoken opponent—until the last minute—of the country entering the Great War. As La Follette discussed how to finance the war effort, he said some widely quoted things that were viewed as disloyal and pro-German, including comments about the passengers on the *Lusitania* violating the law by sailing on a ship with explosives: "The comparative small privilege of an American citizen to ride on a munition-loaded ship . . . is too small to involve this government in the loss of millions and millions of lives." Newspapers went wild with stories of La Follette's "traitorous" speech, and Burnquist and other Nonpartisan League critics used the remarks to brand Townley's movement pro-German and un-American. The *Fairmont Daily Sentinel*, still a year away from its daily coverage of flu deaths, wrote, "A great career . . . has been turned to ashes because Senator La Follette lost his head and betrayed his country in its hour of need. Too bad! Too bad!"

Newspapers weren't the only ones venting outrage. When Burnquist declined the invitation to speak at the Nonpartisan League's March 1918 convention, in his letter to league officials he specifically referenced the September meeting: "The cheering and applauding of the unpatriotic utterance of Senator La Follette at your last convention put a stamp of disloyalty on it [the league] that can never be erased." His letter, widely covered in the newspapers, went on to set up his strategy for blunting the Nonpartisan League challenge to his reelection bid: "He who in normal times needlessly arrays class against class is most often the ambitious demagogue, but any individual who will do so when our nation is in a life-and-death struggle is knowingly or unknowingly a traitor to his state and country. . . . For me there are during this war but two parties, one composed of loyalists and the other of disloyalists."

While Burnquist's letter grabbed the headlines, the Nonpartisan League made news of its own in St. Paul by endorsing Charles August Lindbergh Sr. to top its ticket and challenge Burnquist in the Republican gubernatorial primary. The dashingly handsome Lindbergh was just shy of sixty and ran a small farm near Little Falls. His son, Charles Jr., then just sixteen years old, would become a hero nine years later for his solo flight across the Atlantic Ocean.

When he accepted the Nonpartisan League endorsement, the elder

Fight for Democracy in Europe

Vote for Democracy in Minnesota

Charles A.

LINDBERGH

FOR

GOVERNOR

RALPH E. CRANE
Lieutenant Governor

THOMAS V. SULLIVAN, Attorney General

S. O. TJOSVOLD, Auditor

ALBERT H. FASEL, Treasurer

FRED E. TILLQUIST, Railroad and Warehouse Commissioner

HERMAN MUELLER, Clerk of Supreme Court

Candidates in Republican Primaries.

Prepared and Issued for the Above Candidates by C. W. Barnes, 975 Fairmont Ave., St. Paul, Minn.   JOHN J. WILLINGER CO. 46

Charles A. Lindbergh's campaign for governor in 1918 called on voters to "Fight for Democracy in Europe. Vote for Democracy in Minnesota." *Courtesy of Minnesota Historical Society Collections*

Lindbergh had just wrapped up a ten-year stint in Congress and had written a book in 1917 called *Why Is Your Country at War and What Happens to You after the War, and Related Subjects*. In it, he blamed the "Money Trust" and other profiteers for promoting the war, branding them "the real disloyalists." To root out "these traitors, the profiteers," Lindbergh called for nationalizing essential industry, like France, Britain, and Italy had done.

Months before Lindbergh was tapped to run for governor, Lenin and his followers had overthrown the Russian government, and the Bolsheviks were in charge of the land once ruled by tsars. On the campaign trail, Lindbergh would assert that Russia's failure to put key industries under government control "led to that nation's collapse." Economic management, he said in his St. Paul acceptance speech, was as important as military strategy to win the Great War.

He also challenged Burnquist and McGee's loyalty crusade. Those "seeking to perpetuate themselves in special privilege and in office" fear the will of the majority and raise false issues of "loyalty," denying constitutional rights to honest and sincere citizens, Lindbergh said. "We must put into practice at home those principles for which we have sent our boys to fight abroad. . . . It will avail little to win a war for democracy abroad if in the prosecution of that war all the traditional rights and privileges of the people of this nation have been surrendered and abrogated." Lindbergh told the Nonpartisan League convention that "this is the time to test our sincerity. We must guard against any acts in state or national life which would in any way place doubt upon our honesty or cast reflection upon our motives."

In response, incumbent governor Burnquist opted for a kind of rope-a-dope, Rose Garden strategy to fend off Lindbergh's primary challenge. As the campaign unfolded, Burnquist vowed to "make no political speeches" but to "accept, as far as possible, those invitations to deliver patriotic addresses."

Lindbergh had three months until the June 17 primary to make his case in a campaign that would quickly turn nasty. In some ways, he was an ideal reform candidate—well-liked, experienced, and voicing ideas of economic change that appealed to farmers and workers alike—but his antiwar positions gave Burnquist's team an opening for attack. "Sincere, selfless, hard-working, quiet yet extremely forceful, he was respected by all who knew him and his integrity was beyond question," historian Morlan wrote about Lindbergh in 1955. "A fighter for principles in which he believed, Lindbergh was one who asked and gave no quarter. . . . Yet there was a sense in which Lindbergh was perhaps an unfortunate choice, for, rightly or wrongly, he was extremely vulnerable on the war issue."

At an early campaign stop in Willmar on April 25, 1918, Lindbergh attracted a crowd so large that his event was moved to the fairgrounds. With supporters wearing Red Cross and Liberty Loan buttons, he trumpeted the American war effort as a way to secure democracy across the globe. The Nonpartisan League plans to nationalize industry would secure that loyalty at home. His campaign grew to feature parades with hundreds of flag-fluttering cars—flying both the stars and stripes and Nonpartisan League banners. "They were snowballing affairs," Morlan said, "adding a car at every farm—one parade in Meeker County claimed to be twelve miles long." A crowd of fourteen thousand attended an all-day picnic on June 14 in Wegdahl, a western Minnesota town between Granite Falls and Montevideo. But the Lindbergh campaign ran into plenty of backlash, too.

Anti-Nonpartisan League merchants would close stores when rallies were scheduled. Some towns blocked streets. In Red Wing, Home Guards broke up a parade. In other towns, Lindbergh's campaign was met with fire hoses, ripe tomatoes, tipped-over cars, and yellow paint—the cowardly color aimed at reminding folks about his early antiwar views. In Stanton, a small town south of the Twin Cities near Northfield, an effigy of Lindbergh was hanged from a telephone pole in front of the bank. "It is a striking commentary on the times that a widely known and respected citizen who had served his state ten years in Congress should now be stoned, rotten-egged, hanged in effigy, and subjected to an unending torrent of abuse," Morlan wrote. "Towns and even whole counties were barred to this candidate for the Republican nomination for governor, and he was constantly followed by detectives."

Lindbergh didn't back down, though. According to biographer Lynn Haines, Lindbergh once came out of a meeting to find his driver had been pulled from his car and badly beaten. "By sheer force of will and in a quiet penetrating voice, Lindbergh made the men listen to reason and they fell back. He helped his friend into the car and they went off," Haines wrote in his 1931 book, *The Lindberghs*. "They had

Charles A. Lindbergh Sr. hanging in effigy from a telephone pole in Stanton, Minnesota. *Courtesy of Minnesota Historical Society Collections*

Campaign poster for Joseph A. A. Burnquist's 1918 run for governor. *Courtesy of Minnesota Historical Society Collections*

gone but a few rods when the mob began to shoot at them. Lindbergh turned to his friend and said, 'We must not drive so fast.' And with the rain of bullets hitting the car, continued, 'They will think we are afraid of them if we do.'"

In Duluth, Lindbergh found the doors locked at a hall in which he was scheduled to speak. The *Duluth News Tribune*'s May 29, 1918, edition covered the story: "Lindbergh wanted to speak here. No one cared to hear him. The city objected to the disgrace. It has entertained too many returned soldiers, bearing the wounds of battle, to be willing to act as host to a friend of the Kaiser."

Burnquist, meanwhile, backed up his vow to avoid political speeches, insisting he was confident that "patriotic people" would reelect him on his loyalty. He portrayed the air of a wartime chief executive while his minions encouraged local groups to hold "loyalty meetings" where the governor would speak nearly every day leading up to the primary.

"It can truly be said that the coming state-wide primary in Minnesota is one of the most important, if not the most important election that any state ever held," the *Nonpartisan Leader*, the league's official voice, wrote on June 10. "It will be the first test of the ability of farmers and city working people to cooperate and take over the functions of government for *producers*, who constitute two-thirds of the people, and who are consequently entitled to rule." The Nonpartisan League's journal predicted the state Republican primary would hold national consequences: "If organized farmers and organized labor can carry Minnesota, they can carry any state in the Union. Carried to its logical conclusion, this sort of cooperation will eventually mean the election of a president of the United States and of a majority in both branches of Congress."

Not everyone was so buoyant. The *Minneapolis Journal* said: "The nomination of Lindbergh would be more than a disgrace—it would be a great misfortune. The only way to be for your Country, State and City in 1918 is overwhelmingly to vote down Socialism, wherever it shows its head." The *Journal* went on, "Republicans and Democrats alike should vote in the primary for Burnquist, in order that the stigma of disloyalty may not rest upon this state."

Across the river, the *St. Paul Dispatch* headline on June 17, Election Day, stated: "Patriots Battle in Primary to Rout Non-Partisans." And on Election Day, with a war raging in Europe and with Russia in the first months following revolution, the voters in Minnesota decided the status quo was the way to go.

"The League and its candidates had put up a valiant fight against tremendous difficulties, but the odds proved too great," Morlan wrote. Burnquist beat Lindbergh, 199,325 to 150,626. The sky-high voter turnout of nearly 350,000 more than doubled the previous record of 168,308 set in 1916. Many of those were Democrats crossing over to vote in the open primary. Lindbergh won thirty of eighty-six counties and lost six by fewer than a hundred votes and ten others by fewer than three hundred votes.

For the general election five months later, Nonpartisan delegates and organized labor, meeting separately in St. Paul, endorsed a Tracy hardware store owner named David Evans to run for governor as an independent. An earlier attorney general's ruling had determined that state election laws could limit independents, insisting that only candidates running for established parties could have their names printed on ballots. So labor leaders and Townley's Nonpartisan League opted to call their third-party candidate part of the "Farmer-Labor" party.

Burnquist won again, defeating Evans 166,611 to 111,966; Democrat Fred Wheaton finished third with 76,838 votes. The governor was reelected without winning a majority of the votes cast.

The Farmer-Labor Party would not officially form for a few years, and its merger with state Democrats would have to wait until 1944. But the seeds were sown for what today is part of the state's powerful Democratic-Farmer-Labor Party, now known as the DFL. "The Farmer-Labor Party had been conceived if not yet born" in 1918, wrote Morlan.

The 1918 general election on November 5 attracted less attention than the contentious June primary. After all, the fires torching northeastern Minnesota and the influenza epidemic killing hundreds across the state, "failed to distinguish between 'bond slackers' and 'patriots,'" wrote historian Carl Chrislock. "Like most disasters, they pointed to cooperation as a condition for survival." But two moments in August 1918 are worth reprising from the campaign that pitted loyalty versus alleged disloyalty and returned Joseph Burnquist to the governor's office.

In Rock County in the southwestern corner of the state, a Luverne

Loyalty Club was formed to topple the growing Townley movement. Nonpartisan League members were required to take an oath of allegiance to the United States and renounce Townleyism. League membership shrank from 382 to a dozen, many of whom were unceremoniously "deported" to Iowa. One of those ushered out of the state was fifty-five-year-old German American farmer John Meints, who returned to Luverne in August 1918 to help his sons with threshing. The loyalty club got word of his presence, and a mob tarred and feathered him and drove him across the border to South Dakota on August 19.

A few weeks later, a mob calling itself the Knights of Liberty organized in Duluth. These knights roughed up a Finnish immigrant and alleged draft-dodger, who pleaded that his alien status protected him from being drafted. He was soon found hanging from a tree, although authorities said they couldn't determine whether he was lynched or committed suicide.

Governor Burnquist stayed mum after the Luverne farmer was tarred and feathered. But he issued a statement when the Finn was found dead. "The public welfare demands that persons suspected of disloyalty be given a fair trial," the governor said. "And, if guilty, be punished by the lawfully constituted authorities, and that mob violence shall not be tolerated."

Gunnar Bjornson, the editor of a popular weekly newspaper called the *Minnesota Mascot*, had supported Burnquist in his primary fight with Lindbergh. But the editor mocked the governor for his late anti-mob violence decree. "The governor of the state of Minnesota has come out against mob rule," Bjornson wrote. "After due deliberation, he had decided he does not want any more men tarred and feathered or horsewhipped or deported, beaten or disgraced or shamefully treated, without due process of law."

"The governor," Bjornson went on, "has made the discovery that there is a law against dragging a man out of his home and beating him up and subjecting him to all kinds of indignities. Mobs have been doing—free and unmolested—so many Hun stunts in this state that we had almost come to believe the mob was a new form of law and order enforcement." The editor said Burnquist, McGee, and the rest of the Public Safety Commission "have been silent" on mob atrocities "for so long that we really did not know what to think about it. . . . But the governor has saved the day—also he has saved the constitution."

Bjornson urged Burnquist to go to every corner of the state to speak out against the mobs: "We hope that hereafter there will be no more stealing of banners, no more tearing off of the United States flag from cars that carry a Nonpartisan League banner, no more of the dirty, sneaking yellow paint brigades, no more tar and feathering . . . no more deporting of citizens, nor more of the hundred and one different kinds of outrages that have gone unmolested and unnoticed, if not encouraged, by state and county officials."

Bjornson's angry diatribe appeared in the *Minnesota Mascot* edition printed October 11, 1918. The next day, fires up north would consume Cloquet, Moose Lake, and more than two dozen other villages.

People drove their cars into the lake to escape the flames around Moose Lake.
Courtesy of Minnesota Historical Society Collections

CHAPTER 14

Kettle River; Moose Lake; Cloquet

THE NURSE WANTED TO HUSTLE HOME to her family's farm a mile west of Kettle River. Luckily, the doctor convinced her otherwise, telling her he feared "the fire might take a turn to the worse." Dr. Franklin Reuben Walters never made a more accurate diagnosis.

At twenty-one, his nurse Ida Salmi was the oldest child of John and Olga Salmi's ill-fated family. Her mother and four siblings died when fire swept across the fenced road in front of their farm on that dreadful Saturday, October 12, 1918. Only little Eino, age three, had somehow survived by the Kettle River bridge, where his father later found him. That father, John, who was among the first Finnish settlers around Kettle River in 1888, suffered burns and contracted the flu and several recurring bouts of pneumonia, which killed him five years later.

At the time of the fire, Ida's closest younger sister, Lydia, had been working as a clerk at Michaelson's store in Kettle River and living as a boarder with the Leppas. Ida, two years older, was working at Moose Lake's tiny hospital—with a bed count of two on October 12, 1918. One patient had just been on the operating table.

On that Saturday, Ida and Dr. Walters made a house call, checking in on a sick Mrs. Jarvi. As they headed back to Moose Lake, Ida noticed "the smoke was extremely thick in the Kettle River area," where she still lived with her parents and siblings on the family farm. In a story published fifty years later in the *Moose Lake Star Gazette*, Ida explained how Dr. Walters insisted she stay with him in Moose Lake because the fire was unpredictable—and growing. "That evening as the smoke grew thicker and thicker we were eating our supper," Ida recalled. "But we were forced to flee the hospital even before many of us had a chance to finish" the food.

Ida said Dr. Walters found himself in an agonizing quandary. His two hospital patients were quite ill. He threw caution to the wind— wind that would soon be blowing eighty miles per hour and uprooting trees. "Doctor Walters decided to load them all into his car with some children and make a dash for Sturgeon Lake," about six miles south and, he hoped, out of the fire's path. "He never made it there," Ida said.

Fire had crossed the road south, so Dr. Walters circled back to Moose Lake, then a village of five hundred people nestled on the northeastern side of Moosehead Lake. By the time he got back to town, the car was starting to catch fire. Walters barreled straight ahead and drove his car right into the lake. Ida remembered how everyone, including the two sick patients, "had to drop into the icy water to keep from burning."

Hundreds of people from Moose Lake were in or at the lake. One guy found a bucket for his aunt to sit on and splashed her with water when her clothes ignited. People tried to filter the air by breathing through handkerchiefs and towels. "It seemed like every soul from Moose Lake was there, in or near the water," said Tillie Odberg West-man, who was fourteen at the time. The cottages at Hart's Resort soon began to burn, "and we actually watched flames leap over the lake and ignite buildings on the opposite side. The entire heavens were a huge ball of flame and, within minutes, the entire city was blazing." A hard-ware store that sold ammunition began popping as shells exploded, sounding "like cannon fire," Tillie said, "or a battlefield."

Along with other nurses from the hospital, Ida made it to the other side of the lake. From there, she watched the town of Moose Lake burn—"from a smoky gray, to a bright glowing red and then to black dotted with spots of flame." The fire that torched Kettle River at 7:00 PM swept eastward at a speed of more than twenty miles per hour. Just after 8:00 PM, when electrical power failed and the pumps fizzled out, firefighters surrendered their frantic bid to save Moose Lake. "The fire swept mainly from the southwestern part of town," Ida said, "burning everything but a few buildings on Soo Hill and a brick school building."

Through the smoke, Ida and the other nurses saw a farmhouse still standing and went there to spend a restless night. In the neighboring woods, a Northwestern Telephone Company lineman named George Vader attempted to keep communications going with Barnum, five miles north. His voice faded as the connection crackled and disappeared. His body was found in the woods during the days that followed.

Richard Hart, the mayor of Moose Lake, spent that Saturday in Kettle River with his brother, Charles. They owned the Hart Brothers Lumber Company. As the fires burned themselves out, he trekked back to Moose Lake by late Saturday night, sizing up the damage and dead bodies on Dead Man's Curve. The mayor found his house standing in Moose Lake, but not much else. The railroad office and telegraph facilities were charred and smoldering. The mayor walked another six miles to Sturgeon Lake, where he telegraphed Governor Burnquist in St. Paul: "WE MUST HAVE FOOD AND CLOTHING FOR THREE THOUSAND PEOPLE AND THREE HUNDRED CASKETS AT MOOSE LAKE AT ONCE," the telegram said, in all capital letters and replete with typos. "ENTIRE COUNTY BURNED AND PEOPLE SUFFERING. ALL COMING TO MOOSE LAKE FOR AID. WE MUST ALSO HAVE FINANCIAL AID. THIS APPEAL IS URGENT."

The next morning, Tillie Odberg said the scene reminded her of "pictures of war-ravaged cities in Europe." Kettle River was completely burned, down to the gutted bank building. Moose Lake, down the road, had a few buildings left amid ruins. Ida Salmi made it back to "what was once Moose Lake." She found her sister, Lydia, who had endured the hell of Dead Man's Curve. "Someone told us that a train was waiting to take us" to Duluth or Superior, Wisconsin.

The trains, whose sparks had ignited the deadly fires, had also saved hundreds. Three relief trains had taken more than three hundred people out of danger that Saturday night from Moose Lake and Sturgeon Lake. They continued to ferry people like Ida and Lydia Salmi to hospitals and Red Cross facilities in the twin ports of Duluth and Superior.

A Minnesota Forest Fires Relief Commission later estimated that at least half of the 453 lives lost in the fires on October 12, 1918, died in the Moose Lake and Kettle River area. Among them were at least 15 volunteer firefighters west of Kettle River, 75 to 100 people at Dead Man's Curve, 67 near what was called Eckman's Corner, 37 in root cellars at the Niemi, Soderberg, and Williams farms, and countless others in various buildings, wells, streams, fields, and woods.

The disaster at the Niemi farm—about five miles west of Moose Lake—might be the most heartrending of all the numbing tales of loss. Hulda Portinen Koivisto, who lost seven of her eight children on October 12, 1918, shared her memories with Edwin Manni fifty-seven years later for a story that ran in the *Moose Lake Star Gazette* in 1975.

"The forenoon was beautiful," Hulda said. With eight kids ranging from age one to thirteen, she and her family tackled the Saturday chores and washed clothes. They knew fires were burning a couple miles south at Tomczak's mill. When they realized the danger was approaching, they wrapped valuables in a bedspread and buried them in a half-acre potato field. A child's bike, some furniture, a buggy, and a wagon would somehow remain unburned on a nearby rock pile. The family planned to escape to the south because they didn't see any more smoke coming from the direction of Tomczak's mill. "Suddenly, the wind shifted and increased in velocity and it was obvious disaster was upon us," said Hulda, who was thirty-six at the time. "Despite the shock, confusion and fear, survival was a decision to be made in seconds."

Her dad, Henry Portinen, ran over and encouraged the children to join him at his home nearby. Only seven-year-old Arnold ran through the swampy area with his grandfather. They made it to the gate, where his grandfather's burned body was later discovered. An uncle, Urho (Corny) Portinen, tossed Arnold and another nephew in a Model T. A huge gust of wind lifted the car, throwing it on a stone fence. The three survived in a low spot in a nearby field.

By 7:00 PM on that day of horror, one of the Koivistos' neighbors, Ida Niemi, had hustled the children to her root cellar for what she believed would be safety. With winter coming on, the cellar was jammed with potatoes, but fifteen people managed to squirm inside: seven Koivisto kids—Leonard (twelve), Ellen (eleven), Ester (nine), Ethel (nine), Elsie (five), Wilbert (three), and Evelyn (one); Ida Niemi (fifty) and four of her children, Helmi (fourteen), Alexander (twelve), Bernhardt (ten), and Martha (five); and three members of the neighboring Berkio family, Christina (fifty-seven), Clara (sixteen), and Reino (seven).

Hulda, her husband, Nick, and one of the Niemi boys, John, stayed outside, wrapped themselves in blankets, and tossed bucket after bucket of water on the root cellar door. "With the terrific wind, dust, smoke, and burning debris landing on the root cellar roof, it was a constant battle to keep the fire out," Hulda said.

Every root cellar had an air vent. "Finally in all the confusion, it dawned on us to call down this vent to inquire about the welfare of the people inside," she said. They received no answer, so they opened the door. "You can imagine the horror when we discovered all of the people we had desperately tried to save were dead—suffocated from lack of oxygen. Even some of the potatoes were baked. There was nothing more to be done for them."

Hulda and Nick pulled the bodies from the cellar, arranged them in a long row, and placed their arms across their children's bodies— "hoping and praying for some sign of life, with no success." They remained with the bodies until Sunday afternoon, when guardsmen stopped at the farm after retrieving bodies from roadsides. All the bodies were brought to the new Elm Tree Hotel, which had avoided the flames in Moose Lake.

When Hulda heard her children would be buried in the mass grave, she threw a fit. She was a devout Christian and told three officers that her children would be buried in the family plot at St. Peter's Lutheran Cemetery in Moose Lake "even if she had to push them there in a wheelbarrow." The guardsmen yielded to her request. Coffins were furnished, and army trucks had to stop at each stream crossing to unload because the bridges were burned. But Hulda's children were buried in the family plot at St. Peter's, as were the three Berkios. The Niemis were buried in the mass grave.

Hulda's father was never seen alive again after Arnold lost sight of him at the farm gate. Presumably his body went in the mass grave. Hulda's mother, Lydia, badly burned, died three weeks later at St. Mary's Hospital in Duluth. And eighteen-year-old John Niemi, who tossed the buckets of water on the cellar door, died from influenza and smoke inhalation that November.

*

Twenty miles southwest of Duluth, Cloquet was the largest lumber town around, with about eight thousand people on the south bank of the St. Louis River. Through the mounting smoke, the incessant wail of sirens and whistles punctuated Cloquet as darkness fell the night of October 12, 1918.

Anna Dickie Olesen, the wife of Cloquet's school superintendent, had just finished her after-dinner coffee with Dr. Mabel Ulrich, a physician and bookstore owner who was scheduled to be the guest speaker at the Cloquet Mothers' Club meeting at the high school. Olesen, a fiery orator, would go on to make history in 1922 as the first woman to run for the US Senate with the backing of a major party. Nearly two decades later, Ulrich would spearhead the Works Progress Administration's writers' program in Minnesota during the Great Depression. But on this night in 1918, the two were in a fight for their lives. Anna was thirty-one and Mabel was forty-one. Peter Olesen, the superintendent, ran in—breathless—and interrupted their coffee chatter. There would be no Mothers' Club meeting, he said. The fire was coming across the hills from the south.

Rudolph Weyerhaeuser and Sherman Coy, the manager and secretary of the Northern Lumber Company in Cloquet, had just returned from a business trip. Weyerhaeuser was the fifty-year-old son of St. Paul lumber baron Frederick Weyerhaeuser—a German emigrant who came to Minnesota in 1891 and built an empire that spanned to the forests of the Pacific Northwest. He'd put Rudy, the sixth of his seven children, in charge of the lumber company in Cloquet.

After a nervous dinner at the Coys', the two men headed to see what was happening in town. A block into their curiosity mission, they saw what Coy later described as "a huge sheet of flame over the hill" behind Weyerhaeuser's home. As they walked further toward their lumberyard on the west edge of Cloquet, flames had reached within a few feet of the lumber piles. "I turned in the alarm from the box right there . . . and had the engineer blow the siren and keep it up," Coy said. Those piercing sounds from the mill sirens and warning whistles could be heard for miles around—creating an eerie soundtrack to a beyond-eerie scene.

Weyerhaeuser, Coy, and the Cloquet fire department attempted to douse the lumber piles, but the fire equipment became mired in a ditch and more horses were needed to pull it out. Five men and two hose carts finally squirted some water on the now burning stacks of lumber, but the wind was blowing up to more than seventy miles per hour. "We're gone," Coy told his boss. Weyerhaeuser sent him home to save his family.

Lumber heir Rudolph Weyerhaeuser (right) with his brother J. P. Weyerhaeuser, circa 1925. *Courtesy of Minnesota Historical Society Collections*

Again, the trains returned to rescue people. Lawrence Fauley, the agent in charge of Cloquet's Union Depot, hustled to get word to nearby rail centers to send trains to aid in an evacuation. A Great Northern railroad superintendent in Superior held four trains in Cloquet and one in Brookston for evacuees. Altogether, four trains had been assembled that afternoon, including passenger coaches and freight trains with boxcars. Cloquet mayor John Long helped Fauley organize all the trains. By midnight, they would carry more than seven thousand people out of the inferno and into safety.

As the sirens screamed, telephone operators remained at their switchboards and police alerted citizens to get to the relief trains. At a general store on the east side of town, owner John Blomberg kept calling Fauley at the depot to get the latest updates on the fire burning at Weyerhaeuser's lumberyard to the west. One of Blomberg's customers, a curmudgeon named Johnny Bull, slowly ate his pie and muttered, "This town ain't going to burn." By 9:00 PM, he might have felt differently. No one at the depot answered the phone. Old Bull decided it was time to leave.

Orlo Elfes, the editor of the Cloquet *Pine Knot* newspaper, burst into his home on Third Street and told his wife, Ada, and their fourteen-year-old daughter, Kathryn, "We've got to get out of here. The whole damned town is going!" Kathryn remembered "a shower of burning boards was flying around" as they made their way to the train station. When they found an empty boxcar, her father lifted her in. Her mother, Ada, protested: "I can't get in that! I've never been in a boxcar." She was a society woman; boxcars were for hobos. But Kathryn later recalled how her father, exasperated, picked up his wife "and threw her in with more speed than grace."

The Olesens, with daughter Mary and Mabel Ulrich, plowed through the wicked winds toward the relief trains. They joined a phalanx of wide-eyed refugees—all stunned. "Some went in automobiles or horse-drawn wagons, but most walked; several invalids were pushed in wheelbarrows, including a young woman who had given birth that day," Francis Carroll and Franklin Raiter wrote in their book, *The Fires of Autumn*.

Anna Olesen would long remember the streets chock-full of abandoned cars, wagons, and baby carriages left behind as people scurried to escape on the depot platform. Only women and children were allowed on the passenger train. Some families chose to ride the freight trains to stick together. A pair of Great Northern ore trains, consisting of seventy-five cars, loaded up nearly five thousand people and chugged toward Superior.

By 10:30 PM, with the west end of town burning out of control, the last train moved up the track so it could wait as long as possible. The last two boxcars caught on fire. Horses thrashed, buildings burned, and the sirens kept up their racket. Fauley, the depot agent, finally grabbed a lantern and jumped on the cowcatcher in front of the train to illuminate the way through the smoke. As that last car pulled out of the station, Mayor John Long jumped aboard. Or at least, that's how the legend grew. Fauley's role as hero would later unravel.

But in the moment, besides the sight of flames and the sound of sirens, there was the smell. Evelyn Elshoss recalled in an essay her view from the corner of a boxcar: "Bodies are packed all about me. My nostrils are filled with the stench of the barnyard, of too permeating perfumes, of unbathed bodies, or garlic, and of tobacco."

Train workers with lanterns had to check every bridge on the way to Superior and Duluth, including the trestle spanning the St. Louis River at Jay Cooke State Park. Pearl Drew, who hours earlier had penned a "don't worry" letter to her soldier husband in France, remembered the train grinding to a halt right on the middle of the bridge. "Of all the places we had stopped, this seemed the worst," Pearl said. "Fire was everywhere—flames licking from the deep gullies to the very tracks we were on." Death, she was sure, was close. An awful death.

But in the end, only six people in the city of Cloquet died in the fire, joining about one hundred who perished in the rural areas outside the lumber hub. That compares to roughly eight thousand people who were rescued, most of them on relief trains.

Anna Olesen had jumped on the train taking women and children. She clutched her ten-year-old daughter, Mary, to her side. They stepped off in Superior, Wisconsin, with hundreds of other stunned and exhausted survivors. "And there we waited for our men," she said. "We waited hour after hour, and finally the trains came bringing our men, and I saw the families that were united."

The next morning, she went to Red Cross headquarters and asked how she could help. "They did not, perhaps, recognize that I was a fire sufferer," Olesen said. "And I stood behind the table and helped pass out clothes to our people who the day before were happy and comfortable with the world's goods."

Sherman Lockwood Coy, Rudy Weyerhaeuser's Cloquet sidekick and assistant manager at the Northern Lumber Company, sat down and typed up a letter to his brother, Ted, on October 19, 1918. "Life this past week has been nothing but a dizzy whirl," he wrote. "I don't know how to express it—but I can't believe that a week has gone by since our awful calamity." He marveled at the "surprisingly small" loss of life in Cloquet, crediting the Great Northern and Northern Pacific railroads as "lifesavers." After regaling his brother with stories of "thrilling escapes," he got to the bottom line. "Our financial loss is very large, for me," Sherman Coy wrote, "but I'll be able to get along all right, and that is absolutely nil in comparison to getting out with all my family."

He underlined "all"—and recounted lifting his two-year-old daughter, Mary, from her crib. "The poor little innocent thing had no clothes saved but a pink dress and her pajamas." The family scrapbooks and photos were all destroyed, as were all his records and yearbooks from Yale University. "But what is that after all?" he wrote to his brother. "There are no plans for the future yet. I don't know what will become of us—whether I'll stay here or not. It's very uncertain. . . . The town cannot be what it was in our lifetime. No trees are left, and no vegetation and it's like a bleak wilderness."

CHAPTER 15

Minneapolis; St. Paul

WINFIELD STEPHENS started the decade of the 1910s selling cigars in Minneapolis. By 1918, Win (a nice nickname in wartime) was thirty-two and had become one of the city's first big-time car dealers. He worked for Pence Automobile Company, headquartered in a glitzy showroom at the tony corner of Hennepin Avenue at Harmon Place in Minnesota's largest city.

Clarence Wigington started the decade as a struggling architect, designing a potato chip factory in Sheridan, Wyoming. By 1918, he was thirty-five and had become a draftsman and designer in the St. Paul city architect's office—the first black municipal architect in the nation. He would go on to design the iconic Highland water tower plus schools, libraries, and an airport building in Minnesota's capital city.

These two men in their mid-thirties from such different spheres joined the countless number of Minnesotans thrust into the limelight when the Great War, flu epidemic, and forest fires converged on the state in 1918.

In May of that year, Governor Burnquist tapped Stephens to command the Minnesota Motor Reserve Corps, a military-style swarm of volunteers in every county who offered to drive their own vehicles to move troops within the state and respond to disasters. This was no run-of-the-mill carpool outfit: Stephens oversaw a brigade of ten battalions, 143 officers, and 2,583 men. New York, Massachusetts, Texas, and Pennsylvania had volunteer motor corps, too, but Minnesota's adjutant general Walter Rhinow insisted that "in no instance" were they comparable to Minnesota's imposing statewide operation melding motor cars and police work. "Minnesota is the only state in the Union which has a uniformed and thoroughly military body of business and professional men who have offered their own motor cars for any duty the state may see fit to call them on," Rhinow said in his official report from 1918.

The businessmen and doctors who signed up had to be at least twenty-six years old and were not quite volunteers. Officers received two dollars a day and enlisted men earned a buck a day. Nicknamed the Marines of Minnesota because they were often first on the scene, the Motor Reserve Corps was originally formed in 1917 as part of the new state Home Guard, a military organization created to protect state resources while most men of fighting age were at war against Germany across the ocean or drilling and training in stateside bases. When the United States entered the Great War in April of 1917, Minnesota's National Guard suddenly fell under federal control. It was wartime, but the switch left a void that was quickly filled with the Home Guard and its motoring sidekicks.

Rhinow's report said the Minnesota Motor Reserve Corps started humbly, "the idea being to secure a few cars in each county" which would be under the sheriff's direction. "The idea was a good one but did not go far enough," Rhinow said. "There was no discipline, nor any means of enforcing it."

Enter Win Stephens, who offered to overhaul the organization into a military-style operation with him in charge. Rhinow and Governor Burnquist enthusiastically embraced the car dealer's plans in May 1918—as did Public Safety commissioner John McGee. He figured the men and their cars could help his crackdown against sedition and disloyalty. Within three months, Stephens had used his recruiting network of auto dealerships throughout the state to create five battalions of men offering their vehicles and outfitting themselves in uniforms at their own expense.

Their first test, and chance to secure the public's favor, came when a tornado tore through Tyler on the South Dakota border on August 21, 1918, killing thirty-six and injuring more than two hundred people.

Officers of the Minnesota Motor Reserve Corps in Fairmont, Minnesota. Winfield Stephens is at the far right. *Courtesy of Minnesota Historical Society Collections*

"Driving over roads that in some places were almost impassable as the result of the storm, a 'train' of motor cars roared their way along the roads from the Twin Cities to the stricken village, bearing medical supplies, equipment and other sorely needed articles," the adjutant general said, in a rosy report no doubt aimed—in vain—at securing permanent funding and authority.

The Motor Corps was never formally established with legislative action. But when fires ravaged northeastern Minnesota in October 1918, "this organization earned its mettle," Rhinow reported. The first battalion, made up of men from Minneapolis and Wayzata, "bore its way into the north all night," arriving in Moose Lake on the morning of Monday, October 14. "Without stopping for rest or anything to eat, the majority of the men were dispatched immediately into the gutted district to care for the sick and recover the bodies of the dead," Rhinow's report said.

Photographs showing motor corpsmen tending to coffins at the mass grave in Moose Lake back up the adjutant general's report. The volunteers moved the bodies, dug the graves, and transported refugees, food, and clothing. "They did work that was almost superhuman in quantity and was heroic in quality," the report concluded. "Time was nonexistent for them and because they were the only means of transportation in the larger section of the burned territory, they were going day and night."

More than a modern-day version of the Federal Emergency Management Agency, or FEMA, the Motor Corps didn't limit its scope to disaster relief. Corpsmen were tapped for tracking down car thieves and serving as agents in the field, backing up McGee's patriotic zealotry by showing up at Nonpartisan League rallies, among other supposed threats. "The Motor Corps," the adjutant general's report said in its penultimate sentence, "made their presence known among the lawless and troublesome elements in the state."

On one hand, it's hard to dicker with a group of volunteers offering to drive a dozen hours from their homes and offices in Minnesota to round up and bury charred corpses up north. But as an offshoot of the Home Guard, the Motor Corps' military-style operation created some suspicion at home. Wasn't this the kind of thing that citizens in other countries feared: state-sponsored police squads?

"The Home Guard was meant to ensure public safety and protect citizens' lives and property," Minnesota historian Peter DeCarlo says. "Unofficially, the Home Guard was created to enforce the [Minnesota Commission of Public Safety]'s orders, many of which infringed on the rights of citizens." The commission, and its point man John McGee, established the Home Guard in the spring of 1917. From the outset, its mission was polarizing. The Public Safety Commission "employed the Home Guard as a de facto police force to quell labor disputes," DeCarlo says on the MNopedia.org state history website, pointing to strike-breaking duty at the walkout of Twin City Rapid Transit workers in late 1917. Home Guard troops dispersed crowds and closed off the streets in a six-block area of downtown St. Paul when thousands of pro-labor advocates gathered.

With the temperance movement gaining strength in the years before Prohibition was ratified as a constitutional amendment in 1920, Home Guard troops were credited with forcing bars to close in Blooming Prairie—a southern Minnesota hot spot for booze in Steele County between dry Mower County and surrounding, so-called wet counties. Regulation of alcohol sales was among the duties thrust upon the Public Safety Commission when it was formed in 1917.

On July 1, 1918, eight cars from the Home Guard's Motor Corps zoomed south from St. Paul to Blooming Prairie, fifteen miles north of Austin. Rhinow, the adjutant general, was there and no doubt Governor Burnquist, McGee, and Stephens were complicit in the raid.

Motor corpsmen assist in burying the dead from the fires. *Courtesy of Minnesota Historical Society Collections*

Finding what they viewed as illegal activities, the Home Guard troops closed four Blooming Prairie saloons and posted sentries at their doors. One of the bar owners sued, saying his constitutional rights were getting stomped on. "The Home Guard was a wedge that further divided opinion on issues like sedition and free speech, labor and business, loyalty and disloyalty, and race," DeCarlo insists. "Many people felt it was necessary; others thought it infringed on the rights of citizens."

Notwithstanding its unofficial role as the enforcement arm of the Public Safety Commission, the Home Guard served as a quick fix to respond to natural disasters within the state borders after the

National Guard was put under wartime federal control. Operating under the governor's purview, the guard's shelf life was short; formed in April 1917 and formally disbanded at the end of 1920, the force was mostly inactive once the war ended in late 1918. At its peak, the Home Guard included twenty-three brigades and 7,300 men, including the Motor Corps. It was the Motor Reserve Corps that made the Home Guard one of the most nimble and mobile military forces around. By the time fires broke out up north in the fall of 1918, the Motor Reserves Corps had two hundred private vehicles under its canopy.

Over the course of that fateful weekend in October, telegraphs saying the fire was burning out of control came into St. Paul from Cloquet and other towns, which one by one lost telegraph service until only Duluth and Two Harbors were reporting. Burnquist and his Home Guard chief, Adjutant General Walter Rhinow, acted fast. They first dispatched Home Guard troops from Aitkin and Brainerd, sending them east into the maelstrom to the jeopardized Aitkin County communities of Lawler and McGregor.

Other members of the Home Guard were alerted and swarmed toward the disaster from St. Paul, Minneapolis, Hinckley, Sandstone, Pine City, North Branch, and Duluth. Many began to relieve firefighters in Carlton and what was left of Moose Lake. Several cars, offered up among Company A of the Duluth Motor Patrol, caught fire as they tried to rescue fire victims whose weekends in the countryside had turned black. In some cases, the guardsmen and Motor Corps drivers were among those fleeing for their lives upon confronting the intense heat.

Within days, the brass was heading north. Along with getting medicine, clothing, and food to the disaster, the Motor Corps shuttled General Rhinow and two aides between Aitkin, McGregor, Automba, Kettle River, and Moose Lake. Governor Burnquist traveled to the grim scene in a special train.

Moose Lake, or what was left of it, became the Home Guard's makeshift headquarters. A school and church were among the only structures left amid the charred ash, and the high school in Moose Lake morphed into an emergency hospital. Rhinow quickly called in more home guardsmen and Motor Corps volunteers from Hinckley and Pine City. By the Monday following Saturday's fire, National Guard troops from the Twin Cities arrived in Moose Lake. Two companies of the Motor Corps joined them that Tuesday. Their task was grisly: putting names to the burned corpses. More than seventy people had died near Moose Lake alone, and the Home Guard helped bury them in the town's mass grave.

As grim as that scene must have been, there was also some sense of derring-do and sophistication at play as the Motor Reserve Corps descended. The fanciest cars of the era arrived, piloted by well-to-do men. "Rescuers moved swiftly through the countryside in luxurious touring cars," said Arnold Luukkonen, the late Bemidji-based historian and expert on the 1918 fires. "Drivers were repeatedly forced to use all their skill to keep their machines moving." Some forded streams in their Fords where bridges had burned. Others raced through walls of flame. And the looters and gawkers were close behind, requiring the Home Guard to set up perimeters, restrict access, and serve as sentinels.

Among the other jobs of the motor patrolmen was passing out flyers with sanitation, military, and medical advice. After all, the influenza epidemic had already started to spread across Minnesota. With refugees packed in poorly heated buildings, the virus picked up steam and made a bad situation a deadly one for both relief workers and fire victims. Gauze masks were distributed and field hospitals set up in Aitkin, Cloquet, and Moose Lake.

Three senior members of Rhinow's staff—Major William Garis, Captain J. W. Edwards, and Colonel LeRoy Godfrey—rotated fresh Home Guard troops into the area. The Motor Reserve Corps' mobility and rapid response made such a massive operation possible to mount. "Without the speedy relief provided by the Motor Corps, it is doubtful that many people would have been able to survive both the fire and the aftermath of disease and hunger," Luukkonen said. "The Motor Corps of the Minnesota Home Guard performed splendidly." He went on to describe their contributions as "almost super-human labor."

Rhinow, their general, said, "Had it not been for the Motor Reserve, Minnesota Home Guard, the splendid work done by the other organizations would have been seriously hampered, if not completely nullified." Luukkonen wrote in 1972, "The spirit that motivated these volunteers is something rarely seen in comparable units today." Most were paid "precious little" and received scant praise "except for the gratitude of the refugees." At least two motor corpsmen died in accidents during the rescue operations, and several of their vehicles were destroyed.

Yet the Home Guard and its subset of drivers had plenty of critics, worried about the quickly cobbled-together force of state-run police. And the Home Guard's lack of inclusiveness was also troubling to many—including Clarence Wigington, the rising architect in St. Paul who was fast becoming a community leader.

The Kansas-born Wigington spurned a family friend's offer to pay for dental school and opted instead to clerk for a prominent Omaha architect. He climbed from student to junior draftsman and launched his own firm in 1908. He would become the first black architect to design a home in Omaha. Wanderlust sent him to Wyoming, where he designed a potato chip factory in Sheridan but didn't find much other business. By 1914, Wigington, wife Viola, and young daughters Muriel and Sarah moved to St. Paul, where opportunities seemed brighter.

At Viola's urging, he took the architectural draftsman test in 1915 and earned the highest score, which led to a job at the city architect's office in St. Paul—marking the first time, nationally, that a black man found work as a city architect. In 1918, Wigington designed the Homecroft School in St. Paul—and watched world events unfold.

Wigington was thirty-five when the United States joined the Great War, and he promptly tried to join the National Guard. He was denied a military appointment based on his skin color. A year after the Public Safety Commission created the Home Guard to ensure public safety and protect lives and property on the home front, Wigington successfully petitioned Governor Burnquist to create an all-black Sixteenth Battalion of the Home Guard. "In the racist climate that prevailed, a 'separate but equal' unit was the most feasible option," historian Peter DeCarlo writes.

In the April 6 edition of the *Appeal*, a black community newspaper in St. Paul, a photo of Wigington—bespectacled and wearing a tie and jacket—topped a recruitment blurb:

Through the efforts of Clarence W. Wigington and others, the Governor and Adjutant General of the State of Minnesota have given official authority for the immediate organization of a company of Home Guards among the colored citizens of St. Paul.

Sixty names have been subscribed already. We want forty more. A meeting will be held one day next week, the date and place to be

Clarence "Cap" Wigington (far right), with the Sixteenth Battalion of the Minnesota Home Guard, 1918. *Courtesy of Linda Garrett*

announced later in the daily papers. If you are interested, send your name and address at once to C.W. Wigington.

Racial relations in Minnesota still had a long way to go. This was only two years before three black circus workers were lynched in Duluth. But forming a black Home Guard battalion, with the governor's blessing, was a small step toward feeling part of Minnesota for a growing black community of about eight thousand people. That still represented a tiny sliver of the population, roughly one-third of one percent of Minnesota's 2.4 million people. But they were joining the mainstream.

Wigington launched Companies A and B on April 20, 1918, with leading black men from St. Paul's Rondo neighborhood meeting at the nearby state capitol. A week later, Companies C and D were sworn in at Minneapolis City Hall. With all black officers leading the companies, more than five hundred men of color signed up for the Home Guard's Sixteenth Battalion, which included its own medical corps, band, and drum corps. Veterans of the Spanish-American War of 1898 kept the home guardsmen well drilled.

On Memorial Day 1918, the all-black Home Guard battalion marched in parades in both St. Paul and Minneapolis, receiving hearty applause when they appeared alongside their white Home Guard counterparts. As the troops escorted black draftees to train stations and appeared at patriotic rallies, the battalion—and Wigington in particular—connected the small black community with the Burnquist administration and other state power brokers. And Wigington earned a new nickname in the process. Everyone started calling him "Cap," reflecting his captaincy.

CHAPTER 16

Lawler; Moose Lake; Automba; Cloquet

THE SHERIFF OF AITKIN COUNTY, at the far western edge of the charred expanse left by the fire, was named Isaac Egbert Boekenoogen. The son of Dutch descendants, Boekenoogen was forty-two years old, tall, slender, brown eyed, dark haired, and exhausted. As the chairman of the Red Cross in the village of Aitkin, he'd been working tirelessly.

He went at it—finding shelter and clothing for refugees—so late one night in the nearby torched town of Lawler, he forgot to secure a bed of his own. As a last resort, the newspaper reported, someone brought to the cook's tent one of the crude, hastily hammered-together boxes that were being used to bury the fire dead. Sheriff Boekenoogen climbed in the makeshift coffin and slept soundly. He awoke around dawn just as the cook came in to make breakfast. The cook "saw the form of the sheriff rising in the dim daylight," the newspaper reported. "He took to his heels and has not been seen since."

Sixty miles east along Pike Lake, where fire tore through on its way to Duluth's outskirts, an explosives company worker named George Beers spent the hellish days around October 12 doing all he could to keep the flames away from thirty tons of blasting powder stockpiled for use in the iron ore mines of the nearby Iron Range. "He saved the explosives in the very teeth of the fire storm, but his house was destroyed and his family forced to flee for their lives," according to historian Arnold Luukkonen.

The Red Cross set up camps throughout northern Minnesota to help fire victims as well as home guardsmen assisting in the efforts. *Courtesy of Minnesota Historical Society Collections*

The fire could be fickle, sparing explosives but destroying homes. Perhaps the cruelest twist-of-fate tale to emerge from the ashes of October 12, 1918, involved the postmaster in Automba, John Arvid Kerttu.

Passport records show he was born March 13, 1876, in Haaparanta, Sweden, and sailed from Goteborg for America in the summer of 1901. Five years later, he became an American citizen in Duluth. He was described as five foot three, stout with brown hair and eyes, a round-ish face, and a reddish complexion. Kerttu worked as a taxidermist and artist in Duluth before becoming postmaster in Automba in the fall of 1915. He also had a store in town with a lunchroom, where he became a broker of timber deals for pulpwood and other business matters—a lucrative position for a successful immigrant in his forties.

When the fires began to grow on October 12, 1918, Kerttu loaded up his wife, Elisabeth, and kids Theodore (ten), Lilly (eight), and Raganor (one) into Alex Mattson's car, which was ferrying people out of Automba. Kerttu opted to stay to collect important business papers and the cashbox from his store. He stayed too long. The road to Kalevala that provided an escape route for his family was now blocked with flames. So Kerttu started across the clearing southeast of town. At the east end of the rail yard, surrounded by fire, he lay down against a huge sawdust pile.

Refusing to submit to the agonizing fate of burning to death, he pulled out his pistol and shot himself in the head. When his body was found, the revolver was in his hand. His cashbox and papers were next to him. He was untouched by fire: the flames had somehow never ignited the mountain of sawdust that became his premature deathbed.

*

In countless cases, amazing stories of surviving the fire were followed by the numbing reality of the influenza epidemic. "The days, weeks and months that followed were heartbreaking, hectic and strenuous to say the least," Tillie Odberg Westman recalled fifty years later. "The influenza epidemic followed and many died as a result."

Saima Anttila had just turned eight. Her dad, Charles, was a Finnish-born pulpwood cutter and sawmill worker. He and his wife, Nannie, lived with their five kids near Esko, six miles east of Cloquet. On that fateful Saturday in October 1918, Charles was off fighting the fires but hurried home when he noticed the wind turning north. "He just made it in time to help us, just before the porch collapsed," Saima recalled years later as part of Carlton County's oral history project. Their house on Erkkila Road had caught fire and Charles punched out the window and pulled Saima, her siblings, and Nannie out.

"It was a terrible feeling to face the sparks, burning wood and trees," she said. The family dived into roadside ditches five times to find fresh air amid the smoke cloud. At one point, two huge bundles of hay from a neighbor's shed landed on top of Saima and her sister. The rest of the family had dashed ahead toward a bridge spanning Crystal

Creek. Panicked, Charles realized two of his girls were missing and sprinted back. "He discovered my younger sister, Lila, pulling me to safety, since I had already lost consciousness," Saima wrote in *The Fire that Changed My Life*.

Charles carried a girl under each arm back to the bridge, where several stunned neighbors had gathered. They considered running to a schoolhouse across the road, but flames soon engulfed that structure. So they huddled in a potato field and winced from their burns. "The fiery hay stack had burned our legs, hair, arms, faces, and my side," Saima said. "We had gallon-sized blisters on our legs."

They eventually found their way to the armory in Duluth and St. Luke's Hospital: "They clipped our clothes off with a scissors because they were so badly burned on our skin." In the children's ward, a nurse cut off what was left of their hair. The hospital treatments that followed were horrible: "Every morning they tried to clean our bloody scars that were dirty from the potato field." Medicine was scarce, so nurses used cotton batting at night and would peel it off in the morning and dress the wounds with paraffin wax. A doctor explained that amputation was the only alternative to the painful wax process.

Lila and Saima were at St. Luke's for five months. Less than a month into the stay, on November 8, Saima learned her mother had died from the flu. Her baby brother, George, died from the flu about ten weeks after their mother.

"When my sister and I were finally released from the hospital in the spring, we found out we didn't have a home," she said. They moved into Charles's sister's house on Reservation Road about ten miles east of Esko. Eventually, Charles hammered together a shack back on their charred land north of the town. "It was very sad to go home," Saima said in an audiotaped oral history, later transcribed and preserved at the Carlton County Historical Society in Cloquet. "No Mother, no toys, no little kids to play with. I cried for many years afterwards."

*

Many people blamed the Germans for both the flu and the fire. Rumors swirled that German spies had sneaked the influenza virus into the country to gain a diabolical edge in the Great War. No proof ever surfaced.

Another story circulating fast—but equally unsupported by facts— accused German spies of arson, saying they deliberately set the Clo-

Moose Lake's Main Street was in ruins after the fire, but the rebuilding efforts started almost immediately. *Courtesy of Minnesota Historical Society Collections*

quet fires to halt the production of wooden boxes and crates used to ship war materiel to the American Expeditionary Forces across the ocean. Arnold Luukkonen called that story "more the product of the hysteria surrounding the fire than any secret orders from the Kaiser."

Medical officials, meanwhile, continued to tamp down flu fears, concerned that such anxiety would hurt morale and, thus, the war effort. On November 8, the headline of the Carlton County *Vidette* newspaper reported "probably a dozen deaths" from the disease.

"Hospitals have been pretty well crowded and the ones who have been fighting it have made a heroic struggle to stamp out the disease," the newspaper reported.

Dr. R. G. Spurbeck, who had been commissioned a captain for the Minnesota National Guard, oversaw 220 flu cases at the converted hospital in the Garfield school in Cloquet. His military appointment might make one skeptical of his rosy assessment of the situation. The *Vidette* told its readers that, despite "a few deaths, . . . Captain Spurbeck announces that the situation is being rapidly controlled." He predicted a 60 percent drop in cases "in a week or so."

The *Vidette*'s upbeat flu coverage ran side by side with a story carrying a headline that "Moose Lake will rise from the ashes." It quoted a gubernatorial appointee promising every farm would be rebuilt, every cow and pig replaced for "helping to feed the nation."

"The best government in the world is at the helm, and this government has the means and inclination to see that every farmer of this burned district gets back all he lost in the fire," the newspaper declared, adding, "the patriotic spirit that actuates the American people all through the broad land" has prompted hundreds of thousands of dollars in contributions. "Moose Lake will rise from the ashes, like the Phoenix of old, and in another year or two, things will be better than they were before, except, alas, for those poor people, some 170 of them, in the country west of Moose Lake, who suffered a terrible death in the fire."

The story concluded with this paragraph: "Our advice is to stick by the ship, stay in Carlton County. We want you here and they may not want you as bad in the next place, and will not throw out as good inducements as we will here."

CHAPTER 17

Cloquet

FROM THE AITKIN COUNTY SHERIFF scaring the daylights out of a cook to the ill-fated suicidal postmaster in Automba to the rumored German arsonists, stories spread across the fifteen-hundred-square-mile burned zone in northeastern Minnesota nearly as fast as the flames had. But in some cases, like the smoldering peat bogs that would burn for months, stories festered and remained untold for decades.

In one long-suppressed case, the actions of railroad personnel— widely heralded as heroic in the immediate aftermath of the fire— were drawn into question. Lawrence Fauley, the agent in charge of the Cloquet train depot, for years had been credited with coordinating the relief trains and jumping on the cow guard of the last train to leave, shining his lantern into the smoky chaos.

Fifty years after the fire, Fauley's true role on October 12, 1918, emerged in a far less heroic version of what took place. Kathryn Elfes Gray was sixty-four in 1968 and still worked as a staff writer at the *Pine Knot*, Cloquet's weekly newspaper that her father, Orlo Elfes, edited at the time of the 1918 inferno.

"The events of the afternoon and night of Oct. 12, 1918, are engraved indelibly on my mind," she wrote fifty years later. "I was 4 days shy of my 15th birthday at the time." Her five-page essay, typed in 1968, sits in a box of the Gray Papers in the bowels of the Minnesota

History Center. A year earlier, she penned a lengthy, more sanitized two-part narrative that was published in the *Vidette* newspaper on the forty-ninth anniversary of the "Night of the Fire." Kathryn wrote that her "first twinge of fear, later to give way to a terrorized panic, began as we were eating supper."

Looking back, Gray says Cloquet was "blissfully unaware" of the scope of the fire that surrounded the community. After all, it was nothing new—"forest fires were an old story. . . . The increasing smokiness and rising wind all afternoon, with the sun like a red ball in the murky sky, hadn't frightened me."

By late afternoon, her parents were whispering about a Brookston refugee train that had rolled through Cloquet. Then the first siren blasted. Her father the editor, Orlo, pulled on high boots and fire-fighting clothes. Things grew louder. "Another siren, a bell ringing, a whistle, the roar of the wind increasing," she recalled.

Her mother, Ada, had planned a busy Saturday. She was the secretary of Cloquet's Mothers' Club, which had a meeting scheduled. Then she planned to go to the Red Cross workrooms at the Masonic Temple to knit socks and mittens for soldiers overseas. The movie theater, she told her daughter, was closed because of the smoke from the fires. "You must stay home," Ada instructed. "But you can pop corn."

That's when her father burst in, breathless, and announced: "We've got to get out of here. The whole damned town is going!" Kathryn put on a skirt and a middy (the squared-off blouses of the era that looked like a sailor's shirt). Her father changed into a suit, and Ada, always stylish with "an impeccable taste in dress," donned a white satin blouse, white gloves, and a veiled, velvet hat. It was what a woman wore in 1918 when she was taking a train ride. As her father kept hollering, "Hurry," Kathryn tried to stuff her cat in a knitting bag. A policeman banged on the door and instructed the Elfes to get to the depot at once. "And over it all, the weird cacophony of sirens, mill whistles, train whistles and bells plus the roar of the demon wind."

That wind had blown the blaze into a firestorm. The electricity failed, and "huge pieces of burning lumber flying through the sky" illuminated the smoky evening. The fires and smoke had choked off train connections in all directions. Great Northern trains could neither come from nor leave toward Brookston—where train sparks had first ignited the fire, seventeen miles northwest of Cloquet. Trains

The "whole damned town" of Cloquet in ruins, October 12, 1918. *Courtesy of the Carlton County Historical Society*

from St. Paul couldn't reach Cloquet, either. They would be stopped in Moose Lake, twenty-five miles south and in the swirl of the flames, where they were commandeered and rerouted to help refugees there. In the Corona Bog west of Carlton, peat was burning deep in the ground, prompting interruption of train service between Cloquet and Brainerd, a hundred miles to its west.

Two iron ore trains, empty and bound back for the mines, sat idly in the Cloquet train yards. "There simply wasn't any place for them to go," Gray said, "and it was a great mercy there wasn't, as they were needed a few hours later."

One of the most popular trains of the era was Gilbert's Train, which Gray called a "varnish train," providing fancy commuter service on the Northern Pacific line. "Handy for Cloquet shoppers," Gray said, it carried folks to Duluth twenty miles east or Carlton six miles south. From there, they could usually connect to bigger, Twin Cities-bound trains. Named after its "genial conductor," George Gilbert, the train had left Cloquet for Duluth around 9:00 AM on that Saturday, October 12, and returned around 6:00 PM just as the fire danger exploded.

Gray recalled that Cloquet mayor John Long arrived at the depot in the late afternoon to assess the train situation—knowing no new trains could be brought in to help, what with the fire consuming the surrounding area. Long had worked in lumber camps and had dealt with other forest fires. He started unloading boxcars stranded in Cloquet, anticipating the space would be needed for human cargo—refugees fleeing the blaze. When one railroad employee hollered at the mayor, "That is railroad property, you will have to answer for this," Gray said that Long yelled back, "All right, I'll answer for it!"

Gray's story wasn't completely rooted in her teenage memories. Years after the fire, Long and his wife were at the Elfes's home, playing cards with her parents. She asked him "point blank" about the oft-repeated story she'd heard about the confrontation with the railroad employee. Long nodded and "admitted it," Gray wrote, "but—eyes twinkling, added 'No one put me in jail for it.'"

Gray said that, all told, there were four trains to shuttle the roughly eight thousand panicked residents of Cloquet toward safety: the two idled ore trains, a third stringing together what she called "a motley collection of boxcars," and Gilbert's Train. Gilbert's was the first to get out of town, carrying only women and children—some six years after similar rules were imposed for lifeboats on the *Titanic*.

"We were pushed away by cries of 'train is full—go to the other train,'" Gray recalled. "We were literally propelled as in a bucket brigade to the waiting boxcars." They were buffeted to the Northern Pacific tracks on the north side of the depot. All around them, buildings were burning. Someone yelled that the Methodist steeple was on fire, joining the Cloquet Hotel, the YMCA, the Masonic Temple, and the hospital in flames.

Gilbert's Train and one of the ore trains had already left and the other ore train was nearly packed. Kathryn and her parents found spots on the fourth boxcar from the end. But even after they crammed into the boxcar, a big problem remained: "There was no engine at the front," Gray recalled. Amid reassurances that "it's coming," her father spotted a switch engine backing up to the Cloquet depot. "We felt the thud as it hit," Kathryn remembered.

Just as the train finally began its escape run out of Cloquet, it ground to a halt. Orlo Elfes jumped from the boxcar. His wife, Ada, was "frantically hanging to his mackinaw collar." Then, depot agent Lawrence Fauley—"his face simply numb with horror"—walked past. Orlo asked the station agent, "When are we getting out of here?" Kathryn Elfes Gray, then a high school sophomore, said it was fortunate that she was among the only people who heard Fauley's reply, "or there would have been a panic." Here's what she heard: "We can't take passengers out on this railroad without standard passenger equipment," Fauley said. "And no orders are coming thru!"

In the throes of thick smoke and raging fire, this depot agent was trying to follow the rules, which forbade passengers from riding in boxcars. He was playing it by the book even though the pages of the book were on fire. "My parents gasped but admonished us to keep still," Gray recalled.

John McSweeney, the Cloquet police chief, came by wearing his trademark fur coat. Her father relayed Fauley's words, that no boxcar with passengers would leave without approval from higher-ups. Then, Orlo Elfes, the newspaperman, asked Cloquet's top cop if he had a gun. McSweeney opened his coat and showed two guns belted into holsters. The editor told the police chief to go point one of his pistols at the engineer's head and demand they roll. Now. "For God's sakes."

"McSweeney strode down to the locomotive cab and swung aboard," Kathryn said. "Then, the train, with its cargo of several hundred people began to slowly move."

Fauley did ride with his lantern on the cowcatcher in front of the locomotive, just as the heroic version of the story goes. And Mayor Long jumped on the last boxcar. But the more complete story only emerged a half century later in Gray's 1968 essay. She told how a loaded gun overcame a bureaucrat's penchant for following rules.

The train pulling the motley boxcars—including those carrying Kathryn and her parents, the mayor, and Fauley—picked up a few more refugees at Johnsons Corner and Scanlan on its way to the Carlton depot some six miles south of Cloquet. That's where a depot clerk named Lee Brower paged Kathryn's father. Brower's father, Adam, was the main agent at the Carlton depot, and Adam and his wife, Cora, were close friends with the Elfes.

Kathryn's father wanted to get on a southbound train heading for the Twin Cities because trains were jammed up in Duluth, to the east. The railroad depot clerk shook his head, saying they couldn't flee south because "Moose Lake is burning and most of the people, too!" They had no choice but to get off the train in Carlton. The younger Brower told the family to go to the home of his parents, who were waiting to host them. As the Elfeses walked through downtown Carlton, all the businesses, schools, homes, and even the jail were filled with fire evacuees. The barber shop, meanwhile, had been quarantined with the town's first influenza sufferer—a young girl, cared for by her mother.

Kathryn remembers her "Papa" telling the elder Brower at his home about how his counterpart depot agent at the next stop up the line initially refused to let a train jammed with refugees escape Cloquet because of some rules technicality. "Mr. Brower listened gravely," she recalled.

After a sleepless night, Kathryn helped Cora Brower bake powder biscuits "to give me something to do, and this alleviated my sobbing." Her father rode back to Cloquet in a car with other men. Kathryn went to the breakfast line the Red Cross had set up at the Odd Fellows hall before returning to the Brower home.

"Finally, Papa walked in, his face black, his shoulders sagging and sat down heavily in the nearest chair, burying his head in his hands.

"A moment of silence and then Mama asked, 'Is anything left?' In a thick voice he answered: 'No—nothing! Ada, we haven't a thing left in the world!'"

Ada demanded he stop that kind of talk. "Don't say that—we still have each other and our little girl. We're alive!"

Kathryn and her mother moved to Duluth while Orlo returned to what was left of Cloquet. A few nights later, Orlo's mood was more upbeat. He had been to Cloquet and jubilantly shared news that the city was preparing to rebuild. "Help is coming in from all over the country," he said. "Cloquet is coming back."

But when she returned to her hometown a few weeks later to see for herself, Kathryn was staggered. "I saw an unbelievable sight of an entire city in ruins. You could see from one end of town to another—gaping basements, ruined walls, smoke-blackened chimneys and here and there bright new shacks that were offices, homes and stores."

In the days after the fire, her father was contacted by a "big wig" from the railroad's St. Paul office. The honcho asked Orlo Elfes, editor of the *Pine Knot* newspaper, to never publish the real story of what went down the night of the fire, when depot agent Lawrence Fauley needed prompting from a police pistol to let the last refugee train leave town. Fauley himself approached the editor and asked him to "forget it."

Not much was left of Cloquet after the fire. *Courtesy of Minnesota Historical Society Collections*

"But he never FORGOT it," Gray wrote in her unpublished essay, fifty years later. "And neither did I." A few years after the fire, in the early 1920s, Kathryn wrote an essay for school about the reluctant depot manager. First, she showed it to her father. "He destroyed the paper and told me not to use it as it would be unkind," Kathryn said. "Even though it was true."

Fauley was a fine man, her father convinced her, who did an excellent job. Ohio born and the youngest of nine siblings, Fauley died in Cloquet six years after the fires, in 1924. He was fifty-eight years old. His death certificate says he died of mitral regurgitation, a condition in which blood flows backward through the heart. He also had pneumonia. By the time of his passing, the heroic telling of Fauley's story was arcing toward legend, as was the narrative spun about Percy Vibert, the area's top forestry warden.

"Due to the quick thinking of Percy Vibert, forest warden, and La[w]rence Fauley, train depot agent, the townspeople were carried south to Carlton, Minnesota, by railroad," according to a 1985 nomination to place the Cloquet City Hall, rebuilt after the 1918 fire, on the National Register of Historic Places. Never mind that, according to Kathryn Elfes Gray, "Percy Vibert and Lawrence Fauley were not in conference that afternoon ordering the trains." Vibert, she said, was rushing to the hospital to get to his wife, Mabel, who had given birth to their fifth child, Roland, a week earlier, on October 5, in Carlton. Percy had dropped off his other four kids with his brother, Fred, at Proulx's Drug Store in Cloquet—not knowing that Fred's car was in the repair shop and couldn't be driven to flee the area.

So the two men credited with heroics included a depot manager who hesitated to let boxcars filled with hundreds of refugees leave town and a forestry warden juggling his personal family concerns.

There's even a park in Cloquet named after Fauley. It sits alongside Highway 33 and Cloquet Avenue with Duluth & Northeastern Railroad steam locomotive No. 16. "This train is a reminder of the heroic train evacuations performed by Cloquet Union Depot Agent Lawrence Fauley who ordered trains from nearby train centers into town for the evacuation of our residents," Cloquet's city website says. "This memorial serves to remind people of the 8,000 people ferried to safety as a result of his efforts."

Some years after the fire, Kathryn Elfes Gray recalled that John

McSweeney, the gun-toting, fur coat-wearing Cloquet police chief, was among those at her parents' house when "the story was told over again, and the then-rising 'myth' of Percy Vibert and Lawrence Fauley ordering trains was sneered at. "It just was not that way," Kathryn wrote. "And John McSweeney and Orlo B. Elfes knew it." She pointed out that Percy's brother, Fred, owned the *Pine Knot* in 1918; Orlo was only the paper's editor, before he purchased it from Vibert seven years later in 1925.

"And that's the way it was," she concluded her 1968 essay, solemnly "avering the foregoing is correct, to the best of my knowledge and memory, and I remember the day and night of Oct. 12, 1918 very well."

Only four people died within Cloquet's city limits. "It seems nothing short a miracle," Kathryn wrote in her 1967 article. With such a high survival rate, heroes must have existed and their stories must be told. But sometimes, the truth behind those stories takes years to surface.

Nicollet Avenue in Minneapolis packed with revelers on Armistice Day, November 11, 1918. *Courtesy of Minnesota Historical Society Collections*

CHAPTER 18

Minneapolis; Hermantown

THE SOUND WAS THE SAME: a wailing siren. But it pierced the darkness a month after, and 130 miles south of, the warning blasts in Cloquet that signaled the fire's menacing arrival on October 12, 1918. Just before 2:00 AM on November 11, 1918, word of a war-ending armistice reached Minneapolis. "A big siren tore the midnight silence, with a roar and a series of crescendo shrieks echoing from the hills of Columbia Heights to the lowlands of the Minnesota Valley," the *Minneapolis Journal* reported. "Victory had been achieved and the boys were coming back from over there."

Lights blinked on in homes, and people poured into the streets. Everyone soon headed through the darkness to downtown Minneapolis, in streetcars, trucks, private cars, you name it. "Milk trucks and milk wagons were pressed into service," the *Journal* reported. "Automobiles came out of their garages and every driver felt it his duty to come downtown, carrying as many wayfarers he could find to pick up."

As crowds swelled, the noise just grew. The newspaper said the din "out-rivaled in noise making any other celebration in the history of the northwest . . . horns, bells, loads of tinware dragged over the pavement at the tails of automobiles and trucks. Drums, rattles, guns—everything blended into a mighty symphony.

175

"Everyone was brimming over with good humor and a feeling of fellowship for every other man, be he the struggling newsboy working his way through the crowd or the sedate banker off the hill blowing his horn till the veins on his neck were wreathed in purple expansion," the *Journal* reported in its issue on November 11, 1918.

At the Leamington Hotel, an old soldier-turned-governor joined the euphoria. Samuel Van Sant was a former Civil War corporal who had become a rich boatbuilder and politico in 1880s Winona before being elected to his first of two terms as governor in 1900. By 1918, the seventy-four-year-old Van Sant was a permanent resident at the downtown Minneapolis hotel.

At 2:00 AM, Van Sant met up with another hotel regular in his seventies, a onetime judge and fellow Civil War veteran named Eli Torrance. Both men had become commanders in the Grand Army of the Republic, the Civil War alumni club. By 4:00 AM on November 11, they'd buttoned up their G.A.R. uniforms and joined an Elks Club parade marching around the block. "We kept going until daylight," Torrance said. "Pretty good for two old soldiers."

As the merriment mounted, Minneapolis mayor Thomas Van Lear issued an order declaring November 11 a holiday and requesting all businesses close their doors to mark the armistice. "Our gallant boys in Europe have brought peace to a war-torn world," Van Lear said. "From the hearts of the mothers of this country, a load of anguish and anxiety has been lifted. Today, in spirit she stands with her boy on the battlefield and thanks the Creator for the blessing of peace."

It must have been a bittersweet moment for Van Lear, an avowed Socialist who had irked John McGee and others on the Minnesota Commission of Public Safety for what they viewed as disloyalty. Van Lear questioned President Wilson's decision to enter the Great War and those who would profit from it. He wondered aloud if the fight for democracy in Europe was ignoring democratic ideals of free speech and dissent back home. McGee branded Van Lear unpatriotic and attempted to get him ousted from his post. In the end, he didn't need to. Voters turned Van Lear out of office a week before Armistice Day, electing one-termer J. Edward Meyers, who ran on a Loyalty Party ticket that pointed out Van Lear's ties with antiwar Socialists. With the war over, all those who's-more-loyal debates gave way to noisy celebrations.

"The day of peace is dawning," the *Minneapolis Journal* editorial declared on November 11. "The world's night of agony is almost over—almost but not quite." Especially up north. Despite the peace, the agony was slow to fade after the fire. Shacks had popped up where family homes once burned. Clothing drives and other aid campaigns eased the hardships, but disease—from the Spanish influenza to diphtheria to tuberculosis—added to the woes.

Seven-year-old Doris Lofald, the youngest of six children, escaped the fire in Hermantown, just five miles west of Duluth. Her family had moved into an aunt's house in town—one of hundreds of fire-victim cohorts cramming into relatives' homes. Within a month, her father and two older brothers were stricken with the "war-time influenza," while she and her ten-year-old brother, Wally, had contracted diphtheria.

"Now all these refugees who had to leave their homes on the outskirts to survive, we didn't have anywhere to put them," said Dan Hartman, a present-day Duluth historian. "Everything you just did to try to combat the flu . . . you now put everyone together, and so the number of cases of the Spanish flu skyrockets in the city of Duluth. It's just the perfect storm of a bad scenario."

But after a long month, word of peace and the brief salve of Armistice Day gave people a reason to smile—even if they could only gaze at the celebration through the window of a sickroom, like the one Doris and Wally shared at their aunt's house in Hermantown. "I remember the day of all the hooting and howling and parades and celebrating," Doris wrote in a 1931 essay published in the *Hermantown Star*.

Her recollections, while less tragic than some, provide a child's perspective on the horrors of 1918. She was a twenty-year-old stenographer when she wrote about her memories as a seven-year-old. Her essay gives a firsthand account of the fire, the flu, the rebuilding, and the recovery that followed.

Doris remembered the blackness of the midafternoon of October 12: "it was not the ordinary darkness of after sundown. There was a terrible blackness at the horizon and every object was weird-looking." Thick smoke blocked the sun, she said, and the western sky "was illuminated by a horrid, gruesome, sparkling glow reaching from the horizon up to the high heavens." The fire was ten miles west of their home, but "the winds brought us the smell of burned buildings, burned soil, burned animals, and even bodies of humans that had been burned and who could not escape the sweeping fire."

Her father, Norwegian-born Michael Lofald, had traveled the seven miles into Hermantown with her brothers, Millard (twenty-one), Victor (eighteen), and Irwin (seventeen). They said they'd be back home by 4:00 PM. When they returned, they parked the wagon with the front wheels slightly turned to hasten an escape. They loaded valuables in the back. "We took many things of little importance, and in our frenzy overlooked many things we should have taken," Doris recalled.

As they left their home, she glanced back at the tall spruce trees nearby, knowing she'd likely never see them again. "I know the older folks must have had a terrible sinking feeling as we drove away and left our home at the mercy of those sparks and flying, burning sections of buildings." She wasn't old enough "to share the sense of desolation they must have had."

The Lofalds' white horses, Queen and Maude, trotted with the heavy load toward Hermantown. By 4:30 PM, the smoke was so thick Doris couldn't see her siblings in the wagon box. They'd grabbed some fresh loaves of bread that her mother, Nattie, had baked that morning along with a jar of butter in a water pail. They used some of the water to extinguish sparks that lit on the horses' manes. Then, "A burning piece of timber came flying and landed among our blankets and quilts and we simply threw overboard the burning mass of flames."

On the run toward town, they saw neighbors' buildings burning, and they narrowly missed careening down a high bank in the dark smoke—saved only by the horses' quickness. "We finally reached our aunt's house," Doris wrote. "I remember how surprised they were to see us . . . and that we were all so sick and tired and smoky—we must have been almost unrecognizable." With all the beds taken, Doris and Wally went to sleep behind the heating stove in the dining room "with only some half-burned quilts over us."

When her father and brothers trekked back to the farmstead the next day, "only a smoking heap of ashes and debris remained" amid the charred foundation where their two-and-a-half-story home stood a day earlier. The men slept in the hay shed, which had somehow escaped the blaze.

"Then in due time, the Red Cross helped to furnish 'shacks,' which were just that," Doris wrote. The newly appointed Minnesota Forest Fires Relief Commission provided materials for building temporary shelters. "Because there were so many in our family, we got two—one we called simply the 'Shack,' and the other the 'Paper Shack' because of the paper board walls."

The cold and rainy autumn came too late to staunch the record dryness that had stoked the fires. Her father and brothers contracted influenza but recovered. More than a hundred other fire victims weren't so lucky and were listed in the Minnesota Forest Fires Relief Commission's final report as "persons who died from Flu and Pneumonia immediately after the fire."

"In the fire area, influenza became part of the misery of the whole experience . . . exaggerated by the onset of chilling rains on October 18," Francis Carroll and Franklin Raiter wrote in a 1983 *Minnesota History* magazine article with a headline—"At the time of our misfortune"—cribbed from a City of Cloquet resolution that thanked people for their help.

Doris remembered wearing clothing donated from the Red Cross and families in New London, Minnesota. After more than a month at her aunt's house, she and her brother recovered from diphtheria and her father and brothers shook off the flu. It was time to go home.

"It must have been sheer bravery on Mother's part to go out there and start all over again from nothing . . . doing without things she had been used to . . . towels or linens or dishes or decent clothing." For six years, they lived in the two shacks. "We as children did not mind or complain," Doris wrote years later, "but it must have been a letdown for the grownups. . . . We put up with a lot and did without a lot, always patiently waiting for the time when we could put a house on that foundation again. It was a long wait, but I think even to this day I can appreciate it all the more because of not having a nice house for so many years."

Her attitude, chock-full with resiliency, was replicated across the fifteen hundred square miles affected by the 1918 fires. Hers is simply one of the fifty thousand tales from displaced Minnesotans who benefited from a massive state-run relief effort.

The speed of the initial response and in assembling the bureaucracy needed to address post-fire demands was staggering in its scale—a blend of military mentality and Red Cross caring. Within four days

of the fire, Governor Burnquist scheduled a Public Safety Commission meeting in burnt-out Moose Lake. The special Minnesota Forest
Fires Relief Commission was created to serve as the umbrella for the
recovery and rebuilding efforts. An initial $300,000 was authorized,
but the aid money flowing through the commission would swell to
nearly $2 million within four months. That's roughly $33 million in
2018 dollars.

But even before relief funds began to flow in, people responded in
inspiring ways. In Duluth, on the eastern edge of the burn zone, three
men huddled on the afternoon of October 12: Major Roger Weaver,
commanding officer of the Home Guard's Third Battalion; fire chief
Robert McKercher; and police captain Henry Tourtelotte, who had
gone to gauge conditions north of the city. By 5:40 PM, the fire chief
asked Weaver for troops and, within an hour, seventy men arrived at
the Duluth Armory, the vortex of the relief effort. "I will never forget the sight at the Armory," volunteer driver Frank Murphy recalled.
"The main floor was filled with cots and people sleeping—some of
them not knowing where the rest of their families were or whether
they were alive or not. It was one wild night."

The St. James Catholic Orphanage and the Nopeming Sanatorium,
the county's tuberculosis hospital west of town, were in jeopardy from
the fire. But fifty Home Guard troops helped evacuate more than two
hundred patients, moving them eight miles to the Denfeld and Irving
schools in western Duluth. Firefighters were able to save the buildings. Duluthians, meanwhile, stepped up to offer their own cars to
bolster the work of the Home Guard's Motor Reserve Corps, shuttling
refugees from the train depot to the armory and hospitals. Standard
Oil Company offered free fuel to help the transportation effort.

Governor Burnquist later insisted that the death toll in and around
Duluth would have been higher if not for the volunteer motor corpsmen driving their own vehicles for grueling stretches. One such volunteer, fleeing the fire that came within a mile of his home in Duluth,
ferried three loads of people on Sunday morning and then delivered
medical supplies to hospitals from noon until 10:30 pm.

In the Duluth Armory, thirty-two-year-old Kate Covey created
an emergency hospital and spent twenty-four sleepless hours making sure it was ready for the flood of fire refugees. When seventy-five
beds were quickly filled, more cots were lined up on the armory's drill

floor. The Red Cross in Duluth converted space into refugee centers at the courthouse, the Masonic Temple, and the Shrine Auditorium. Each venue was assigned a doctor and nurses. Within twenty-four hours, 438 people were treated, according to Carroll and Raiter. By early November, more than 750 fire-affected people had been cared for in Duluth's armory and hospitals, and records show twenty-nine doctors, fifteen nurses, and twenty-one medical aides had come to the victims' aid.

In Cloquet, guardsman Gus Apel set up a dispensary in the Northeastern Hotel, treating refugees and dressing burns for thirty-six hours without sleep. But more than just people needed help in the fire's aftermath. Burned wooden culverts needed to be rebuilt. Roads

The Duluth Armory, along with various locations in the city, was converted into a refugee center in the wake of the fire. *Courtesy of Archives and Special Collections, Kathryn A. Martin Library, University of Minnesota Duluth*

needed to be cleared. Livestock needed feeding. And a pontoon bridge needed to be constructed across the St. Louis River in Brookston, opening routes to both living and dead victims from the fire's starting point. Coffins needed to be delivered and lakes dredged for those who chose death by drowning over burning.

It was grim work that demanded structure. Adjutant General Walter Rhinow set up headquarters in Moose Lake, pulling together nearly three hundred troops, thirteen army trucks, a dozen civilian trucks, and another dozen Motor Corps cars. In the Moose Lake High School, one of the Mayo brothers' physicians, Dr. Frederick Smith, set up a makeshift hospital. The Red Cross built its own temporary hospital in Cloquet, serving 375 in-patient victims, more than a thousand clinical cases, and seventy pregnant women. The Red Cross also employed more than fifty trained social workers, many from Chicago, who helped reunite families and get them shelter and clothing. Their caseload included a whopping 11,382 families who registered for assistance.

Although outside of the fire zone, Duluth's twin port city of Superior, Wisconsin, stepped up, too. Soo Line and Great Northern railroads brought nine thousand refugees from the western reaches of the burned area into Superior. Eighteen locations in the city offered shelter and aid, including the YMCA, the Masonic Temple, churches, schools, and private homes. Superior citizens raised nearly $127,000 in a special relief kitty. Their efforts didn't come without a price, however, as nearly three hundred cases of the flu were reported, two fatal, in the wake of the relief efforts. Governor Burnquist formally thanked Wisconsin for its helping hand in Minnesota's time of need.

In Minnesota, meanwhile, the Fires Relief Commission began to assume more control, easing the financial and personnel demands from the Red Cross. Commissioners juggled both short- and long-term relief for fire and flu victims. Long-term relief plans were put in place with the hopes of returning the area to pre-fire normalcy. Indeed, as Doris Lofald, the girl from Hermantown, put it, "The Forest Fire of October 12, 1918, marks a dividing line in our memories—reckoning something was either 'before the fire' or 'after the fire'—unless it happened to be 'at the time of the fire.'"

The fire relief commission, with a philosophy "to help every man help themselves," established a four-pronged Central Replacement

Committee with district offices in Aitkin, St. Louis, and northern and southern Carlton counties. Local people would hear the appeals and scrutinize applications for replacing what had been lost. Commendably, the commission realized that local people would more fairly and justly gauge their neighbors' requests than social worker strangers from the Twin Cities. Warehouses and offices were set up in eleven burned towns and a dozen smaller communities. When burn victims returned home, they would talk to their local relief representative, detailing the scale of what they'd lost, and the local committees would dole out relief supplies that fit the circumstances. The system worked well.

"It gives me great satisfaction to report that, owing to the generous relief poured into this district from all sections, there has been no suffering from want of food or clothing," Clarence McNair, Cloquet's fire relief commissioner, wrote to Governor Burnquist on October 23, 1918. "And that this relief effort thus far has been wisely and effectively locally administered."

Refugees were provided with food rations, which slowly weaned them from public mess halls and enabled them to cook for themselves. They were also given lumber, hardware, and furniture for shelters—twelve-by-sixteen-foot shacks for smaller families and twelve-by-twenty-foot buildings for larger families.

Pearl Drew, a fire survivor whose husband was fighting in France, recalled how the shacks were like "mushrooms springing up over night, one shack after another dotted the snow-covered city" of Cloquet, she wrote in a 1936 essay. "With smoke curling from the chimneys, they looked quaint and inviting, snuggled in the snow." Long forms had to be filled out to show what was lost and prove that no other funds were available. But by mid-November, a month after the fire, 250 such structures had popped up in Cloquet alone. "To be sure, these were crude and sparse," Carroll and Raiter wrote in *Minnesota History* magazine. "But they were intended as temporary quarters that would enable people to get through the winter." Mild weather allowed for people who'd lost everything in the October fire to get back to their land by December.

With public tax dollars combining with private and corporate donations of cash, supplies, and vehicles, the post-fire response was a true public-private partnership long before that term became popular. To wit: lumber companies gave $175 of rough boards to their employees and allowed them to build structures for themselves and neighbors on company time. The Fires Relief Commission, meanwhile, stepped up with state money in a big way: $873,000 for building materials for fire victims, $264,000 for hardware, stoves, and implements, $161,000 for furnishings and bedding, and $185,000 for clothing and shoes. That doesn't count all the clothing donated from around the state.

Despite all the good-spirited generosity, however, tensions soon rose between the two categories of refugees: farmers and their urban counterparts who worked at or owned businesses in town.

The Fires Relief Commission quickly determined farmers needed more help because they had animals and crops to worry about in addition to their families. Barns and outbuildings needed rebuilding. Lost farm implements needed replacing. Animals needed feed and burned livestock required herd replenishment. Again, outside groups raised their hands to help. State chapters of Guernsey and Holstein cattle breeders lent prize animals to reproduce and build up reduced herds. The US Department of Agriculture and the University of Minnesota joined the effort. All told, the commission forked out $172,000 on wagons, harnesses, and implements, $52,000 on livestock, $118,000 on seed, and a whopping $807,000 on hay and feed.

All that money going to farmers began to irk city dwellers, who argued that they'd lost all their possessions, too, but fewer dollars were flowing their way. "They maintained that it was unfair that one family got a rude shelter, some old clothes, and a few weeks' worth of food while others were . . . virtually re-established in their former agricultural occupations," Carroll and Raiter wrote.

In a report, the commission acknowledged the charges of favoritism, but defended its actions as timely: "Mistakes have been made . . . but if we did not make mistakes, we would really be inactive." Commissioners argued that urban laborers could go back to work once their shelter, clothing, and short-term food needs were met. Indeed, Cloquet lumberyards reopened quickly, albeit at a smaller scale than before the fire. Farmers, on the other hand, needed future crops and fattened-up livestock herds—a longer-term predicament. Commissioners claimed that, thanks to the relief program, 95 percent of farmers returned to their land after the fire. But farmers, too, complained, writing angry letters about losing equipment and livestock confiscated to fight the fires. Disgruntled, they insisted they could be self-sufficient if they just got their stuff back.

Taking into account the concurrent flu epidemic, which further taxed the Red Cross, the Home Guard, and the Fires Relief Commission, the overall relief effort was impressive—warts and all. Within a week of the fire, fifty thousand people became the responsibility of this government, military, and Red Cross network. The general public also did its part, responding to appeals from the governor. "I cannot urge too strongly upon the people of the State," Burnquist said in an October 1918 speech, "the immediate necessity of large funds to care for the personal needs of those suffering and to aid in restoring the settlements that have been destroyed."

Minnesotans responded. Five Minneapolis clothing collection centers opened. Voluntary contributions topped $1.1 million, with checks flowing in from towns, churches, and fraternal organizations. Handwritten notes of encouragement and sympathy typically accompanied those checks. Ordinary citizens sent in as little as fifty cents to as much as a thousand dollars from a man in Olmsted County, two hundred miles south. Within two and half years of the fire, the Forest Fires Relief Commission had collected and shared more than $3.1 million in donations.

Outside Minnesota, Denmark's Prince Axel contacted Burnquist offering help, as did fellow governors. Even the railroads offered free passage for refugees and relief supplies. And Minnesota education leaders organized a statewide clothing drive in late October—sorting and labeling donated items brought to schools. The clothing was distributed out of Cloquet's Garfield School, the only one still standing in the burnt-out city. Private organizations kicked in, from the Shriners to the Masons to the Odd Fellows. Carpenters donated labor to build shelters. Even Clarence Wigington, the St. Paul architect and leader of the state's color barrier-breaking black Home Guard unit, wrote to the governor: "As a citizen and architect," he would be "pleased to be called on at any and all times."

Choreographing this massive relief effort wasn't always easy. It meant coordinating the military's Home and National Guards, the Red Cross, the Minnesota Forest Fires Relief Commission, the state legislature, the railroads, and private individuals. "It was a monumental task," Carroll and Raiter said, "and one for which there could have been no practice planning or anticipation. The need created it."

A year later, Governor Burnquist attended anniversary memorial services in Moose Lake and Cloquet. He thanked those across the state and outside Minnesota's borders for all the aid. "But to the people of Cloquet themselves," the governor said, "belongs the great share of the credit for the magnificent work that has been done."

CHAPTER 19

Minneapolis

OF ALL THE MINNESOTA DEATHS stemming from the fire, flu, and war in 1918, one came as a surprise—especially by how it happened.

Appointed a federal judge in 1923, John Franklin McGee had been on the bench for nearly two years when he left his home at 2712 Pillsbury Avenue in Minneapolis at 10:00 AM on Sunday morning, February 15, 1925, to work in his chambers at the federal building. When he didn't return home that night, his twenty-eight-year-old daughter Dorothy, one of his six children, went to investigate. She got a janitor to unlock his office and found her father dead in a vault. "A revolver was on the floor," the *Minneapolis Star* reported. "A bullet hole was in his forehead."

McGee, the powerful loyalty crusader, 1918 Minnesota fuel administrator, and patriotic zealot who led the Minnesota Commission of Public Safety, killed himself more than six years after all the anti-German witch hunts and civil rights stomping. His long-winded, rambling suicide note blamed his mental health problems on overworking himself as a judge. But he also traced his anguish back to the stormy days of 1918.

"The state of mental depression I am in is difficult for anyone to understand—everything looks dark and the bottom seems to have fallen out," he wrote. "I wonder if it was worthwhile to lead the strenuous life I have led, particularly since 1917 in April," he said, pointing to the time Governor Joseph A. A. Burnquist appointed him to the Public Safety Commission. He wondered whether a more selfish, quiet, and normal life would have been better. "I do not know," McGee wrote. "The people who benefit thereby are willing that one man do that which benefits them and when the emergency is over they forget the sacrifices made for them."

He lashed out when remembering "the war period during which my time was entirely given to the state without a penny of pay," not counting the dollar he earned from the federal government for his fuel administration work—a "trying and strenuous two years . . . that burned up my nerves and weakened me but I would never admit it." For weeks before killing himself, McGee said, he was losing weight, suffering from night sweats, unable to sleep—"staring at the darkness of the room and trying to conceal my condition."

Others noticed him unraveling. His secretary during the previous year, Anna Nash, said he had grown agitated while dictating to her the last couple of weeks. "I had to keep repeating to him over and over again what he had just said," Nash told the *Minneapolis Star*. "He didn't seem to keep his mind on what he was dictating and that annoyed him greatly." He told her repeatedly he was losing his mind and could neither think nor sleep. Federal prohibition director S. B. Quale said McGee had been "talking queerly about himself . . . incoherent at times and rambling."

McGee's family doctor, M. J. Lynch, said he had last seen the judge two days earlier, on Friday. "He was so nervously exhausted that he could not sleep or accomplish the work he had in hand," the doctor said, concluding that "he was not a fit man" and needed extensive rest "or that he would be in a critical mental state." In a convoluted reply, McGee told his doctor he had important decisions to write but couldn't think clearly enough to express legal matters. He added that the government didn't appreciate him and "the people didn't care."

The Public Safety Commission fizzled out in early 1919 after the Great War ended, and McGee returned to his legal practice. Always scheming, he set his sights on a federal judgeship. That meant calming his many critics who remembered McGee's role on the commission as "a ruthless dictatorship perpetuating a reign of terror," as historian Carl Chrislock put it.

After the smoke cleared up north, the flu waned, and the soldiers returned from France, many people looked back on the now-defunct commission and shook their heads. The commission had worked hard at getting Burnquist reelected. It closely monitored the liquor business, went after bond slackers and idlers, harassed immigrants who had delayed naturalization, and hounded anyone with a whiff of pro-German leanings—real or mostly imagined.

At the same time in the early 1920s, Congress received a proposal from President Warren Harding's administration to swell the federal judiciary at the district court level. McGee had been named district court judge in 1897 Minneapolis when he was thirty-six, long before his fiery reign on the Public Safety Commission. He quit that judge job before the end of his first full term, returning to private corporate law. He counted grain elevator companies and the Chicago Great Western Railway as his prime clients.

By the early 1920s, McGee was lobbying to return to the bench—this time for a more prestigious seat as a federal judge. His main advocate was a good one: Republican senator Knute Nelson, the eighty-year-old Norwegian-born former Minnesota governor, legislator, and congressman and the first Scandinavian American elected to the US Senate. Nelson knew a McGee judicial appointment would stir up controversy because of his heavy-handedness on the Public Safety Commission. And President Harding didn't like appointing judges older than sixty; McGee turned sixty-one in 1921, just as the judicial nomination process heated up. It would be the last of Nelson's countless political fights. He died aboard a train heading from Washington back to his home in Alexandria, Minnesota, in April 1923—a month after McGee was sworn in as a federal judge.

The skirmish over the appointment showed how polarizing McGee could be. Presidents typically backed judges sponsored by senators from their own party. The elderly Nelson knew he needed to persuade Minnesota's junior senator, sixty-five-year-old fellow Republican Frank Kellogg, to join him in backing McGee. Then the nomination would sail through Congress. But Kellogg, up for reelection in 1922, refused to commit to support McGee's nomination, knowing it could hinder his campaign. Also up for reelection and hesitant to support McGee was Minnesota congressman Andrew Volstead, another Republican. Volstead, then the chairman of the House Judiciary Committee, was best known for sponsoring alcohol prohibition legislation. (The Volstead Act, as it was known, enforced the Eighteenth Amendment's prohibition of alcohol, from 1920 to 1932.)

In addition to facing reluctance from within the political ranks, McGee's nomination for a federal judgeship received strong opposition from labor unions and from McGee's colleagues within the legal profession. The Hennepin County Bar Association held a poll and McGee earned only 48 of 299 votes—a slight that McGee chalked up to the lawyers' Bolshevik faction. "I don't think you really know how unpopular Judge McGee is in Minnesota," Minneapolis attorney Edward Lee wrote to Senator Nelson that spring.

The judicial appointment was delayed until after the elections of 1922—which saw Republicans Volstead and Kellogg both ousted from office as the Farmer-Labor Party gained popularity. With Kellogg a lame duck, McGee's appointment passed on March 2, 1923, despite a bitter challenge from Republican progressives and Nonpartisan Leaguers. Kellogg warned the vitriolic McGee to avoid criticizing the eleven senators who voted against him. McGee shrugged off the advice, saying he understood proper judicial behavior.

In his nearly two years on the federal bench, McGee spent a dizzying amount of time handing down speedy and stiff sentences against bootleggers and whiskey smugglers in the early years of Prohibition. "With a calendar heavily loaded with booze cases," the *Minneapolis Star* reported, "Judge McGee began work at a sentence a minute clip. At one time he imposed 112 sentences" in eighty minutes. In his suicide note, McGee talked about scoffing at his doctor's rest recommendation. "I thought how foolish to say rest with my desk filled with undecided cases"—80 percent of which were whiskey and narcotics crimes he thought state courts should handle. Such cases "are trying on the nerves with no end in sight."

When the end came with a self-inflicted gunshot to the forehead, McGee was lauded by political cronies and even the bootleggers he went after with a vengeance. One floral wreath at his funeral came from Omaha moonshine maker "Slim Billy" Fox, who said: "I haven't any grudge against him. He was against bootlegging and didn't make any secret of it. He was fighting in the open. He did a lot of good, too." Minnesota Supreme Court chief justice Samuel Wilson said, "Our community has lost one of our most fearless and staunchest supporters of justice." The chief judge said that while McGee was considered a "severe" man because of his "vigorous prosecution of liquor and criminal cases, he was at heart a very kind and considerate man and a very sensitive one."

Minnesota's governor in 1925, Theodore Christianson, served as an honorary pallbearer and said McGee "was a man of much ability, strong convictions and great strength of character. He had no tolerance for what he considered wrong." Christianson admitted to disagreeing with McGee on many issues, "but I have always respected him for his courage and admired him for his independence."

Christianson wasn't the only gubernatorial pallbearer. Former governor Burnquist, McGee's chief political ally, was also invited to serve the honorary role at the funeral at St. Stephen's Church and St. Mary's Cemetery in Minneapolis. Burnquist watched his political career stumble in the 1920s after serving two full terms as governor. His attempts to win Republican nominations for a US Senate seat following Nelson's death and for the 1930 governorship both failed. His relationship with McGee, it turned out, proved toxic.

"[McGee] last basked in the limelight of publicity by reason of his appointment under Governor Burnquist," Lee, the Minneapolis lawyer, said in his letter to Knute Nelson during the confirmation brouhaha in 1922. "Burnquist is almost forgotten politically in Minnesota and one of the things that brought about that . . . was his unfortunate appointment of Judge McGee."

Anna Dickie Olesen, circa 1935, five years after she testified before Congress in support of the victims of the 1918 fire. *Courtesy of Minnesota Historical Society Collections*

CHAPTER 20

Washington; Cloquet

ANNA DICKIE OLESEN was forty-four when she stepped to the podium to testify before a congressional subcommittee on claims. It was the last week of March 1930, and Olesen had become a bit of a celebrity since surviving the fire in Cloquet nearly a dozen years earlier as the thirty-three-year-old wife of the town's school superintendent.

In the subsequent years, the fiery orator had become the first American woman to receive major party backing in a US Senate campaign when she ran as a Democrat in 1922—two years after women won the right to vote. The feminist pioneer from Waterville, Minnesota, had finished third in the election that fall. But she kept up the fight for the victims of the 1918 fire as their legal cases ground through courthouses and countless appeals, through government delays and partial settlements. The federal government had taken over the railroads in 1918 because it was wartime. When some judges and juries found the railroads liable for the massive fires, the government, which insisted the fire was "an act of God," was pitted against the poor immigrants of northeastern Minnesota who had lost so much.

A bill to pay the victims what was still owed slogged on through years of congressional foot dragging. When three days of hearings were finally scheduled in 1930, Olesen joined a delegation from the Minnesota Forest Fire Reimbursement Association, a group that had been lobbying for justice for fire victims. Olesen and her fellow advocates would need another five years until the matter was finally resolved, in 1935—seventeen years after the train sparks ignited the inferno. The $10 million of federal money promised by the settlement wouldn't start flowing for five more years.

But when Olesen stood before the congressional committee in 1930, she was the marquee speaker to testify. Her popularity had swelled as a public speaker on the Chautauqua circuit, often as a side-kick for three-time presidential candidate William Jennings Bryan. The national publicity she attracted for her historic Senate run gave her added clout. And this wasn't her first foray into the political jungles of Washington, DC. As a candidate in 1922, she was among those vociferously opposing John McGee's judicial nomination. She and the eventual winner of the Senate seat—Farmer-Laborite Henrik Shipstead—provided enough pressure that incumbent senator Frank Kellogg agreed to delay action on McGee's controversial nomination until post-election.

Now, Anna Dickie Olesen was back in Washington delivering one of her most powerful speeches, to advocate for the victims of the horrific 1918 fire. First, she acknowledged that only a handful of Minnesotans had trekked to Washington for the hearings. "It cost money to come from Minnesota," she told the committee. "It costs about $100, round trip, in railroad fare alone. Our people are with us in thought and mind."

Then she addressed questions about why hundreds of people in Cloquet and Moose Lake had agreed to settle their claims for half of what they asked for in a government-brokered deal in 1921. "I want to tell you that we signed under duress," Olesen testified. "It was the duress of poverty, the duress of broken hearts, the duress of broken homes. We had no more money to fight; and you, who know something of the psychology of disaster, know that we had fought as long as we could, have suffered what we did."

She then made it clear: she wasn't testifying to appeal to the congressmen's hearts. "I did not come here asking for sympathy . . . we never have asked for sympathy," she said. "We only ask for justice—not sympathy in any way, shape or manner." At the same time, she pivoted her comments, flashing back to October 12, 1918. She made the dispute personal, testifying about what she experienced firsthand.

She might not have wanted sympathy, but she didn't shy away from pulling some heartstrings.

"That fire struck us at the worst possible time," she said, noting that it swept across the region during autumn, "when we had our wood and coal in." Families were preparing for winter: "In our basement, we had over $100 of coal; we had about $20 worth of wood; we had all our canned fruit: I would say there was in our cellar alone $100 to $150 worth of fruit." The same squirreling away of supplies took place across the area: "That is why we suffered so much harder than if the fire had come in the summer or the spring."

Then she deftly reminded the politicians about the horrors of disease—memories that had surely faded during the ensuing decade. "The influenza was raging," Olesen testified. "People were ill all over the country. . . . The winter was coming on. Our boys were in the war." She estimated five hundred young men from northeastern Minnesota had joined the Great War effort.

She told the congressmen what she saw after her husband, Cloquet school superintendent Peter Olesen, rushed into their home, yelling about the fire sweeping across the hills. "I ran out of the doors and took one look," she said, "and if you have ever seen a cyclone of fire, that is what was coming over the hills." She recounted how a windless afternoon had given way to sixty-mile-per-hour gusts, stealing her hat as they dashed to the train depot. "The sand was cutting our faces" as women and children were hustled into rescue trains.

She then shared a vivid memory of a phalanx of empty baby carriages along the fence that ran near the railroad: "They had taken the babies into their arms and to the train, and it was just one long line of baby carriages there along the fence." Everyone stayed cool and collected—"the calm was marvelous"—as men shouted out, "Save the children." And that they did. "We risked everything to get the children out," Olesen told the rapt congressmen. "There were people there that night who never attempted to save a material thing but only sought to save the children. . . . They were heroic.

"No amount of money the government can ever pay us will compensate fully for those hours of anguish while we waited, fearing that our husbands and brothers and fathers would not come to us, and that they might have been destroyed in the city."

Not once, Olesen testified, did anyone whine: "I never heard one person during that night of fire, or in the years of misery that followed, ever murmur or complain about this loss." As she helped refugees the next day in Superior, Wisconsin, she heard people clamoring to get back to work, sharing rumors that the mills might soon reopen. She told the politicians how her family, husband Peter and daughter Mary—who turned eleven two days after the fire—lived that winter in a cloakroom of the Garfield School, one of the few buildings that escaped the flames in Cloquet. "People were living in shacks, here, there, and everywhere," she said. "Building up their little shacks, and suffering, too; living many of them in one room."

The fire victims turned to local lawyers, Frank Yetka and Victor Michealson, to try to ease their suffering. Earlier in the three-day hearings, and through the years of legal wrangling that preceded them, chief government officials had said that money-grubbing lawyers had preyed upon the victims to line their own pockets. They often agreed to work on contingency, taking no money up front—because people were broke—in exchange for large chunks if they won their cases. "But we never felt that we had paid our lawyers too much," Olesen insisted to the committee.

She also took on James C. Davis, the director general of the US Railroad Administration and the former general counsel, who had been the first to testify when the hearings opened. Davis had long insisted the government shouldn't have to pay for an act of God, ignoring Minnesota court decisions that found his administration liable for the fires. "He used the term 'my money,'" Olesen said, drawing her testimony to a dramatic conclusion. "I have no right to take Mr. Davis's money. None of our people have. We have no right to take a cent of government money unless the money is rightfully coming to us."

She argued that the courts had determined the railroads, then under wartime federal government control, were liable. "Our courts in Minnesota said that my little house was burned 100 percent by the agents of the railroad administration," Olesen said, adding that the government settlement had in fact paid for only 50 percent of losses. "When I came to get my money back, I get only half, although my house was burned altogether, not half; they burned all my house, not half. They burned everything we had, not half of what we had, and we feel in right and justice and equity we should have that money back."

It was powerful testimony, but Olesen wasn't done. "I want to say one more thing," she continued. "Our settlers are Polish, Finnish, Austrian, and a good many of them Scandinavian." Those first three immigrant groups, she said, came from countries with oppressive governments. "They fear government up there more than they do in a community that is all of American birth and ancestry. They were afraid of these government investigators.

"When they rallied together that night of the fire, October 12, [1918] to get out the settlers, they were using broken English the best that they could." Her anger was palpable, her defense of her immigrant neighbors heartfelt. "I hate to see it laughed at," Olesen testified. "And I hate to see our courts laughed at. The people need the money very badly."

Then Olesen wrapped up her testimony with her trademark fervor. "Let us not blind justice and forget the poor because some with more money were partly reimbursed for their loss," she said, referring to survivors with better connections who received 50 percent payments in the earlier government settlement. "The poor lost far more than others, and most of our people were of the poor class, just had enough to get along by laboring and struggling hard."

For years following Olesen's strong and personal testimony, the US Treasury Department dug into its files and found each eligible claim and the value of housing, goods, and animals that had been agreed to in the early 1920s. Once the claims were verified and the fire victims located, the government finally began handing out a thousand checks a month starting in November 1935.

All told, nearly $11 million was paid to settle the longstanding claims. Lumped in with another $13 million that had previously been paid via a blanket settlement with the federal Railroad Administration, the government paid out more than $23.5 million to fire sufferers. It marked the first time that victims of a massive forest fire successfully sued railroads for causing the disaster.

On December 6, 1935, Orlo Elfes's *Pine Knot* newspaper in Cloquet printed a special fire-reimbursement edition, with the headline: "The Debt Is Paid." That front page featured a panoramic photo of the sun rising over a largely rebuilt Cloquet. The paper dedicated its jubilee edition to "the scores of people who worked so untiringly and gave their time, services and money to bring about justice for the fire sufferers of 1918 in Northern Minnesota. Their successful effort will ever

Refugees received clothing and bare necessities from relief workers in the immediate aftermath of the fire. *Courtesy of Minnesota Historical Society Collections*

be gratefully remembered." That dedication ran in a box surrounded by an etching of Uncle Sam doffing his hat and outstretching his right arm over the US Capitol building to a father and son—"$10,000,000 PAYMENT IN FULL MINNESOTA FIRE CLAIMS." "That was the day when people in Cloquet danced on Cloquet Avenue," recalled Herbert Hubert, the chairman of the reimbursement committee.

How they went from burnt-out victims in 1918 to dancing in the streets in 1935 is a twisted legal marathon that included Anna Dickie Olesen playing the "Eleanor Roosevelt card." Reflecting her status as a Democratic activist, Olesen attended President Franklin Roosevelt's first inauguration in March 1933, just as another Minnesota fire reimbursement bill was introduced in the Senate. Within eight months, FDR would tap Olesen to be the Minnesota director of the National Emergency Council. The only woman on the national panel, she coordinated FDR's New Deal programs in the state.

Olesen's connections with the fledgling Roosevelt administration meant she also sometimes handled the First Lady's mail. When a poor Minneapolis woman wrote to Eleanor Roosevelt asking when the government would finally pay the fire claims, Olesen was asked to draft a reply. This got her to thinking. "Now that gives me an idea," she wrote in a letter to Frank Yetka, the Cloquet victims' lawyer, on the first day of spring in 1933. "Mrs. R—is a great social justice person. She has a sense of right. It may be that we should get our plea to Mrs. Roosevelt, too."

Whether that back-channel lobbying through the First Lady worked is unclear. But when her husband, Franklin Roosevelt, signed an omnibus claims bill on August 27, 1935, it meant the fire victims had finally won their case against the government—despite opposition from within the president's own party.

Texas Democrat Thomas Blanton had little interest in helping out the Minnesotans. "All this cry of duress raised years after these claimants and their lawyers accepted $13 million in full settlement from the government is an afterthought," Blanton said on the House floor, "is a subterfuge, is a sham, is a camouflaged scheme to get some more millions out of the United States." Congressman Edward Cox, a Georgia Democrat who opposed the New Deal, tried to strip the Minnesota fire reimbursement language from the omnibus claims package. Cox called it "the notorious Minnesota fire-claim case," the work of a "crooked . . . lobby [that] has been maintained here during the whole of the present administration." Cox's motion lost on a vote of 100 to 64. When he demanded a second roll-call vote of ayes and nays, he went down again, 168 to 130. The claims bill passed later that day, August 20, 1935, and FDR signed it into law a week later.

"After so long a fight, such an anticlimax was almost droll," Carroll and Raiter wrote in their book, *The Fires of Autumn*. The authors detailed the lengthy legal battle, one that reflects the tenacity of Olesen and the members of the Minnesota Forest Fire Reimbursement Association and tested the resolve of the Minnesota victims. "It was a bitter and disillusioning experience, which seemed to reveal the iron fist of government exercised against the essentially defenseless citizenry," Carroll and Raiter wrote.

The crux of the seventeen-year dispute was, simply, determining who was responsible for the 1918 fires that destroyed Cloquet, Moose Lake, and dozens of other communities in northeastern Minnesota—whether the fires were the result of an "act of God" or the railroads' fault. From the beginning, most local people blamed the railroads.

On November 1, 1918—just weeks after the inferno—state forester William Cox released a report pointing to careless travelers, landowners, and railroad locomotives. At Cox's urging, Governor Burnquist appointed a Forest Fire Investigation Commission, made up of professors, a state forest ranger, and local people. "We owe the settlers in the burned district" a thorough investigation, the governor said, "to prevent a repetition of the disaster."

After hearings in Duluth, Moose Lake, and Cloquet, the panel sent its report to the governor on November 26. Although it held that Soo Line and Great Northern operators were responsible for some of the fires, the report said dry conditions, slash piles of discarded timber branches, swamps drained for farming, and, mostly, high winds were to blame. "It was little less than a tornado and whipped all these numerous fires into a great conflagration," the report said, adopting the act of God theory.

In the final report of the Minnesota Forest Fires Relief Commission, issued in 1921, the group's secretary, Hubert Eva—a Spanish-American War veteran and National Guard colonel—quoted longtime Duluth meteorologist Herbert Richardson: "For some days before the great fire in question there had been numerous brush and peat-bog fires burning. . . . These were directly traceable to automobilists, and on the part of the farmers and settlers in burning brush to clear land." He didn't mention train sparks.

Despite the two reports assessing accountability to a variety of factors, the railroads began bracing themselves for the blame sure to come their way. After all, the Great Northern and Soo Line were named in the initial Forest Fire Investigation Commission report. Although they had rescued thousands from Cloquet and Brookston, and their special trains proved vital during relief operations, the railroads knew juries of locals would not hesitate to rule against them. So, all kinds of independent investigations were launched, by railroad companies and by the federal government. The waters were muddied by the fact that the federal government had nationalized the rails during the Great War. Operations were still handled by individual railroad companies, but the US Railroad Administration was officially responsible. And the congressional act that created the Railroad Administration said the rail lines must obey the laws of the states they rumbled through.

Within a few years of the fire, some fifteen thousand lawsuits had been filed against railroad companies and the federal Railroad Administration, specifically naming the director general of the administration as an agent of the president. Officials of the Railroad Administration blamed the massive number of cases on "greedy lawyers" in northern Minnesota, who signed up victims on contingent-fee arrangements.

The first victory for the fire sufferers came in 1920 when the Minnesota Supreme Court supported a lower court ruling about a fire along the Soo Line tracks west of Moose Lake that destroyed Jacob Anderson's barn. Neither the weather nor the wind nor other fires in the area could "relieve the railroad company from liability," the state's high court ruled. In one of the next legal victories for fire victims, defendant railroad companies were dismissed and the Railroad Administration was named in their place.

The stakes increased when people in towns and cities, instead of simply rural farmers out in the country, began to sue. Among the first test cases involved A. R. Peterson of Cloquet, who blamed a Great Northern locomotive for sparking an October 10 fire near Brookston. That fire ignited four hundred carloads of lumber stacked by a railroad siding. When the winds whipped up two days later, the massive fire that would level Cloquet was on its way, and the rail crews' failure to contain the initial blaze led to the town's destruction, Peterson argued. A judge agreed with the victim's lawyers, saying that the Great Northern Railway had allowed huge piles of combustible material to collect on its tracks and "negligently failed to extinguish and prevent the spread." The state supreme court would agree.

As hundreds of similar cases piled up, a five-judge panel was formed to handle the load. But the first few lawsuits had taken years to navigate through appeals. Court officials said the backlog of cases, including 850 out of Moose Lake alone, would take a decade to sort through.

Eventually, the government—all the way up to President Warren Harding—hit upon a settlement strategy. For the 278 Cloquet cases winding through the courts, the victims would get 50 percent of their estimated damages, while the plaintiffs in the more than 2,500 remaining cases yet to be decided would receive 40 percent of their claims. "Gentlemen, this is the best I can do; take it or leave it," James C. Davis, the director of the Railroad Administration, later recalled saying.

Duluth attorney Hugh J. McClearn, of the Dodge and Blacklock law firm, sent a letter to his clients on November 19, 1921, urging them to accept the government's deal. "We are now definitely and finally informed that the Government will not voluntarily pay more than 50 percent to any fire sufferer," he wrote. "If the court decided in cases now before them, some claimants would undoubtedly get judgments for the whole amount of their loss," the lawyer said. "Some, however, would get nothing. . . . For these reasons, we feel that we should recommend that you accept the 50 percent settlement and we will endeavor to get your money to you as promptly as it is humanly possible."

"Many of the fire sufferers," he added, "are desperately in need of money." For the cash-strapped victims of the fire, getting fifty cents on the dollar in cash, rather than waiting years with no guarantee of receiving anything, proved too tempting. The people of Cloquet and other burn victims were angry but worn down. "They had their choice," Davis said. "If that is coercion, there was coercion."

A. R. Peterson, the Cloquet property owner who won a $30,000 judgment against Davis, had to settle for less than $12,000, after interest costs and insurance claims were subtracted from his 50 percent. Peterson's Cloquet case had endured three trials and was combined with 277 similar cases. When the people won, the Railroad Administration appealed to the Supreme Court. When that avenue was exhausted, the federal government simply failed to fork over what it was found liable to pay. The take-it-or-leave-it 50 percent settlement offer was left on the table.

Cases from within the Fond du Lac Reservation boundaries were even more complicated because the 130 Ojibwe who sued didn't own their land, which had been held in trust dating back to treaties from the 1850s. That meant lengthy delays in the Indian cases, and claimants had to wait for years to get their money, after white victims were paid off first.

In all, the government paid nearly $13 million to victims under terms of the settlement. In 1921, Davis, the federal government's railroad point man, had warned President Harding that the damages could reach $15 million. The district courts of Minnesota had set the total damages at nearly $30 million—less than half the $73 million the plaintiffs had tallied up for their losses. The Railroad Administration wound up paying about 48 percent of the total amount the state courts had awarded—leaving $17 million in damages unpaid. Davis insisted it was a fair settlement for an act of God. He believed local lawyers had tricked the plaintiffs into believing they'd get more from the federal government.

People felt betrayed. If the settlement had come quickly, that would have been one thing. But dragging it out for four years of litigation, only to settle for fifty cents on the dollar was "altogether too low," Duluth judge Herbert Dancer said.

But the people weren't done. When Davis made his "take it or leave it" offer, he underestimated the grit of the people with whom he was dealing. "These were Indian people, successors of the area's earliest inhabitants," Carroll and Raiter wrote. "These were immigrants, homesteaders, farmers; these were lumberjacks, log drivers, sawmill operators; these were people who had settled towns and carved out farms from forest . . . risked their lives cutting and moving timber." They had endured cold winters and hot summers and survived the fires of 1918—"the worst nature had to offer," Carroll and Raiter said. "These people were too tough to be intimidated by a government lawyer."

So when a new Minnesota Forest Fire Reimbursement Association was formed in 1928—a decade after the flames—Anna Dickie Olesen told the young Cloquet lawyer Frank Yetka: "We must push now—no let up. We can win this time." It would take another seven years after bills were introduced in late 1929 requesting the government pay off the remainder of the damages left on the table after the Railroad Administration settlement. Two years in, Olesen would deliver her personal appeal to the US House subcommittee. And the claims ran smack-dab into a cost-cutting drive that President Herbert Hoover hoped would stanch the economic wounds inflicted by the Great Depression.

Fuming over the lack of congressional action, Yetka wrote to Olesen in 1932, "I have made up my mind to get on the offensive whether it hurts or not and if it takes dynamite to loosen some of the obstacles out of our way we will have to do it." In parentheses, he added, "By this I mean verbal dynamite, of course."

When President Franklin Roosevelt was sworn in in 1933, Olesen was on hand. Minnesota governor Floyd Olson visited with FDR that May. A thirteen-page document was drawn up, rehashing the fire stories, the court cases, the Railroad Administration's settlement, and the four additional years of legislative stalling. FDR's attorney general Homer Cummings wrote a memo to the president saying there appeared to be no legal liability forcing the federal government to settle the dispute. "Nevertheless," Cummings wrote, "the contention that there is a moral and equitable obligation on the part of the Federal Government in the matter is not devoid of merit." He recommended further study and consideration.

Finally, on August 27, 1935, Roosevelt signed the omnibus claims bill with nearly $11 million of unpaid damages for Minnesota fire sufferers. It was time to dance in the streets of Cloquet.

Although it took nearly two decades to receive adequate compensation from the government, the citizens of Cloquet began rebuilding the downtown almost immediately. *Courtesy of Minnesota Historical Society Collections*

Amy Robbins Ware, in her Army Educational Corps uniform, 1918. *Courtesy of the Robbinsdale Historical Society*

CHAPTER 21

Robbinsdale; Brizeaux-Forestiere, France

WHEN RED CROSS CANTEEN WORKER, airplane spotter, and nurse Amy Robbins Ware returned to Minnesota from the trench-pocked battlefields of France in 1919, she published her war diary of poetry and prose. Titled *Echoes of France*, the little book reminded those back home, those who endured fire and flu, that their mayhem was dwarfed by what she saw in Europe.

"Mrs. Ware's transcript of the Great Struggle has the advantage of being personal; she saw, experienced . . . this renders her account authentic, gives it vividity," University of Minnesota professor Richard Burton, chairman of the English department, wrote in 1920 for the book's introduction. "Many a beautifully written book falls on lackadaisical ears, for it is about nothing in particular; a noise in a vacuum," Burton said, insisting that Ware's book was different. "This unique, conventional, honest setting down of actual and stirring occurrences, since she went through with it, had the enormous asset of being participant in the mightiest international movement in all human history. . . . It is by the reduplicated testimony of millions of eye witnesses like Mrs. Ware that we stay-at-homes can get a synthesis on the whole, and re-live its scenes through the imagination."

Nearly a century later, Ware's book allows one to flash back to that first week of October, when the dry conditions in Minnesota were turning into a kindling box, when the influenza was coursing through Martin County and the rest of Minnesota, and when a nineteen-year-old with a bullet hole in his lung arrived at Evacuation Hospital 11 in the Brizeaux-Forestiere in the Argonne region of France's bloody Western Front. "How well I remember, dear lad, the night I came to you out of the agonies of that unspeakable hell," Ware wrote, "in which you had been changed from the gay boy you must have been, to the wonder-man for whom I came to care so tenderly. You said you had no mother, and I,—I have no son!"

She had just turned forty-one, a well-to-do woman from Minnesota's elite and a descendant of Mayflower pilgrim John Howland. Amy's father, Andrew Robbins, founded a first-ring Minneapolis suburb in 1893—naming Robbinsdale after himself. Her mother's brother, lumber baron Thomas Barlow Walker, created a museum for his art collection—naming the Walker Art Center after himself.

Although her parents were living in Willmar, Amy Robbins was born in 1877 amid all the art in her uncle's Minneapolis home. Ware studied violin at age eight and later earned bachelor's and master's degrees from the University of Minnesota, studying architecture, archaeology, wood-carving, and drama. "She early found that keenest joy which arises from the intellectual stimulus that comes through comprehensive study, research and investigation," according to a 1923 book, *History of Minneapolis, Gateway to the Northwest.*

The draw of war raced through her veins. Both her mother and grandmother, Adelaide Julia Walker and Mary Shaw Robbins, served as Civil War nurses. Her great-great-grandfather, Captain Andrew Shaw, fought against the British in the Revolutionary War. And when her dad, Andrew Bonney Robbins, was seventeen, he joined the Eighth Regiment of Minnesota Volunteers in 1862. He fought in the Civil War in Tennessee as well as in the US–Dakota War back home on the plains. "Her family history indicates . . . it was but natural when her own country became involved in the great World war that Mrs. Ware should at once devote herself to the cause," according to that 1923 historical profile.

After training in Morse code and radio telegraphy, Ware sailed to France on March 14, 1918, on the *La Touraine*, delicately crossing the Atlantic, which hid German submarines in its depths. After teaching radio operations and using those skills to observe air battles, Ware volunteered to go to the Western Front on September 18, 1918. There, at the evacuation hospital, she met the unnamed nineteen-year-old with the punctured lung.

"The incessant thunder of the dread barrage shook the very tent-pole where you lay all white and breathless of your ghastly wounds," Ware wrote in her diary on October 4. "You thought I was an angel on that night and your transfigured smile gave my heart pause, as I sought your fluttering pulse, and bent to catch the whispered word which seemed so near your last."

The Red Cross had recruited twenty thousand registered nurses during World War I to staff hospitals and ambulance companies and to try to combat the influenza's lethal spread. Ware belonged to a different group; she was among more than 120 Minnesota women enrolled to be clerks, searchers, canteeners, social workers, supply-truck drivers, nurses' aides, recreational volunteers, stenographers, secretaries, and chemists. In Amy Robbins Ware's case, that meant canteen work during the day and teaching radio skills to potential air combat observers at night. It also meant nursing in a pinch, such as holding the hand of the wounded nineteen-year-old in Evacuation Hospital 11.

She thought he'd die the night she first encountered him: "Yet in the morning when I made my rounds you were still there. Each weary day that dragged its tedious course, I held you steady while the tortures that meant life to you, tore my very soul to shreds.

"Your head pressed tight against me and your hands gripped in mine we fought it out together, you and I. You never flinched just drew your breath in those great agonizing gasps, while the cold sweat drenched my shoulder.

"You were so young, so brave," she wrote, "I *could not* let you die."

When the wounded soldier was transferred the next day, "you smiled up at me from the stretcher there, that strange sweet smile that seemed scarce of this earth." He insisted he was in no pain, but Amy Ware "shuddered when I thought the drug that held your pain in leash might loose its hold before you came to that far haven that I could not even know."

Amy married a lawyer named John Ware in 1907. They had no children, and records show she divorced him. In the autumn of 1918, near the bloody Western Front, this wounded boy on the stretcher, twenty-two years her junior, must have triggered something maternal. "Dear boy, you might have been my son," she wrote. "And I have never known if you survived that journey, or whether you lie buried there in that sad France, which I should love more tenderly, if you were sleeping there."

CHAPTER 22

St. Cloud; Minneapolis

ALMOST AS IF they were on the same timetable, the influenza pandemic began to fade just as the Great War ground to a close in late 1918. But one of the nightmares lingered a bit longer than the other.

"Happily the first definite steps have been taken towards a permanent peace," the Rev. Charles Grunewald, one of St. Cloud's leading Catholics, wrote in his December 1918 "My Message," the official publication of the St. Cloud Diocese. "But the pest, under the guise of the Spanish influenza, is still with us, and we hope and pray that nothing worse will follow," he said. "Whole families have been wiped out of existence. No locality has been spared, and those who congratulated themselves upon having escaped have since fallen prey to its ravages."

To Grunewald, a superintendent of Catholic schools in St. Cloud—a deeply Catholic pocket in central Minnesota—the influenza outbreak was more than a fast-moving virus killing millions. "These visitations are sent to make a guilty race realize its wrongdoings," he said in his message, pivoting to a less dark offshoot of the misery: "This terrible visitation has at least given the world an opportunity of witnessing the indomitable courage, the spirit of heroic self-sacrifice, the limitless charity of our . . . priests, our consecrated nuns and our laity." Excluding Bishop Joseph Busch, the good father didn't want to name names because "it would be insidious to single out any particular one, where so many gave cheerfully of their personal service." He didn't name one Benedictine nun, Sister Julitta Hoppe, but indirectly thanked her for an "unremitting ministration of charity."

Born in 1875, Hoppe was the seventh child of German immigrants Henry and Theresa Hoppe. They lived in the German town of New Munich in the heart of Stearns County, about thirty miles west of St. Cloud. Records show both her parents had emigrated from Westfalen, Prussia. Henry sailed to New York in 1851; Theresa listed 1860 as her immigration year. They settled and farmed in central Minnesota around the time of statehood in 1858. They were buried three years apart—Henry in 1899, Theresa in 1902—in New Munich's Immaculate Conception Cemetery. With all the anti-German rhetoric fueled by the Great War, it's worth emphasizing that Sister Julitta was, like so many, just one generation removed from Germany.

Sister Julitta's door-to-door care for the sick during the influenza waves that swamped Minnesota shines as merely one of countless examples of the goodness that penetrated an otherwise awful year. While the war raged "over there" where her parents spent their youth, Sister Julitta put to use her education as a member of the first graduating class, in 1911, from St. Raphael's Training School for Nurses in St. Cloud. With a kerosene lamp to guide her and lumber wagons to transport the flu-stricken, Sister Julitta cared for more than two hundred patients. She didn't feel like she was doing enough. "While the flu was raging in St. Cloud, it seemed that every family was involved," she recalled in 1959. "With mothers and five or six children in bed, all who needed to have care—temperatures taken, heads bathed, applications given—we could not get very far."

Feeling overwhelmed, Sister Julitta and her fellow nun, Sister Cunegund Kuefler, went to the boss: Bishop Busch. He agreed to provide the diocese civic center, the St. Cloud Institute, as an emergency hospital. "We drew a curtain through the center, dividing the large room into two wards, with the mothers and children on the one side and the men and boys on the other," Sister Julitta said.

St. Cloud, like the rest of the state, was walloped by the flu. On October 16, the *St. Cloud Daily Times* reported: "scores of cases through out the city. One prominent citizen said last night that he believed there were over two-thousand cases in St. Cloud." A leading doctor in town, T. W. Hovorka, died at six o'clock that night. Another

Sister Julitta Hoppe (left) with Sister Glenore Riedner at St. Cloud Hospital.
Courtesy of the Sisters of Saint Benedict's Monastery

"prominent physician said that he visited a family yesterday where the father, mother and six children were down with influenza," the St. Cloud newspaper reported. "The question on every one's lips is what are we going to do about it?"

Schools and churches were shuttered. Funerals were held quickly and privately. And Sister Julitta went to work at the makeshift hospital at the St. Cloud Institute. "We got very little rest that night as the patients needed care," she said. "Sister [Cunegund] and I alone cared for almost 200 before we asked for help."

They set up a bathtub on the stage of the center's auditorium, where volunteers bathed children after writing their names on pieces of tape adhered to their shoulders. "Otherwise we would not have known one from another," Sister Julitta said. Pregnant mothers became a particular concern. "Mothers with child were in a dangerous condition," she said. "I had to do a Caesarean myself. . . . If the mother was dying, I would take the infant just before she took her last breath. Some of the infants had already been dead. Others were baptized before they died."

Sick doctors made matters worse. And when undertakers became stricken with the flu, too, "there was no one left to bury the dead," Sister Julitta said. "Often there were three or four bodies needing burial. We wrapped them in sheets dipped in formaldehyde and put them in the coldest place until they could be buried. We did the best we knew how."

On November 1, the *St. Cloud Daily Times* reported, "Deaths directly due to the epidemic of Spanish flu in the city, during the last ten days have reached the appalling total of seventy-two." The story ran on page five—lest the numbers prompt a war effort–dampening panic.

Twenty miles north, at the cemetery in the tiny Stearns County town of Opole, Thomas Opatz and Edward Zwack dug a small grave for a baby struck down by the flu. "I wonder who is going to be next?" Opatz asked, according to Rev. Robert Voigt's church history. "As fate would have it, a few weeks later, he (age 17) was the one going into the grave."

Opatz, the seventh of eight children of German immigrant farmers in Stearns County, died November 19. In Spring Hill, thirty-five miles northwest of Opole, a twenty-eight-year-old farmworker named Hubert Thelen died from influenza on December 19—two days before his twenty-three-year-old wife, Carla Elizabeth, succumbed to the deadly virus. Their deaths punctuated the "extreme danger and serious nature of the prevailing epidemic . . . forcefully brought to the people of this community," the *Melrose Beacon* reported, the day after Christmas, 1918.

At the time of Hubert Thelen's death, the newspaper said, "his wife's condition was such that she could not be told of her husband's and she passed away not knowing that her husband had preceded her to the Great Beyond." They had been married four years. Her death was the third in her family in three months. They left behind a two-year-old daughter and four-month-old son. "To the bereaved relatives and to the two small children, who have so suddenly been deprived of the care of their kind and loving parents," the *Beacon* said, "is extended the sincere sympathy of the entire community."

Then, while communities struggled to deal with the continuing losses in late 1918, the flu's grip slackened—almost as quickly as it had grabbed the globe by the throat earlier that spring. In the last week of October, 21,000 Americans died—including 800 in one day in New York City. "But in November the epidemic began to recede as mysteriously as it arrived," Philip Bourbon wrote in the *Washington Post* in 1991. "It seemed ironic that just as the guns of World War I were falling silent, the plague too had virtually spent itself."

All told, the 1918 influenza pandemic was so staggering that the numbers only partly capture the horror. In the month of October alone—while the fires raged across the bogs and farmsteads of northeastern Minnesota—196,000 US citizens died from the flu. That one-month death toll is more than twice the number who would die in this country during the first decade of the AIDS epidemic.

In 1918, the planet housed roughly 1.8 billion people—nearly one-fourth of its 2018 population, estimated at 7.5 billion. According to science journalist Gina Kolata, about one in five people globally came down with the flu in 1918, including 28 percent of Americans.

Some experts say the number who died from the flu ranged anywhere from 20 million to more than 100 million, globally. The true number of flu deaths will never be determined. No formal count was conducted, and there was no test in those days to confirm who had the flu. But even taking the low estimate of 20 million, that's double the estimated 10 million military deaths during World War I. Although estimates vary, the number of combined military and civilian deaths in the First World War was about 15 million people. The number of combat deaths in World War II neared 16 million—still not as lethal as this quick-killing pandemic whose symptoms and scope were equally appalling.

Historian Alfred Crosby says we can dispute the numbers, but we can't argue that the virus "killed more humans than any other disease in a period of similar duration in the history of the world." Of all the gruesome statistics, Crosby unearthed perhaps the most telling by accident. A university professor at Washington State, Yale, and Texas, Crosby once confronted a bookshelf lined with world almanacs. He grabbed a 1917 volume and looked up US life expectancies: 48.4 years for men and 54 for women—or just over 51 years. In 1919, that number climbed to nearly 55 years—53.5 for men and 56 for women. In between those two years, with the 1918 influenza snuffing out so many young lives, the average US life expectancy was 39.4 years, dropping about a dozen years in a single trip around the sun.

A more Minnesota-based statistical anecdote comes from Rose-lawn Cemetery in Roseville. In the fall of 1917, fifty-two people were buried there. The number nearly doubled to ninety-two in the deadly autumn of 1918—with flu and pneumonia popping up as the cause of death over and over again in the cemetery's records. By 1919, as some flu cases lingered on, the fall burial total dropped back to sixty-three.

And the scope of the 1918 flu strain was as staggering as its death toll. Eskimo villages were ravaged and some almost disappeared. Far from the igloos, one in five Western Samoans died. Eight million Span-iards got sick. In May, the British Grand Fleet was docked because 10,000 sailors were stricken. In the grisly competition with the "war to end all wars," the flu held up mightily. At one stage in France, Amer-ican hospitals counted 70,000 flu victims on top of nearly 100,000 men wounded in combat. And the other side suffered just as much.

German general Erich von Ludendorff called the virus the Flanders Fever and blamed it for his failed July offensive that could have swung the war in Germany's favor. His soldiers were hungry in the muddy trenches and now the flu further damaged their morale and weakened their bodies. "It was a grievous business having to listen every morn-ing to the Chiefs of Staff's recital of the number of influenza cases, and their complaints about the weakness of their troops," the German general groused, according to Kolata.

The death curves from the 1918 flu pandemic look like Ws, with the lethal peaks including babies and toddlers younger than five, older people in their seventies, and the in-their-prime group aged twenty to forty. Scientists have since determined that the 1918 virus triggered a massive immune system response in its victims. That reaction itself decimated sufferers' lungs, as the response attacked more than the virus. Those with the strongest immune systems, people aged eigh-teen to forty, thus died more often.

In her book, *Flu: The Story of the Great Influenza Pandemic of 1918 and the Search for the Virus That Caused It*, Kolata described the horri-fying process people went through as the virus took over their bodies.

The sickness preyed on the young and healthy. One day you are fine, strong, and invulnerable. You might be busy at work in your office. Or maybe you are knitting a scarf for the brave troops fighting the war to end all wars. Or maybe you are a soldier reporting for basic training, your first time away from home and family.

You might notice a dull headache. Your eyes might start to burn. You start to shiver and you will take to your bed, curling up in a ball. But no amount of blankets can keep you warm. You fall into a restless sleep, dreaming the distorted nightmares of delirium as your fever climbs. And when you drift out of sleep, into a sort of semi-consciousness, your muscles will ache and your head will throb and you will somehow know that, step by step, as your body feebly cries out "no," you are moving steadily toward death.

It may take a few days, it may take a few hours, but there is nothing that can stop the disease's progress. Doctors and nurses have learned to spot the signs. Your face turns a dark brownish purple. You start to cough up blood. Your feet turn black. Finally, as the end nears, you frantically gasp for breath. A blood-tinged saliva bubbles out of your mouth. You die—by drowning, actually—as your lungs fill with a reddish fluid. And when a doctor does an autopsy, he will observe your lungs lying heavy and sodden in your chest, engorged with a thin bloody liquid, useless, like slabs of liver.

Vomiting, dizziness, labored breathing, and profuse sweating joined another distressing symptom: purplish blisters appeared on oxygen-starved skin, according to *Smithsonian* magazine. "Blue as huckleberries," was the way Dr. William Henry Welch, a leading pathologist, described the bodies upon which he performed autopsies back in 1918.

This flu strain killed 2.5 percent of those who caught it—compared to the typical one-tenth of one percent of flu-stricken people who die from the disease. "This must be some kind of new infection," Welch said. Experts still aren't certain how the 1918 strain morphed into such a deadly virus. "No one knows for sure where the 1918 flu came from or how it turned into such a killer strain," Kolata said.

But could it happen again? According to John M. Barry, author of *The Great Influenza*, "every expert on influenza agrees that the ability of the influenza virus to reassert genes means that another pandemic not only can happen. It almost certainly will happen." Those experts say that if a similar plague killed a similar slice of the US population, about 1.6 million Americans would die. That's more than die in a single year from heart disease, cancers, strokes, chronic pulmonary disease, AIDS, and Alzheimer's disease combined.

Modern medicine, of course, has come up with flu vaccines—which target certain strains—as well as anti-influenza drugs and scores of antibiotics to prevent and treat the pneumonia and other secondary infections that killed so many in 1918. Still, as science writer Robin Marantz Henig says, "We like to believe such plunder is an ancient relic; whatever was killing people so ruthlessly in 1918 must be something we can treat by now.... But in the face of a virus that kills so rapidly, all the antiviral drugs in the physician's armamentarium would be impotent. If a strain similar to the 1918 variant were to emerge today—a strain that, last time around, killed literally overnight—some experts believe that even modern medicine would be helpless to prevent many related deaths."

CHAPTER 23

Blooming Prairie; Cloquet

EIGHTY YEARS AFTER THE FIRE, almost to the day, Beatrice Parks Gellerman died on October 6, 1998, at age one hundred in Blooming Prairie, Minnesota—more than two hundred miles south of the shack she called home after the inferno leveled her Cloquet home. Her obituary ran on the fire's eightieth anniversary, October 12, in the *Austin Daily Herald*.

The obit didn't mention the fire, but Bea's story of love and resilience captures the spirit of post-fire Cloquet as well as any. And, luckily for those interested in the stories of 1918, she left behind a manuscript in the archives of the Carlton County Historical Society.

"The day was the 23rd of December, 1918," she wrote, opening her recollections. "The Armistice (the end of World War I) had been signed in November and Floyd was home on leave from the Navy." Bea was twenty. Floyd was twenty-four.

"We were living in a shack, 16 by 20 feet, heated by a wood stove." A little addition had been hammered on one end of the shack, with a wood-burning range, a wood box, and a few shelves. "We had just enough kettles, silver and dishes for the five of us." Her father, John, was a lumber worker. He and his wife, Clara Mabel, had three kids: Bea (twenty), Lucile (sixteen), and little Merton (two). The shack, built with government-issued pine, contained one double bed, a couch that could sleep two, and a trundle bed that tucked under the double bed by day and could be pulled out at night for Merton. "The sleeping area was enclosed by a rough board partition about six feet high with a curtain in the doorway."

Bea's boyfriend, Floyd, a railroad operator's son and grandson of German immigrants, had enlisted in the navy on April 6, 1917—the day the United States entered the Great War. Floyd's mother was a schoolteacher, and they were living in similar temporary housing three miles southeast of Cloquet in Scanlon.

As romantic reunions go, Floyd's leave started well but soon grew frustrating. He'd purchased a diamond engagement ring for Bea at Tiffany's in New York when his ship docked there. They were engaged, "spending as much time as possible together," she wrote, "but due to the lack of sleeping space in either home, we walked back and forth between the two homes."

This being late December in northern Minnesota, they likely held hands kept warm by mittens or gloves on their long, crisp walks. If they spent the day in Scanlon, Floyd would walk Bea the three miles home to Cloquet and then march back through the cold to Scanlon to sleep. If they spent the day in Cloquet, the sailor would make that same cold walk home. "It was not what an engaged couple had in mind," Bea wrote, "after having been parted by the duration of the war. In Cloquet, there wasn't even a movie where one could spend the evening." After all, this was only a couple months after the fire devastated the town, leveling most everything except the Garfield School and the paper and lumber mills.

On the afternoon of December 23, 1918, on yet another walk between Scanlon and Cloquet, Floyd must have been ready to explode. So he asked: "Why don't we just get married and go to Duluth for our honeymoon?"

Now they had something to talk about. First, they would consult Bea's folks, John and Clara. "Mother was plenty perturbed," Bea recalled. "She had visions of a nice wedding the following summer in a new home that was already planned—after Floyd was out of the Navy." Her father, on the other hand, empathized with his future son-in-law, who was spending his leave trudging back and forth through the cold. "Dad could see how we felt and said, 'When would you like to get married?' Floyd said, 'Tomorrow!' His leave was almost over."

Hastily constructed buildings using government-issued materials provided temporary shelter and accommodations in fire-stricken areas of northern Minnesota. *Courtesy of Minnesota Historical Society Collections*

A plan was hashed out: Rev. William Williams, their Presbyterian pastor, was living in a forestry station four miles outside Cloquet. "There being no cars or telephones," Bea's father agreed to walk over and fetch the reverend first thing the next morning—Christmas Eve.

The groom, meanwhile, would walk to Scanlon to invite his parents to the wedding. Then he would hop the train to Carlton, purchase a marriage license and a wedding ring, and come back to Cloquet on the next train, due to chug in at about noon to what was left of the depot. The night before their wedding, the couple slept together—sort of. In the shack of his soon-to-be-in-laws, Floyd slept "under the table with a minimum of bedding."

The next morning, a Tuesday, "we put the plans into motion." Floyd's mother, Jenny, was baking items for a holiday celebration when her son informed her of the amended schedule. "She put her Christmas bread and rolls in the breezeway to bake later. Then they got ready." Milo, Floyd's nineteen-year-old brother, would serve as best man. He went to alert their father, Henry, who was working as the Western Union operator in Cloquet.

Back at the shack at 910 Carlton Avenue, "things were really going in high gear," Bea recalled. Her mother and sixteen-year-old sister, Lucile, were busy scouring the shack: "Everything movable went out in the back yard in the snow so the rough board floor could be scrubbed." Bea's great aunt, Flo, had sent a braided rug after the fire, and that was placed in front of a homemade chest of drawers. As the rest of the furniture was moved back into the cleaned shanty, Bea got dressed.

Her options were narrow. She had two dresses: the one she was wearing when she fled the fire and a new dark blue jersey dress with a rounded neckline and braided fabric in front, which she had purchased in Duluth—a twenty-mile train ride away. Her skirt was layered with an overskirt called a peplum. "There wasn't much choice as to what to wear," she said. She accessorized with a lavalier necklace Floyd had given her. For his part, Floyd buttoned up his navy dress uniform.

"One thing I remember clearly was the fresh fragrance of the shack," Bea wrote, sixty-five years later. "New, green, unfinished pine, a fresh scrubbed floor, and a cozy fire in the little heater." Just before noon, Floyd returned from his errands and walked into the Parks' shack. Then Bea's father and the minister—"dressed in a plaid wool shirt, high topped boots, and jacket"—crowded in. Floyd's parents, brother Milo, and sister Doris elbowed into place, next to Bea's parents, her sister and bridesmaid, Lucile, plus her little toddler brother. "Merton was all dressed up in a sailor suit and was cute as a button," the bride recalled, "sitting on a shelf that usually held the wash basin, and intensely interested in the whole proceedings."

Two families, two months after the disaster, crowding together in the warm, pine-scented shack. "The ceremony didn't take long," Bea recalled. "We stood on the rug in front of the chest."

When it was over, Floyd slipped a five-dollar bill to the minister, who was filling out the marriage certificate. Rev. Williams later gave the certificate to the bride in a little booklet. "That evening when we looked at the book there was a $5 bill in an envelope with 'Bea' written on it," she said. The pastor had refunded the five dollars, making the ceremony "a very simple inexpensive wedding," she wrote.

Now all that was left was the honeymoon. Floyd had invited Milo and Lucile along for dinner in Duluth, and the newlyweds and their guests headed to the makeshift depot and waited for the Great Northern train to Duluth, a run they called the "Wooden Shoe." "On the train, Milo and Lucile had come prepared with a bag of rice and they proceeded to embarrass us and amuse the passengers by pouring rice down our necks," Bea remembered. "Floyd's sailor collar made a good funnel for that. The conductor came down the aisle and told Floyd: 'The monkey business would have to stop.' Floyd politely told him we were all in favor of that. But it didn't stop."

When they arrived in Duluth's Union Station, Floyd and his new bride gave their siblings the slip and enjoyed their wedding dinner at the McKay Hotel—just the two of them at last. "To this day," Bea wrote in 1973, "I don't know where [Milo and Lucile] had dinner before going back to Scanlon and Cloquet on the evening train."

The newlyweds had Christmas breakfast in Duluth and returned to the city after spending the day with their families. "We spent several days in Duluth, getting our pictures taken." Bea purchased a plum-colored wool suit with a sealskin collar and a new blouse to go with it.

When they trekked back to Cloquet, they received good news. The Parks' neighbors, the Wights, had traveled to Little Falls for Christmas and told Bea's father that Floyd and Bea could live in their shack for the rest of Floyd's leave: "It was a cozy little shack being 12 by 16 feet overall in size."

Floyd wired the Navy Department to ask for an extension of his leave, listing as the reason: "he had just gotten married." War over, extension granted, the couple had a few more days together before he left by train headed east, stopping in Niagara Falls, of all places. He loved to tell people in the years to come how he'd spent his honeymoon at the roaring falls—all by himself.

The Gellermans would have one son, Laurence, and two daughters, Doris and Joanne. Over the years, Floyd worked for the Wood Conversion Company in Cloquet, as a secretary of the YMCA, and as a stamp dealer. He died in the central Florida town of Sanford in December 1969, fifty-one years after his hastily planned wedding in Cloquet.

The Gellerman wedding illustrates how life goes on after any disaster. Amid all the sadness, mass burials, influenza-wracked coughing, and shell-shocked veterans returning home, joyous moments endured.

Four weeks after the fire, the Carlton County *Vidette* promised in a headline: "Moose Lake Will Rise From Ashes." Charles Mahnke, a governor-appointed local member of the Minnesota Forest Fires Relief Commission, promised every farmhouse would be rebuilt, every cow and pig replaced: "We are going to put you back as well off as you were before," Mahnke said. "And we are going to do more than that."

In some ways, he was right. The relief commission helped replace farming implements and rebuilt barns and shelters. Within a year of the fire, the *Moose Lake Star Gazette* reported that more than 90 percent of the people "are back on their farms or in new homes." Livestock was replaced with top-notch dairy cows thanks to assistance from the Minnesota Guernsey and Holstein breeders' groups, along with the University of Minnesota and US Agriculture Department.

Not all the help came from outside the region. These largely Finnish communities brought from the Old World a strong sense of cooperation and working together. Cooperative stores and farming societies sprouted up. In fact, Cloquet was considered the largest cooperative society in the nation by the late 1930s.

Farming in Carlton County grew by 50 percent in the 1920s, with records showing 2,899 farmers in 1930 compared to 1,938 in 1920. And those gains came despite a wrenching agricultural depression in the 1920s that presaged the Great Depression following the 1929 stock market collapse.

Schools reopened in early 1919, although teachers held back some children. "The reason I could not promote many was poor attendance, we having lost much time on account of the Forest Fire of Oct. 12 and sickness," teacher Nora M. Thorstenson of the Mansikka school, District 16, near Kettle River wrote in the spring of 1919. "The term was so short this year, attendance poor, that we could not do all the work we wished and are very much behind, but the children are hard workers and I am sure they will get along fairly well."

Train and telephone services were back within a matter of weeks of the fire. The relief commission helped merchants get back on their feet instead of simply swamping the region with donated goods. But notwithstanding all the happy weddings and rebirths, some towns

Floyd and Beatrice Gellerman were married in a hastily arranged wedding in the winter of 1918, and they remained together until Floyd's death in 1969. *Photo courtesy of Darlene Marsters*

would never be the same. Bain, Lawler, Harney, and Automba really never recovered.

The fires of 1918 were considered a watershed event even for Duluth's once-robust economy. "There's a fairly decent argument that this is a major turning point in the city of Duluth—historically speaking, you can pinpoint a lot of the city's decline" to 1918, said Dan Hartman, a former employee of the St. Louis County Historical Society and an expert of the region. Duluth's population had climbed steadily since 1860 and nearly doubled between 1900 to 1920, to about 100,000 residents; those numbers suddenly leveled off through the 1920s and '30s. And the optimism of the first part of the century no longer ran unchecked, Hartman said. The city's economy and population would later be buoyed by World War II and the Cold War, but it slipped again in the 1960s and 1970s before stabilizing in more recent years.

Today, one hundred years after the 1918 fire, Dan Reed is one of fewer than ten people living in the once-thriving, now nearly dormant lumber town of Automba. The catastrophic fire was an event that changed the area forever. "The timber dried up," he said. "But worse yet, everybody shifted to farming and then came the farm depression of 1924 and things kept getting worse and worse before the stock market crashed. People were driven off the land again in major economical dislocation." By the 1950s, the farms and creameries—buoyed by the cooperative spirit of the Finns and their fellow immigrants—were back on the rebound.

The lumber industry might have been doomed even before the fire. America's tree-felling business moved west like its immigrants had. The region where the cry of sawmills once buzzed loudly soon quieted into ghost towns. The Weyerhaeusers, whose family member Rudy was in Cloquet when the fires swept in, had already invested heavily in operations in Idaho and Washington state. "By 1918, the white pine forests of northern Minnesota, and certainly of the St. Louis River valley, had only a few years left to sustain full-scale logging operations," Carroll and Raiter wrote in *The Fires of Autumn*.

"Don't Lose Courage," the Carlton County *Vidette* pleaded on October 18, 1918, assuring readers that Cloquet would return—better than ever. And the optimism wasn't all pipe dreams. Cloquet had displayed plenty of luck when the fires swept in, pushed by fierce winds out of the northwest. That wind direction and the topography along the steep, curving banks of the St. Louis River diverted the fire's path enough to minimize the death toll and spare much of Cloquet's lumber sector. The Northwest Paper Company, the Cloquet Tie and Post Company, and local toothpick and box factories survived.

Those secondary businesses fared better than the big lumber companies. And some of the lumber businesses did better than others. The Weyerhaeusers' Northern Lumber Company lost two sawmills, 65 million board feet of cut lumber, and shops, barns, offices, and power plants. Others were hardly damaged. The Weyerhaeusers, still controlling large forests of timber in northern Minnesota, merged with the Cloquet Lumber Company before it went belly-up. With a shot in the arm to the tune of nearly $170,000 from the Railroad Administration, the Northern Lumber Company was back in the black by 1921. Although in steady decline in assets and cut lumber through the

The Cloquet Lumber Company mill somehow survived the 1918 blaze. *Courtesy of the Carlton County Historical Society*

1920s, two large lumber companies remained solvent in Cloquet for more than a decade after the fire.

In order to stay afloat, they developed commercial uses for jack pine, balsam, birch, and aspen and further diversified by creating a fluffy insulation material that looked like sheep's wool and pulp paper. The Wood Conversion Company was born as a brainchild of one of the Weyerhaeuser grandchildren in 1921 on the same St. Louis riverbank parcel where the Northern Lumber Company had burned. That wood-products firm remained strong and resilient for decades. Cloquet would never be the booming lumber and sawmill center it had been before the fire. But pulp, paper, and toothpick factories would continue to produce products and provide jobs for the rest of the twentieth century.

The extent to which one can say Cloquet rebounded from the fire is a matter of degree. A week after the fire, lumber baron Frederick Weyerhaeuser came to visit the city and described it as "one of the saddest looking sights I ever saw—nothing but black ruins and desolation for as far as one could see." His lumber company employee Sherman Coy had written in an October 19, 1918, letter to his brother, "the town cannot be what it was in our lifetime. No trees are left and no vegetation and it's like a bleak wilderness."

The numbers bear out Coy's grim assessment. The 1910 census showed 7,000 people in Cloquet, and it is widely held that between 8,000 and 10,000 people lived there in 1918. By 1920, the population had fallen to nearly half that number, to 5,127. By 1930 and 1940, census totals ticked upward to 6,782 and 7,302, respectively—meaning it took decades to approach pre-fire population levels.

In Carlton County, where many more lives were lost around Moose Lake and Kettle River, the population bounced back faster than in Cloquet. County numbers swelled from 17,559 in 1910 to 19,391 in 1920—just two years after the devastation.

A year after the fire, when Governor Burnquist returned to the site of the mass grave in Moose Lake, the graveyard was blanketed with flowers for the first anniversary. The governor praised the "spirit of determination" and "the generous aid which came from all parts of the state, as well as from other states," but he offered special tribute to the people of Cloquet for their "magnificent work" in reviving the area. The Cloquet City Council shared a resolution at the ceremony, thanking neighbors from Carlton, Duluth, and Superior, plus the governor, the legislature, and the Red Cross, "for all that they have done for us at the time of our misfortune."

During those darkest days, the people of northeastern Minnesota—largely immigrants from Finland, Poland, Germany, and Scandinavia—had displayed such gumption that it offset much of the misery. "There were innumerable instances of the most splendid heroism and the noblest self-sacrifice," Herbert Richardson, Duluth's longtime weatherman, wrote in April 1919 for the American Geographical Society. "Thousands of people would have perished," he said, without the soldiers, motor corps, train crews, and volunteer citizens who scoured the countryside for days following October 12, 1918. Automobile rescue efforts, a relatively new thing in 1918, were "rendered especially hazardous," he went on, "when even to use lights was almost futile because of the dense, suffocating, and blinding smoke and flying sparks and brands."

Century-old memories of families suffocated in root cellars, burned in wells, killed on Dead Man's Curve, or stricken with the deadly influenza virus or of the shell-shock and wounds of World War I slowly faded. Those flashbacks were too painful, so everyone looked to the resiliency of Minnesotans after the horrors of 1918—traits that

Governor Burnquist told the crowd at the first anniversary ceremonies "did much to awaken courage and hope when the people . . . were in despair." Writing just months after the fires, Richardson insisted: "No danger was too great. It was a sublime exemplification of true Americanism in a time of gravest peril."

Aina Jokimaki.
Photo courtesy of the family

Epilogue

IT WOULD BE TOO DIFFICULT to tell what happened to all the people who survived 1918 Minnesota and are mentioned in this book. John McGee's suicidal end and others' post-fire, post-flu, postwar narratives have already been described. But following are seventeen brief after-stories from some of the 1918 characters who etched their names into state history, when that trident of woe—war, fire, and flu—thrust itself in Minnesota's gut.

*

Aina Jokimaki was seventeen when she survived the fire five miles west of Moose Lake. But she lost her mother and six siblings. She married Carl Johnson in 1919 and raised nine children. She named two of them—Elma and Fred—after siblings lost in the fire. Her feet remained discolored from the 1918 burns. "They were white and never tanned and she always covered them with heavy socks," said her son, Ray Johnson, who at seventy-four still farms the land his great-grandfather Erik first claimed in the 1880s. He said his mother never talked much about the fires, but he would listen to the stories she finally agreed to share with Edwin Manni in the 1970s. Manni said the Johnsons "were blessed with a fine family, a credit to any community," which included a number of great-grandchildren. He thanked Aina "for her patience in furnishing this information, to be recorded for historians and researchers, painful as it may have been for her." Aina died in 1979 at seventy-seven and was buried in Eagle Lake Cemetery in Cromwell, Minnesota.

*

World War I canteen worker, nurse, and poet Amy Robbins Ware lived just more than a decade after her service in France, experiences she captured in her *Echoes of France* war diary. She died at fifty-one from a cerebral hemorrhage at Minneapolis's Abbott Hospital on May 5, 1929. She "had gained national prominence in her work on international relations" following the war, according to her front-page obituary in the *Minneapolis Morning Tribune*. The General Federation of Women's Clubs named her vice president of its international relations panel. President Warren Harding sent her a letter of commendation for her brochure, "The Permanent Court of International Justice as the First Step Toward the Prevention of War." The daughter of Robbinsdale's founder, Amy had been working in real estate and insurance before her death. She had no children and was buried at Lakewood Cemetery in Minneapolis.

*

Eino Salmi was three years old when the fires swept through Kettle River. The wagon carrying his mother, Olga, and four siblings was overcome with flames, killing them all. Eino, somehow, had gotten separated from the rest. His father found him the next day near what was left of the Kettle River bridge, where some men had kept him safe the night of October 12, 1918. Eino later joined the navy during World War II, moved to California, and lived until 1960. He's buried in the Los Angeles National Cemetery.

*

Pearl McIver, the University of Minnesota nursing student who took off her mask and cuddled flu-suffering children during the 1918 epidemic, graduated with a nursing degree the next year. She moved to Washington in 1922 and joined the US Public Health Service, where she worked for thirty-five years before retiring as chief of the division of public health nursing. Named a member of the American Nurses Association Hall of Fame, she is credited with creating nursing programs at local and state levels that employed more than thirty-five hundred nurses during the Great Depression. Pearl earned the first Public Health Nurse Award in 1956—an award later renamed in her honor after her death at eighty-two in Washington, DC, in 1976. She never married, and records show she sailed out of New York City aboard the *Queen Elizabeth* in 1948 during her eight-year stint with the Veterans Affairs Department's public health nursing corps.

*

Mary McCarthy, the six-year-old orphaned when her family contracted influenza on a Seattle-to-Minneapolis passenger train in 1918, continued her eastward trek later in life. After attending Vassar College in Poughkeepsie, New York, she moved to New York City and blossomed into a sharp-tongued American literary critic and author of more than two dozen books, including the 1963 bestseller *The Group* and her 1957 memoir, *Memories of a Catholic Girlhood*. When she died in New York City in 1989 at seventy-seven, the *New York Times* called her "one of America's pre-eminent women of letters." She was married with one son and split time between Maine and Paris. According to Goodreads.com, her debut 1942 novel, *The Company She Keeps*, and writings in publications such as the *Nation*, the *New Republic*, and the *New York Review of Books*, "initiated her ascent to become one of the most celebrated writers of her generation." In 1984, she was awarded both the Edward MacDowell Medal for outstanding contributions to literature and the National Medal for Literature.

*

The diary-writing Thortvedt sisters near Moorhead—Dora and Florence—went different directions after 1918. Dora married a neighbor boy, Ted Bergh, in 1923, and they moved to western North Dakota to live as ranchers. Ted died from tuberculosis in 1926. Dora returned to the Clay County farm before dying from encephalitis at fifty-one; she is buried behind the Concordia Lutheran Church in Glyndon. Her younger sister, Florence, moved to Minneapolis and married Emil Mathison later in life. They had no children. Census records show her working as a presser in a garment shop and living as a lodger on Laurel Avenue North. By 1940, she was working as a receptionist. She died in Moorhead in 1997 in her mid-nineties. Their older brother, Goodwin, returned from World War I and farmed grain near Glyndon. A bachelor farmer, he lived until 1962, when he died at seventy-five. He's buried next to his sisters.

*

The Honkala sisters, Esther and Helen, who at ages five and three, respectively, had been left for dead in a smoldering carriage, became two of the longest-surviving fire victims. Helen married Oscar Repo, worked as a cook and housekeeper in New York during the Great Depression, and farmed with her husband for twenty years near Floodwood, Minnesota. She died in a Duluth nursing home in 2002 at eighty-six. Her older sister, Esther, also farmed near Floodwood before moving with her husband in 1962 to Cloquet, where they operated the Luoma Sauna for more than a decade. A mother of ten and a champion Scrabble player, Esther moved to Hermantown and then Duluth, where she died at ninety in 2004. Together, the sisters produced more than fifty great-grandchildren.

*

Iowa born, Carleton College educated, and University of Minnesota Law School trained, Joseph Alfred Arner Burnquist served as a Republican state legislator from 1909 to 1911 before being elected lieutenant governor in 1912. He became governor in 1915 when Governor Winfield Hammond suffered ptomaine poisoning and died of a stroke. Burnquist won reelection in 1916 and then again in the trying year of 1918. Attempts to win Republican nominations in the 1920s for a US Senate seat and the 1930 governorship both failed. After returning to his law practice, Burnquist did stage a comeback, serving as Minnesota's attorney general from 1939 to 1955. "Fortunately for his place in history, his sixteen-year tenure in that [attorney general's] office was considerably less stormy than his two terms as governor," historian Carl Chrislock wrote. "Accolades rather than brickbats accompanied his final retirement from public life in 1955." Indeed, conservative Republicans urged him to seek a third term in 1956 at age seventy-seven—forty years after he left the governor's office. He declined. He and his wife, Mary Louise, had four kids. Burnquist died in 1961 at age eighty-one and is buried at Lakewood Cemetery in Minneapolis, along with at least six other former governors.

*

Anna Dickie Olesen, the Cloquet superintendent's wife, lobbied for years on behalf of her fellow fire survivors. In 1922, two years after polling places opened to women, she became the first female with major party backing to run for the US Senate. "I was and am ready to accept on equality with men whatever the fortunes of politics may offer," she said on June 20, 1922, in a story that ran in the *New York Times*. The *Washington Herald* said, "Small in stature, she proved her-

234

self a forensic giant." She wound up third in her historic Senate run, and Minnesota would wait eighty-four years before Amy Klobuchar's election to the US Senate in 2006 broke the gender barrier. Franklin Roosevelt repaid Olesen's party loyalty with a spot on the New Deal's National Emergency Council; she was the only woman on the policy panel. After spending years in Minnesota towns including Waterville, Cloquet, and Northfield, Anna moved to Georgia. When her first husband, Peter Olesen, died, she married Chester Burge, a man nineteen years younger than her, who had been charged and acquitted in his first wife's murder. He'd also been charged and acquitted, on appeal, of sodomy with his black chauffeur. Two years after they wed, Burge died when their home exploded in Palm Beach, Florida. Olesen died at eighty-five in 1971 after a fall and is buried in the Sakatah Cemetery in Waterville.

*

Ida Salmi Kohtala, the young Moose Lake nurse who survived the fire when the doctor she was working for drove his car into Moosehead Lake, was buried in the Holy Trinity Lutheran Cemetery in Kettle River in late August 1969—more than a half century after her mother and four siblings perished in the 1918 fire. She was seventy-two. Census records list her as a housekeeper in 1920 and show she went on to have six children. She's buried next to her husband, Jacob Kohtala, who died fewer than five months later, in 1970. He worked as a bridge construction carpenter and was employed by the Kettle River Co-op Creamery.

*

Dr. Franklin Reuben Walters and his wife, Ebba, scuttled their plans to build an expanded Moose Lake hospital after the 1918 fires. Funds were too limited. They left the area instead, resettling in Battle Creek, Michigan.

*

Nick and Hulda Koivisto—after seven of their eight children perished in the Niemi root cellar during the fire—went on to have four more children. Hulda died in 1968 at age eighty-six. She's buried in the St. Peter's Lutheran Cemetery in Moose Lake, the same graveyard she insisted be the resting place for her dead children despite orders that they be buried in the mass grave. Her husband, Nick, lived to the ripe age of ninety-six in 1973.

Their lone surviving child from the fire, Arnold, worked as a gardener at the Moose Lake State Hospital before moving to Castro Valley, California, south of Oakland after World War II. He died in 1992 at eighty-one.

*

Sister Julitta Hoppe, who cared for St. Cloud's flu-stricken in 1918, spent six decades as an active hospital worker, most of it as an administrator, surgical supervisor, and superior of the sisters stationed at St. Raphael's Hospital. She became one of the original planners of the St. Cloud Hospital, finding land and drawing up plans for the new, larger facility. "These 24 acres were out in the country, away from everybody," Sister Julitta said. "There was little prairie over toward the north, and we decided to take land that far." Despite many additions to the hospital, the original part that Sister Julitta designed still stands. The Hoppe Auditorium at the St. Cloud Hospital was named in her honor. When she died on February 26, 1971, at ninety-five, she was the oldest member of the Saint Benedict's Monastery in St. Joseph, Minnesota.

*

Sherman Lockwood Coy, the assistant manager of the Northern Lumber Company in Cloquet, wrote his brother a letter the week after the 1918 fire, describing the uncertain future and the "bleak wilderness" left with no trees. "I don't know what will become of us—whether I'll stay here or not," he wrote on October 19, 1918. Census records, at least, show he was living in Cloquet in 1920, 1930, and 1940 before moving to Libertyville, Illinois, around the time of World War II. He died in 1946 and was buried at Woodlawn Cemetery in Winona, Minnesota, his wife Kate's hometown. Kate was buried beside him twenty-three years later.

And their little toddler, Mary, who escaped with nothing but her pajamas and pink dress? Mary Coy Pritchard attended Smith College in Massachusetts and returned to Cloquet in the 1930s to work as a stenographer at her father's lumber mill. She lived until 2012 before dying in her longtime home of Liberty, Missouri, when she was ninety-six. She was instrumental in launching one of the first Habitat for Humanity chapters in the nation; the organization built more than two hundred homes for low-income families around Kansas City.

Acknowledgments

A NETWORK OF HISTORY BUFFS across Minnesota made this collection of stories possible. Dan Reed, the Finnish storytelling *kalle* in Automba, tenderly handed down sacred stories. Natalie Frohrip not only runs a great museum in the Moose Lake train depot that survived the fire, she pointed me to Chuck and Shirley Eckman one day over lunch. An hour later, I was stepping into the Soderberg cellar on Chuck's invitation. I bumped into Kimberly Etter at the Moose Lake museum during the ninety-seventh fire commemoration in 2015, and she became a trusty researcher on the project.

In Rochester, Carol Alley scoured the Mayo Clinic archives and the Olmsted County Historical Society's records, sending an inches-thick file of documents, ranging from letters from Will Mayo to poems written for the St. Marys School of Nursing yearbook. In one of her many countless encouraging emails, she said: "No need for reimbursement—Mayo copied the documents for free. . . . Happy sorting, organizing, and thinking!"

David Simpkins, editor and publisher of the Sauk Centre *Herald*, shared digital copies of the paper, where Albert Betz's flu-death story lay hidden. George Glotzbach provided a steady stream of New Ulm history, and Dr. Ellen Vancura filled in some family history about her relative, Ben Seifert, who died in World War I.

Retired naval reserve chaplain David Thompson in Rosemount provided World War I statistics, along with Doug Bekke, curator of the Minnesota Military Museum at Camp Ripley.

In Fairmont, Martin County Historical Society executive director Lenny Tvedten collected all the flu stories in the *Daily Sentinel* from October 1918 and sent them my way, along with county history and flu research he conducted. Copies of Dora and Florence Thortvedt's handwritten diaries came thanks to Mark Peihl, archivist of the Historical and Cultural Society of Clay County in Moorhead. The sisters' great-niece Becky Jetvig filled in some holes on their later lives.

Steve Penick, archivist at the Stearns History Museum, provided volumes of Stearns County clippings from 1918, including the tale of the indefatigable Benedictine nun Sister Julitta Hoppe. Lynette Anderson, a volunteer at the Minnesota History Center, shared the story of her great aunt from Hermantown, Doris Lofald Archibald, who died in 1990. Darlene Marsters, a close friend of Beatrice Gellerman's late daughter Doris, responded to an out-of-left-field call to her Afton church and sent along a sweet photo of Floyd and Bea, the couple that married after the fire. Other photo wranglers included Sister Mariterese Woida at the Saint Benedict's Monastery, Pete Richie of the Robbinsdale Historical Society, Rachael Martin at the Carlton County Historical Society, and University of Minnesota Duluth ace archivist Patricia Maus.

Descendants of 1918 survivors helped round things out, including Aina Jokimaki's son Ray Johnson and grandson Kevin DeLacey. Longtime friend and *Minneapolis Star Tribune* researcher John Wareham, World War I expert Randal Dietrich, and Brian Horrigan at the Minnesota Historical Society offered constant help, along with society coworkers Jennifer Rian, Marisa Rose Gonzalez, and Anne Levin.

I relied heavily on the exhaustive 1990 book *The Fires of Autumn*, which was the result of a Herculean, ten-year effort by Francis Carroll and the late Franklin Raiter. Carroll, a retired history professor at the University of Manitoba, sent an encouraging email that said, among other things: "We hoped that our book would inspire others to write about the fire. . . . You will be able to turn up new material and come up with a different view of the fire than we did. And you will be able to put this event in the context of what else was taking place."

Edwin Manni's 1978 collection of fire stories, "Kettle River, Automba, Kalevala and Surrounding Area," proved equally invaluable.

Last but certainly not least, the idea that 1918 Minnesota could morph into a book came from Josh Leventhal at the Minnesota Historical Society Press. Thanks, too, to the press's former director, Pamela McClanahan, and to hawk-eyed manuscript editor Shannon Pennefeather.

This book is dedicated to my wife and sounding board, Adele; my first grandchild, Lillian Judith; and all the Minnesotans who endured the horrors of 1918 and upon whose resilient shoulders we stand a century later.

Notes

Opening Quotes and Introduction

Lyrics from "High Hopes," *Monterey*, Milk Carton Kids (2015), used with permission. Amy Robbins Ware quote from page 137 of her book *Echoes of France*. Richardson, "The Northeastern Minnesota Forest Fires." Adjutant General Rhinow's 1918 report. Anna Olesen's 1930 speech to Congress is excerpted in *Fire Storm* by Skalko and Wisuri.

Soderberg family history: Wold, *The Other West Side Story*, 106-7; Moose Lake Area Historical Society, *1918 Fire Stories*, 51; ages and names: *1918 Fire Stories*, 151; stories: Illikainen, *Firebeast*, 104; *Superior Telegram*, Oct. 18, 1918, 7, "Emma Naomi Soderberg Samuelson," Find a Grave, http://image1.find agrave.com/cgi-bin/fg.cgi?page=pv&GRid=118743727&PIpi=90679947.

Eckman family history: Chuck Eckman, interview, Sept. 15, 2016; Wold, *The Other West Side Story*; Illikainen, *Firebeast*, 20; *Superior Telegram*, Oct. 16, 1918, "Agnes Eckman Peterson," Find a Grave, http://www.findagrave .com/cgi-bin/fg.cgi?page=gr&GRid=133105035.

World War I statistics: Doug Bekke, curator, Minnesota Military Museum, Camp Ripley, Little Falls, MN; David Thompson, retired Naval Reserve chaplain, Rosemount, MN. Additional World War I information from Crosby, *America's Forgotten Pandemic;* Barry, *The Great Influenza;* and "The Great Pandemic of 1918: State by State."

Record dryness up north, death toll, other statistics, financial totals, and scope of fire: Gray, "Are You a 49'er?"; Skalko and Wisuri, *Fire Storm*, 15;

Carroll and Raiter, *Fires of Autumn*; Richardson, "The Northeastern Minnesota Forest Fires," 9, 10, 13; and Minnesota Forest Fires Relief Commission, Final Report, 6, 12. Kettle River plaque says thirty-eight towns were destroyed and 52,000 people were displaced. Log drive and Automba: Dan Reed interview, recorded by author, Sept. 16, 2016. The *Kalevala* quote can be found in Friberg's translation or at Niina's Spirituality blog, http://niinac.blogspot.com/2010/10/kalevala-studies-part-1-poem-50.html.

Aina Jokimaki's family history at ancestry.com; her story appears in Manni, *1918 Forest Fire Stories*, 99–100. John Peura's account is in Manni, 110; also see "Suoma Josephine Himango Jokimaki," Find a Grave, http://www.findagrave.com/cgi-bin/fg.cgi?page=gr&GRid=131720364&ref=acom.

Chapter 1

Betz's World War I draft registration record at ancestry.com; his death record in the Veteran's Grave Index, Minnesota Historical Society, http://people.mnhs.org/finder/vgri/49717?return=q%3Dalbert%2520betz; Iris Betz's music teaching: 1920 census.

For flu information, see Barry, *The Great Influenza;* Crosby, *America's Forgotten Pandemic;* Stanford University, "The Influenza Pandemic of 1918"; and PBS, *American Experience*, "Influenza 1918: The First Wave": http://ec2-184-73-243-168.compute-1.amazonaws.com/wgbh/americanexperience/features/general-article/influenza-first-wave/.

Sauk Centre *Herald* editions from October 1918, provided by the paper's current editor and publisher, David Simpkins. A calendar of 1918 (https://www.timeanddate.com/calendar/?year=1918) shows that Betz died on a Tuesday; his remains arrived a week later and were buried on Friday, Oct. 25, 1918.

Minnesota demographic information: Minnesota State Demographic Center, "Minnesota Now, Then, When . . . An Overview of Demographic Change," Apr. 2015, https://mn.gov/admin/assets/2015-04-06-overview-MN-demographic-changes_tcm36-74549.pdf.

Tillie Odberg Westman's account, including the mass grave: Manni, *1918 Forest Fire Stories*, 104–6. For more on the mass grave, see *1918 Forest Fire Stories*, 84. World War I stats can be found at US Department of Veterans Affairs, America's Wars fact sheet: http://www.va.gov/opa/publications/factsheets/fs_americas_wars.pdf.

Tyler tornado information: Minnesota Department of Natural Resources, "Minnesota Tornado History and Statistics," http://www.dnr.state.mn.us/climate/summaries_and_publications/tornadoes.html.

Duluth newspapers: Krueger, "Duluth's Worst Year," and *Herald* clip on grave digging provided by Moose Lake Area Historical Society.

Chapter 2

Thortvedt diaries courtesy of Mark Peihl, archivist, Historical and Cultural Society of Clay County, Moorhead. For more on early Thortvedts: Patrick Springer, "New Exhibit Depicts Norwegian Immigration to Clay County," *Grand Forks Herald,* Nov. 9, 2015, http://www.grandforksherald.com/news/region/3878551-new-exhibit-depicts-norwegian-immigration-clay-county.

World War I death toll: "List of Wars by Death Toll," http://webcache.googleusercontent.com/search?q=cache:EosWkmmncTYJ:research.omicsgroup.org/index.php/List_of_wars_by_death_toll&num=1&client=safari&hl=en&gl=us&strip=1&vwsrc=0.

More World War I history: "Lusitania," History Channel, http://www.history.com/topics/world-war-i/lusitania; Minnesota vote: Dr. Eric Ostermeier, "U.S. Senate Race Ends Up 12 Votes Shy of '62 Gubernatorial Margin of Victory Record," *Smart Politics,* Jan. 8, 2009, https://editions.lib.umn.edu/smartpolitics/2009/01/08/us-senate-race-ends-up-12-vote/; Wilson-Jackson: President Woodrow Wilson House, "1916 Election," http://www.woodrowwilsonhouse.org/1916-election; Wilson losing Minnesota: Wikipedia, "United States Presidential Election, 1916," https://en.wikipedia.org/wiki/United_States_presidential_election,_1916; Wilson electoral vote totals: Atlas of U.S. Presidential Elections, "1916 Presidential General Election Results," http://uselectionatlas.org/RESULTS/national.php?year=1916; Wilson quote and other insight: Barry, *The Great Influenza,* 120–24.

German population: Ehsan Alam, "Anti-German Nativism, 1917–1919," MNopedia, http://www.mnopedia.org/anti-german-nativism-1917-1919. For Minnesota Commission of Public Safety in New Ulm, see Chrislock, *The Progressive Era* and *Watchdog of Loyalty;* Paul Nelson, "New Ulm Military Draft Meeting, 1917," MNopedia, http://www.mnopedia.org/event/new-ulm-military-draft-meeting-1917. On Bremer, schools, Germania bank, Meints: Alam, "Anti-German Nativism."

Chapter 3

Lutra Krigsholm's account: Reed, *Automba*, 103. Some census records show a Krixholm spelling but we used Reed's local knowledge.

Weather: Skalko and Wisuri, *Fire Storm*, 15; Richardson, "The Northeastern Minnesota Forest Fires," 9, 10; Carroll and Raiter, *Fires of Autumn.*

Evelyn Lyngen Mead account: Manni, *1918 Forest Fire Stories*, 132-34; Smith: Carroll and Raiter, *Fires of Autumn*, 5; other fires, Brookston start, gun analogy, railroad culpability: *Fires of Autumn*, 6-9, 26-30, 78-82, 87-88, 98-99, 129, 133; Columbus Day: http://print-a-calendar.com/holiday/columbus-day/1916.

Richardson, "The Northeastern Minnesota Forest Fires." For more fire sources, see Carroll and Raiter, "At the Time of Our Misfortune," 271n.

Chapter 4

Pearl Drew's account: Skalko and Wisuri, "Fire Storm," 92-96; Argonne background: Maps of the World, "Battle of the Argonne Forest—1918," http://www.mapsofworld.com/world-war-i/battle-of-argonne-forest.html.

Evelyn Lyngen Mead account: Manni, *1918 Forest Fire Stories*, 132-34; Soderberg history: see notes for Introduction; Esther Honkala Luoma: *Duluth News Tribune*, Oct. 29, 1991; Luoma family history: Genealogy .com, "Ted Luoma and Esther Honkala of Floodwood, Minnesota," http://www.genealogy.com/ftm/l/u/o/Dawn-S-Luoma/WEBSITE-0001/UHP-0073.html; Esther Alma Luoma obituary, *Duluth News Tribune*, http://www.duluthnewstribune.com/content/esther-alma-luoma.

Brown Road divide: Reed, *Automba*, 113; Helen Honkala history: Find a Grave, "Helen Sylvia Honkala Repo," http://www.findagrave.com/cgi-bin/fg.cgi?page=gr&GRid=87199423&ref=acom.

Chapter 5

For more on Pearl McIver, see her essay on her nights in the children's flu ward, "1918 Influenza Epidemic at University of Minnesota Hospital," http://editions.lib.umn.edu/ahcarchives/wp-content/uploads/sites/7/2009/09/McIver1958.pdf; Erik Moore, "Pearl McIver," Academic Health Center History Project, Sept. 29, 2009, http://editions.lib.umn .edu/ahcarchives/2009/09/29/pearl-mciver/; "Honoring ANA's Hall of Fame Inductees," *The American Nurse*, http://www.theamericannurse .org/2014/07/03/honoring-anas-hall-of-fame-inductees/.

Flu in Wells, MN, Bracken profile, stats: Jordan, *The People's Health*, 77-78, 140-45, 410-17; more flu, shortage quote, Bracken's frustration, early stats, elevator rules: see study comparing Twin Cities approaches: Ott, et al., "Lessons Learned."

For flu at the University of Minnesota, including twenty-one nurses, see Brady, "The Great Flu Epidemic"; flu in Minneapolis: University of Michigan Center for the History of Medicine, "Minneapolis, Minnesota."

Background for Bracken at Uppingham: John Huntley Skrine, *Uppingham By the Sea: A Narrative of the Year at Borth*, http://www.amazon.co.uk

/Uppingham-Sea-Narrative-Year-Borth-ebook/dp/B004TP9RJW; Boeck-man: Jordan, *The People's Health*, 410; more stats, including Dilworth and quote on trains: Jordan, *The People's Health*, 413.

For more on Sundwall: Brady, "The Great Flu Epidemic," and "John Sund-wall," University of Michigan Faculty History Project, http://um2017.org/faculty-history/faculty/john-sundwall/memoir.

Mary McCarthy's account: see her book, *Memories of a Catholic Girlhood,* 8, 9, 12, 13, 16, 17, 34-37, 40, 41, 44, 45, 54, 55. For more on McCarthy: Susan Perry, "Mary McCarthy, Minneapolis and the 1918-19 Flu Pandemic," MinnPost, https://www.minnpost.com/second-opinion/2012/03/mary -mccarthy-minneapolis-and-1918-19-flu-pandemic and McCarthy bio, Goodreads, https://www.goodreads.com/author/show/7305.Mary _McCarthy.

Chapter 6

For Native American flu stats: Crosby, *America's Forgotten Pandemic,* 228; Mille Lacs history: Westerman and White, *Mni Sota Makoce*, 24; Mille Lacs Band of Ojibwe, "Our History," http://millelacsband.com/about/our -history; jingle dress history: Child, *My Grandfather's Knocking Sticks*, 125-50; fire at Fond du Lac: Carroll and Raiter, *Fires of Autumn*, 24-25, 31-37, and Anderson, "The 1918 Fire on FDL"; Manni, *1918 Forest Fire Stories,* 38-41; more Fond du Lac history: Fond du Lac Band of Lake Superior Chippewa, "Onigamiinsing Dibaajimowinan—Duluth's Stories," http:// www.duluthstories.net/.

Chapter 7

Lutiant LaVoye: Child, *My Grandfather's Knocking Sticks*, 150-60; Camp Humphreys: "1917-1918: Establishment of Camp A. A. Humphreys," Fort Belvoir website, http://www.belvoir.army.mil/history/Humphreys.htm; her Washington boardinghouse still stands and was worth an estimated $700,000 in 2017: realtor.com, http://www.realtor.com/realestateand homes-detail/213-14th-St-SE_Washington_DC_20003_M65951-73230.

For more on Indian boarding schools, see: "History and Culture: Boarding Schools," Northern Plains Reservation Aid, http://www.nrcprograms .org/site/PageServer?pagename=airc_hist_boardingschools, and Mary Annette Pember, "Tiny Horrors: A Chilling Reminder of How Cruel Assimilation Was—and Is," *Indian Country Today*, Jan 1, 2013, http:// indiancountrytodaymedianetwork.com/article/tiny-horrors-chilling -reminder-how-cruel-assimilation-was—and-146664.

New York Times letter: "The German Plague," *New York Times*, Oct. 20, 1918, column six: http://query.nytimes.com/mem/archive-free/pdf?res

=9B06E4DC113BEE3ABC4851DFB6678383609EDE; flu history, including Bayer suspicions, American Protective League: Kreiser, "1918 Spanish Influenza Outbreak."

John Franklin McGee in Washington and backlash: Chrislock, *Watchdog of Loyalty*, 78-79, 298-300; Greg Gaut, "McGee, John Franklin, (1861-1925)" MNopedia, http://www.mnopedia.org/person/mcgee-john-franklin -1861-1925 (which lists multiple additional sources); McGee speech to Senate: Chrislock, *Watchdog of Loyalty*, 299, and Haines and Haines, *The Lindberghs*, 281-82; additional McGee information: Shutter and McLain, *Progressive Men of Minnesota*, "John Franklin McGee," Genealogy Trails, http://genealogytrails.com/minn/hennepin/bios_m.htm.

Chapter 8

New Ulm history: Ubl, *The Matter Lies Deeper*, and Hoisington, *A German Town*, including Fritsche's 1914 trip (122); Tyler, "William Pfaender and the Founding of New Ulm"; Chrislock, *The Progressive Era*, 12, 22, 70, 71, 102, 134, 140-44, 151, 180; Chrislock, *Watchdog of Loyalty*, 47, 120, 133-36, 151-53, 179, 224, including Burnquist quote (179) and "Pfaender was incendiary" (141); Rippley, "Conflict in the Classroom," includes "traitor . . . shot" quote (174); Braun, *Marking Time*.

Deadliest wars: Ejaz Khan, "10 Deadliest Wars in Human History," Wonderslist, http://www.wonderslist.com/10-deadliest-wars-in-human-history/; Zimmermann: "Arthur Zimmermann," *Encyclopedia Britannica*, https://www.britannica.com/biography/Arthur-Zimmermann; Nelson quote: Nelson, *I Will Hold*, 12; Brown County war dead: Ubl, *The Matter Lies Deeper*, 527; transit strike: Nathanson, "Remembering the Other Lowry."

Seifert's death: "New Ulm Soldier Called by Death," *New Ulm Journal*, Apr. 10, 1918, https://www.newspapers.com/image/80060142/; "Corp. Benjamin J. Seifert," Find a Grave, http://www.findagrave.com/cgi-bin/fg .cgi?page=gr&GRid=33232388; "Christian Seifert," My Heritage, https://www.myheritage.com/names/christian_seifert; additional Seifert details courtesy Brown County Historical Society, relative Dr. Ellen Vancura, and George L. Glotzbach, "The History of Corp. Benjamin J. Seifert, New Ulm's First WWI Casualty," *Mankato Times*, June 27, 2016, http://mankatotimes.com/2016/06/27/the-history-of-corp-benjamin-j-seifert -new-ulms-first-wwi-casualty/.

Chapter 9

Lydia Salmi Ivonen's account: Moose Lake Area Historical Society, *1918 Fire Stories*, 104-6; Ailie Leppa Nikkila's account: Manni, *1918 Forest Fire Stories*, 84-85; Ida Salmi Kohtala's account: Manni, *1918 Forest*

Fire Stories, 119-20; Eino Salmi: ancestry.com, link: http://tinyurl.com
/EinoSalmi.

Finnish-Minnesota history: Kolehmainen, "The Finnish Pioneers of Minnesota"; Brown Road divide: Reed, *Automba,* 113.

Dead Man's Curve: Carroll and Raiter, *Fires of Autumn,* 73, 75, 92-93, 107;
Ida Hiipakka spelling and death record: ancestry.com, http://tinyurl.com
/IdaHiipakka; story of her Ely class ring: Manni, *1918 Forest Fire Stories,*
120. Stella Paapanen's burial is in question: Carroll and Raiter said she
was placed in the mass grave in Moose Lake, while Find a Grave puts her
at Holy Trinity Lutheran Cemetery in Kettle River: http://tinyurl.com
/StellaPaapanen.

Chapter 10

The excerpted poems from the 1919 St. Marys School of Nursing yearbook
came courtesy of the W. Bruce Fye Center for the History of Medicine at
the Mayo Clinic in Rochester. The Fye Center was the source for much of
the material in this chapter, including quoted letters. See also Clapesattle, *The Doctors Mayo,* 569-71. Mary Ledwidge background: ancestry.com,
http://tinyurl.com/MaryLedwidge.

For more of Rosenow: his research article, "Prophylactic Inoculation Against
Respiratory Infections," appeared in the Jan. 4, 1919, *Journal of the American Medical Association* (31). An editorial criticizing that research appeared
in the same issue (44-45). Quotes from Crosby, *America's Forgotten Pandemic,* 277, and Barry, *The Great Influenza,* 268, 317, 407.

See also Clapesattle, *The Doctors Mayo;* John M. Eyler, "The State of Science, Microbiology, and Vaccines Circa 1918," Public Health Reports,
https://www.ncbi.nlm.nih.gov/pmc/articles/PMC2862332/; S. H. Shak-
man, "Tribute to Edward C. Rosenow," Institute of Science, http://www
.instituteofscience.com/rosenow.html. Rosenow's house is mentioned in a
"Pill Hill" preservation document: http://www.mnhs.org/preserve/nrhp
/nomination/85003768.pdf.

Mayo and St. Marys Hospital history: Saint Marys School of Nursing
Alumni Association, "History," http://www.mayo.edu/saint-marys-school
-of-nursing-alumni-association/about/history; "Saint Mary's Isolation
Hospital During the Influenza Epidemic," Edith Graham Mayo Papers,
Mayo Clinic Historical Unit, 110-11; "A Century of Caring, Saint Mary's
Hospital of Rochester, Minnesota, 1889-1989," and "Mayo Clinic Histor-
ical Suite and the Plummer Building," (2015), Mayo Foundation for Med-
ical Education and Research; Saint Marys Hospital, *News Bulletin,* 1, no.
1 (May 1, 1942), and 1, no. 4 (Aug. 1942); for Mangners' price: "St. Marys
Hospital Annals—1918"; Kate Roberts, "Mayo Clinic," MNopedia, http://

www.mnopedia.org/group/mayo-clinic; Thomas Edward Keys, "Mayo Family," *Encyclopedia Britannica,* https://www.britannica.com/topic /Mayo-family#ref264054; Allen J. Aksamit, "Appendix: Catholicism, the Mayo Clinic, and the Future of Medicine," *Humanum* (Fall 2013), http://humanumreview.com/articles/appendix-catholicism-the-mayo-clinic -and-the-future-of-medicine; a fiftieth anniversary story ran in the *Spencer (Iowa) Daily Reporter,* June 3, 1956: https://news.google.com /newspapers?nid=1907&dat=19560603&id=JGwrAAAAIBAJ&sjid =29kEAAAAIBAJ&pg=2926,3997100&hl=en.

Letters from Mayo and others: courtesy of the Mayo Historical Suite, Mayo Foundation, and W. Bruce Fye Center for the History of Medicine, Mayo Clinic. Civilian deaths: see flu time line at PBS, *American Experience,* "Influenza 1918": http://ec2-184-73-243-168.compute-1.amazonaws.com /wgbh/americanexperience/features/transcript/influenza-transcript/.

Chapter 11

Buczynski unpublished manuscript, "Thank You, Mother, For Being My Hero" (note: he uses Leon while census records use Leo Soboleski); 1920 Census: ancestry.com, search "Albena Soboleski" for family roster; *Moose Lake Star Gazette,* Feb. 27, 1919, as reprinted in Illikainen, *Firebeast,* 37–38; Homicz: "John Victor Homicz," Find a Grave, http://www.findagrave.com /cgi-bin/fg.cgi?page=gr&GRid=92139040&ref=acom; Hay reference: Reed, *Automba,* 104; see also Manni, *1918 Forest Fire Stories,* 93 (fire noise), 120–21; Nanticoke: "History of Nanticoke," http://www.nanticoke city.com/history.htm; Jusola: ancestry.com, http://tinyurl.com/Jusola; Homicz family roster: Moose Lake Area Historical Society, *1918 Fire Stories,* 147. The 1919 *Moose Lake Star Gazette* reports Homicz buried in the Polish cemetery, but Illikainen says in *Firebeast* that the family was buried in the mass grave in Moose Lake.

Chapter 12

Martin County history: Martin County Historical Society, "Early History of Martin County and Fairmont," "Martin County—Its History and People Significant in its Development," and "Early History of Martin County." See also: Upham, *Minnesota Place Names,* 351–57; census figures for Welcome: "Welcome, Minnesota," Wikipedia, https://en.wikipedia.org/wiki /Welcome,_Minnesota.

Fairmont Daily Sentinel, Oct. 4, 7, 8, 10, 11, 12, 14, 15, 19, 22, 29, Nov. 2, 4, 5, 14, 18, 23, 1918; *Martin County Sentinel,* Oct. 15, Nov. 5, 1918; Dr. Strobel's World War I registration card and other genealogy information: ancestry. com; for more on gauze masks, see Barry, *The Great Influenza,* 358–59, and Crosby, *America's Forgotten Pandemic,* 101–13.

Chapter 13

1918 Minnesota election: Morlan, *Political Prairie Fire* and "The Nonpartisan League," 224 (Mar. 21, 1918, rally), and Chrislock, *The Progressive Era*
and *Watchdog of Loyalty*; Burnquist's letter declining Nonpartisan invite:
"Burnquist Fights Nonpartisan League," *Warren Sheaf*, Oct. 13, 1918,
http://chroniclingamerica.loc.gov/lccn/sn90059228/1918-03-13/ed-1/seq
-1.pdf; Burnquist on loyalty in 1918 campaign: Chrislock, *The Progressive
Era,* 164–65.

See also Haines and Haines, *The Lindberghs*; Peter J. DeCarlo, "Nonpartisan League," MNopedia, http://www.mnopedia.org/group/nonpartisan
-league; Jenson, "Loyalty as a Political Weapon"; "Townley, Arthur C.
(1880–1959)," Encyclopedia of the Great Plains, http://plainshumanities
.unl.edu/encyclopedia/doc/egp.pd.052; Lindbergh Sr: "Lindbergh,
Charles August (1859–1924)," Biographical Directory of the U.S. Congress,
http://bioguide.congress.gov/scripts/biodisplay.pl?index=L000320.

Townley early life: Morlan, *Political Prairie Fire*, 23; Chrislock, *The Progressive Era,* 110 (socialism quote), 112 (five-foot-ten quote), 164 (Burnquist
"normal times" quote); Lindbergh Sr. quote: Morlan, "The Nonpartisan
League," 223; vote totals: Morlan, "The Nonpartisan League," 231, and
Chrislock, *The Progressive Era,* 179.

Note on eighty-six counties: Lake of the Woods County is the most recently
established and organized county in the state, becoming Minnesota's
eighty-seventh county in 1922: "Lake of the Woods County Courthouse
History," Minnesota Judicial Branch website, http://www.mncourts.gov
/Find-Courts/LakeOfTheWoods/CourthouseHistory.aspx.

"Condition for survival" quote: Chrislock, *Watchdog of Loyalty*, 289; Hammond death: "Minnesota's Governor Dies," *Glasgow (MT) Courier*, Dec. 31,
1915, http://chroniclingamerica.loc.gov/lccn/sn85042379/1915-12-31/ed-1
/seq-1.pdf; Rock County and Duluth vigilantism: Chrislock, *Watchdog of
Loyalty,* 289–90 and *The Progressive Era,* 174; Bjornson's editorial: Chrislock, *The Progressive Era,* 174–75; for a chart of towns and villages burned:
Carroll and Raiter, *Fires of Autumn, 5.*

Chapter 14

Ida Salmi Kohtala's account: Manni, *1918 Forest Fire Stories,* 119–20; ancestry
.com includes her in censuses from 1910, 1920, and 1930, showing her first
as the oldest child, then the lone survivor in home with her father, John,
and finally with her husband, Jack; see also Johnson, "Fires of 1918," and
Lois Johnson, "City of Moose Lake to Celebrate 125 Years," *Moose Lake Star
Gazette*, July 3, 2014: http://www.mlstargazette.com/story/2014/07/03
/lifestyles/city-of-moose-lake-to-celebrate-125-years/1141.html; Dr. Wal-

ters' first name: ancestry.com, http://search.ancestry.com/cgi-bin/sse .dll?db=1920usfedcen&indiv=try&h=26510372; Tillie Odberg Westman's account: Manni, *1918 Forest Fire Stories*, 104-6; eighty-mile-per-hour winds: Manni, *1918 Forest Fire Stories*, 104n; phone lineman Vader's story and Mayor Hart's: Manni, *1918 Forest Fire Stories*, 97.

Niemi-Koivisto tragedy: Manni, *1918 Forest Fire Stories,* 100-102, and *Moose Lake Star Gazette*, Oct. 9, 1975; ages of victims: Moose Lake Area Historical Society, *1918 Fire Stories*, 148, 150.

Speed of fire: Richardson, "The Northeastern Minnesota Forest Fires," 227; Cloquet 1918 population: Carroll and Raiter, *Fires of Autumn*, 187; Olesen's account: Carroll and Raiter, *Fires of Autumn,* 47, and Skalko and Wisuri, *Fire Storm*, 112-15; Ulrich, career: R. L. Cartwright, "WPA Federal Writers' Project in Minnesota, 1935-1943," MNopedia, http://www.mnopedia.org /thing/wpa-federal-writers-project-minnesota-1935-1943; Olesen career: Curt Brown, "Fiery Orator Anna Dickie Olesen Blazed a Path for Women in Politics," *Minneapolis Star Tribune*, Nov. 15, 2015, http://www.startribune .com/fiery-orator-anna-dickie-olesen-blazed-a-path-for-women-in -politics/349039041/; Weyerhaeuser background: "Weyerhaeuser Family Inventory," Minnesota Historical Society, http://www2.mnhs.org /library/findaids/P930.xml; "F. Weyerhaeuser, Lumber King, Dead," *New York Times*, Apr. 5, 1914, http://query.nytimes.com/mem/archive-free /pdf?res=9E07E2DB163AE633A25756C0A9629C946596D6CF; "Frederick Weyerhaeuser," Encyclopedia Britannica, https://www.britannica.com /biography/Frederick-Weyerhaeuser; Rudolph Weyerhaeuser, Coy account: Carroll and Raiter, *Fires of Autumn*, 43-45; Fauley's role, trains, Bull anecdote, Elfes's account: *Fires of Autumn*, 45-49.

Kathryn Elfes Gray account: Gray Papers, "Are you a 49'er?" and Carroll and Raiter, *Fires of Autumn,* 47-49; Elshoss quote: "My Experiences in the Cloquet Fire of 1918," Carlton County Historical Society, and *Fires of Autumn,* 49; Pearl Drew quote: "The Forest Fires of 1918," Carlton County Historical Society, and *Fires of Autumn*, 49; Cloquet death toll discussed: *Fires of Autumn, 56;* Sherman Coy's letter to his brother: "Fires of 1918, Personal Narratives," Carlton County Historical Society.

Note on speed of fire at sixty-five miles per hour: Kreuger, "Duluth's Worst Year."

Chapter 15

Wigington: "Clarence Wesley (Cap) Wigington (1883-1967), Architect," Nebraska Historical Society, http://www.e-nebraskahistory.org/index.php ?title=Clarence_Wesley_(Cap)_Wigington_(1883-1967),_Architect; story in *Appeal:* "Home Guard Notice," Apr. 6, *1918,* http://chroniclingamerica

.loc.gov/lccn/sn83016810/1918-04-06/ed-1/seq-3/; Peter J. DeCarlo, "Six-teenth Battalion, Minnesota Home Guard," MNopedia, http://www.mnopedia.org/group/sixteenth-battalion-minnesota-home-guard; Paul Nelson, "Wigington, Clarence (1883-1967)," MNopedia, http://www.mnopedia.org/person/wigington-clarence-1883-1967; Wigington profile: Curt Brown, "A Life by Design," *Minneapolis Star Tribune*, Feb. 25, 1998.

Win Stephens and the Motor Corps: Adjutant General Rhinow report; Peter J. DeCarlo, "Minnesota Motor Corps," MNopedia, http://www.mnopedia.org/group/minnesota-motor-corps; Luukkonen, "Brave Men in Their Motor Machines"; 1910 census shows Stephens selling cigars; more on Stephens: "2370 Highway 100 So.—Win Stephens Buick," St. Louis Park Historical Society, http://slphistory.org/hwy1002370/; see also Carroll and Raiter, *Fires of Autumn*, 70; DeCarlo, "Minnesota Home Guard," http://www.mnopedia.org/group/minnesota-home-guard.

Tyler tornado information: "Minnesota Tornado History and Statistics," Minnesota Department of Natural Resources, http://www.dnr.state.mn.us/climate/summaries_and_publications/tornadoes.html.

Blooming Prairie: Kay Fate, "Blooming Prairie Was a Hub of Liquor Sales," *Post-Bulletin* (Austin, MN), July 27, 2012, http://www.postbulletin.com/austin/news/blooming-prairie-was-hub-of-liquor-sales/article_79b5282c-446f-5e40-804f-bca86ba14e50.html; see also Carroll and Raiter, *Fires of Autumn*, 217-20.

Black demographics: Shandira Pavelcik, "Minnesota," Black Demographics, http://blackdemographics.com/states/minnesota/.

Chapter 16

Aitkin County sheriff anecdote: Moose Lake Area Historical Society, *1918 Fire Stories,* 82, and Reed, *Automba,* 112; ancestry.com confirms spelling, birth date on World War I draft card: http://search.ancestry.com/cgi-bin/sse.dll?indiv=1&db=WW1draft&h=29706626&tid=&pid=&usePUB=true&_phsrc=dKr2&_phstart=successSource&usePUBJs=true&rhSource=60525.

Beers' explosives: Luukkonen, "Brave Men in Their Motor Machines," 6; Kerttu's sad story: Manni, *1918 Forest Fire Stories,* 122, and Illikainen, *Firebeast*, 47; passport application: ancestry.com; Dan Reed interview, Sept. 15, 2016.

Tillie (Odberg) Westman account: Manni, *1918 Forest Fire Stories*, 104-6; Saima Anttila Lumppio account: "Esko's Corner," 162-63.

German rumors: Kreiser, "1918 Spanish Influenza Outbreak," and Luukkonen, "Brave Men in Their Motor Machines," 4. *Vidette,* Nov. 8, 1918, provided by Moose Lake Area Historical Society.

Chapter 17

As a longtime Cloquet journalist, including a stint at the (Cloquet) *Pine Knot* her father edited for years, Kathryn Elfes Gray wrote several accounts—including the unpublished essay "This is the Way it Was," Sept. 5, 1968, in the Gray Papers at the Minnesota Historical Society. See also, "Are You a 49er?" and "My Story of the Cloquet Fire," Gray Papers. See also Carroll and Raiter, *Fires of Autumn*, 46–49, 185.

Cloquet fire deaths: four reported in National Register nomination below; Richardson, "The Northeastern Minnesota Forest Fires," 227, says "five lives" and "fewer than six"; Carroll and Raiter, *Fires of Autumn*, 56.

Fauley mentioned in new Cloquet City Hall nomination for National Register of Historic Places: http://www.mnhs.org/preserve/nrhp/nomination/85002312.pdf and park detailed on city's website: "Fauley Park," http://www.ci.cloquet.mn.us/index.asp?Type=B_BASIC&SEC={71F215BF-D1C2-4B8E-B0E4-C0187F39E916}&DE=.

Chapter 18

Armistice Day in Minneapolis: Nathanson, "Remembering Nov. 11, 1918"; Van Sant: Jerome Christenson, "Samuel Van Sant: At the Helm," *Winona Daily News*, May 1, 2013, http://www.winonadailynews.com/special-section/pieces-of-the-past/samuel-van-sant-at-the-helm/article_1f4d71d0-b2ab-11e2-91c7-001a4bcf887a.html.

Torrance: "Ell Torrance," ancestry.com, http://search.ancestry.com/cgi-bin/sse.dll?indiv=1&db=FindAGraveUS&h=70508916&tid=&pid=&usePUB=true&_phsrc=wDf7&_phstart=successSource&usePUBJs=true&rhSource=7316.

Van Lear: Chrislock, *Watchdog of Loyalty*; Lofald, "Remembering the Fire of 1918," a reprint of her Oct. 12, 1931, essay, *Hermantown Star*; more on ancestry.com: http://search.ancestry.com/cgi-bin/sse.dll?indiv=1&db=MNDeaths&h=94516&tid=&pid=&usePUB=true&_phsrc=FRR6&_phstart=successSource&usePUBJs=true&rhSource=6061.

Hartman quote: Krueger, "Duluth's Worst Year"; recovery effort, McNair, Wigington, and Burnquist quotes and eight counties affected: Carroll and Raiter, "At the Time of Our Misfortune."

Inflation calculator: https://data.bls.gov/cgi-bin/cpicalc.pl?cost1=2000000&year1=1918&year2=2016; 11,382 families registered for help: Minnesota Forest Fires Relief Commission, Final Report; Pearl Drew mushroom quote: Carroll and Raiter, *Fires of Autumn*, 184.

Notes

Chapter 19

McGee suicide: mentioned briefly in Chrislock, *Watchdog of Loyalty,* 332; details in *Minneapolis Star,* Feb. 16, 1925, 1-2; Feb. 17, 1925, 2; Feb. 18, 1925, 2; bootlegger's tribute: *Minneapolis Star,* Feb. 19, 1925, 3; see also Shutter and McLain, "Progressive Men of Minnesota," 500.

For more on Knute Nelson: Elmer E. Adams, "Incidents in Knute Nelson's Life," Minnesota Legal History Project, http://www.minnesotalegal historyproject.org/assets/Adams-Nelson%20Incidents%20(1923)--SWE .pdf.

Chapter 20

Anna Dickie Olesen's 1930 speech, excerpted: Skalko and Wisuri, *Fire Storm,* 112; see also Delores De Bower Johnson's essay in Stuhler and Kreuter, *Women of Minnesota,* 226-46, and Carroll and Raiter, *Fires of Autumn,* 47-48, 115, 163-64, 167-69, 184; Brown, "Fiery Orator"; *New York Times* story on her candidacy: "Woman Nominated for U.S. Senator," http:// query.nytimes.com/mem/archive-free/pdf?res=9B04E7DA1231EF33A 25752C2A9609C946395D6CF, and Hvistendahl, "Sensational and Strange Saga"; and "Anna Dickie Olesen," Find a Grave, http://www.findagrave .com/cgi-bin/fg.cgi?page=gr&GRid=155031999.

McLearn letter: courtesy of the Moose Lake museum; James C. Davis: Carroll and Raiter, *Fires of Autumn,* 142, 146-50, 152-55, 162, 215. The book examines the seventeen-year battle with the government over fire claims, in three chapters (129-74); dancing in streets quote (174), Eleanor Roosevelt anecdote (168-69), Cox quotes (171-72), quote on Indians and immigrants (158), Yetka quote on verbal dynamite (167), Cummings's quote (169), Blanton quote (170).

Chapter 21

Ware, *Echoes of France;* Shutter, "Bio of Robbins, Amy (Ware)," *History of Minneapolis,* 3:782-84, http://files.usgwarchives.net/mn/hennepin/bios /1923/robbinsa.txt; "Amazing Amy," Robbinsdale Historical Society, http://www.robbinsdale.org/amazing-amy/; "Amy I. Robbins Ware," Find a Grave, http://www.findagrave.com/cgi-bin/fg.cgi?page=gr&GSln =WAR&GSpartial=1&GSbyrel=all&GSst=25&GScntry=4&GSsr =1281&GRid=31936631&; "Andrew. B. Robbins," Robbinsdale Historical Society, http://www.robbinsdale.org/andrew-b-robbins/.

Burton: "Richard Eugene Burton (1861-1940)," Golden Personalities: Notable People of Rollins and Winter Park, http://lib.rollins.edu/olin/oldsite /archives/golden/Burton.htm; Red Cross history: "Our History," American Red Cross, http://www.redcross.org/about-us/who-we-are/history, and Wagner, "Awfully Busy These Days"; women on home front: Kathryn R. Goetz, "Women on the World War I Home Front," MNopedia, http://www.mnopedia.org/women-world-war-i-home-front.

For summary of Meuse-Argonne offensive: "The Big Show: The Meuse-Argonne Offensive," Doughboy Center, http://www.worldwar1.com/dbc/bigshow.htm.

Chapter 22

Rev. Grunewald's Dec. 19, 1918, *"My Message"* provided by Steve Penick, Stearns History Museum archivist. More on his Church of St. Joseph: "St. Joseph's Church Marks Jubilee," *St. Cloud Times*, Oct. 4, 1966.

Sister Julitta Hoppe: Bauer, "The Influenza Epidemic of 1918"; ancestry .com, http://search.ancestry.com/cgi-bin/sse.dll?indiv=1&db=1880usfedcen &h=32971249&tid=&pid=&usePUB=true&usePUBJs=true&rhSource =7316.

St. Cloud Daily Times: Oct. 16, 17, 18, Nov. 1, 8, 1918; Thelen story: *Melrose Beacon,* Dec. 26, 1918; Opole anecdote: *St. Cloud Visitor,* Sept. 21, 1989, 8.

Flu death toll in October: Henig, "The Flu Pandemic"; one in four sick: "1918 Flu Pandemic," History.com, http://www.history.com/topics/1918 -flu-pandemic; 675,000 US deaths: Kreiser, "1918 Spanish Influenza Outbreak," and Stanford University, "The Influenza Pandemic of 1918"; 100 million in "1918 Flu Pandemic" and Kreiser, "Influenza 1918"; World War I death comparison: "WW1 Casualties," WW1 Facts, http://ww1facts .net/quick-reference/ww1-casualties/, and U.S. Department of Veterans Affairs, "America's Wars."

Crosby quote, flu's scope, anecdotes on life expectancy and German general, plus war dead comparisons and W-shaped curves: Kolata, *Flu,* excerpted in *New York Times,* http://www.nytimes.com/books/first/k/kolata-flu .html; life expectancy: "Life Expectancy in the USA, 1900-1998," http://u .demog.berkeley.edu/~andrew/1918/figure2.html; bubonic plague comparison: Stanford University, "The Influenza Pandemic of 1918"; Minneapolis detail: Roselawn office manager Michelle Lind, interview with author, May 14, 2017; statistics on seventy thousand sick soldiers in France: Bourbon, "When the Flu Gets You Down."

Immune system response: "Researchers Link Deadliness of 1918 Flu to Severe Immune Deficiency Response," Science Daily, https://www .sciencedaily.com/releases/2006/09/060927201707.htm; huckleberries quote: Fincher, "America's Deadly Rendezvous with the 'Spanish Lady'"; one thousand in last week of October: Bourbon, "When the Flu Gets You Down"; 1.6 million deaths today: Kolata, *Flu;* Henig quote: Henig, "The Flu Pandemic."

Notes

Chapter 23

Beatrice Parks Gellerman's "The Wedding," manuscript at Carlton County Historical Society, excerpted in Skalko and Wisuri, *Fire Storm*, 109–11; obituary: Roots Web, http://obits.rootsweb.ancestry.com/cgi-bin/obit.cgi ?Surname=GELLERMAN%2C%20Beatrice&type=Keyword.

Cloquet population, post-fire recovery, Weyerhaeuser quote: Carroll and Raiter, *Fires of Autumn*, 187, 173–75, 183–89; Burnquist quotes, *Fires of Autumn*, 190; Mahnke quote: Carlton County *Vidette*, Nov. 8, 1918; Thorstenson letter courtesy of the Moose Lake museum.

Hartman quoted: Krueger, "Duluth's Worst Year."

Meteorologist Richardson, "The Northeastern Minnesota Forest Fires."

Epilogue

Ancestry.com proved a pivotal tool for these post-1918 sketches.

Aina Jokimaki: interviews with son Ray Johnson and grandson Kevin DeLacey, and Manni, *1918 Forest Fire Stories,* 99–100. (Note: Ray Johnson date of birth is April 24, 1947.)

Amy Robbins Ware: obituary in *Minneapolis Morning Tribune*, May 6, 1929, death certificate, and Curt Brown, "Daughter of Robbinsdale's Founder Was a Well-To-Do-Woman Serving on Western Front in World War I," *Minneapolis Star Tribune*, Nov. 26, 2016, http://www.startribune.com /daughter-of-robbinsdale-s-founder-was-a-well-to-do-woman-serving-on -western-front-in-world-war-i/403154926/.

Eino Walfred Salmi link: http://search.ancestry.com/cgi-bin/sse.dll?indiv =1&db=QGHeadstoneApps&h=1185347&tid=&pid=&usePUB=true& _phsrc=lot14&_phstart=successSource&usePUBJs=true&rhSource=8750.

Pearl McIver: American Nurses Association Hall of Fame bio: http://www .theamericannurse.org/2014/07/03/honoring-anas-hall-of-fame -inductees/.

Mary McCarthy: Goodreads bio, https://www.goodreads.com/author/show /7305.Mary_McCarthy; obituary, *New York Times*, Oct. 26, 1989, http:// www.nytimes.com/books/00/03/26/specials/mccarthy-obit.html.

Thortvedts: archivist Mark Peihl, Historical and Cultural Society of Clay County, Moorhead, provided information, along with great-niece Becky Jetvig; "Florence H. Mathison," ancestry.com, http://search.ancestry .com/cgi-bin/sse.dll?indiv=1&db=FindAGraveUS&h=21475359&tid =&pid=&usePUB=true&_phsrc=lot21&_phstart=successSource&use PUBJs=true&rhSource=7316.

Honkala sisters: obituary, "Esther Alma Luoma," *Duluth News Tribune,* http:// www.duluthnewstribune.com/content/esther-alma-luoma; "Helen Syl-

255

via Honkala Repo," Find a Grave, http://www.findagrave.com/cgi-bin/fg
.cgi?page=gr&GRid=87199423&ref=acom.

Burnquist: "Burnquist, Joseph Alfred Arner 'J. A. A.,'" Minnesota Legislative Reference Library, https://www.leg.state.mn.us/legdb/fulldetail
?ID=11509, and Chrislock, *Watchdog of Loyalty,* 332; "J. A. A. Burnquist
Biography," Governors of Minnesota, Minnesota Historical Society, http://
collections.mnhs.org/governors/index.php/10004146; "Winfield S. Hammond Biography," Governors of Minnesota, Minnesota Historical Society, http://collections.mnhs.org/governors/index.php/10004145. Former
governors at Lakewood include Rudy Perpich, Floyd Olson, John Pillsbury, John Lind, Orville Freeman, and Charles Pillsbury: "Famous Memorials at Lakewood," Lakewood Cemetery, http://www.lakewoodcemetery
.com/History_Famous_Memorials.html; "Lakewood Cemetery," Find a
Grave, http://www.findagrave.com/php/famous.php?page=cem&previous
JumpTo=1&previousFameFilter=&FScemeteryid=82700&jumpTo=4
&fameLevel=all.

Anna Dickie Olesen: "Woman Nominated for U.S. Senator," *New York Times,*
June 21, 1922, http://query.nytimes.com/mem/archive-free/pdf?res
=9B04E7DA1231EF33A25752C2A9609C946395D6CF; Carroll and Raiter, *Fires of Autumn,* 163–69; Chrislock, *Watchdog of Loyalty,* 231, 234,
248, 329; Hvistendahl, "The Sensational and Strange Saga"; "Anna Dickie
Once Prominent Politician," *Northfield News,* Jan. 16, 2009, http://www
.southernminn.com/northfield_news/archives/article_15c56239-065f
-5cb9-ac80-02c031054bda.html; "Anna Dickie Olesen," Find a Grave,
http://www.findagrave.com/cgi-bin/fg.cgi?page=gr&GRid=155031999,
and Brown, "Fiery Orator."

Ida Salmi Kohtala: "Ida M. Kohtala," Find a Grave, http://www.findagrave
.com/cgi-bin/fg.cgi?page=gr&GRid=115261009.

Dr. Walters: Lois E. Johnson, "City of Moose Lake to Celebrate 125 Years,"
Moose Lake Star Gazette, July 3, 2014, http://www.mlstargazette.com
/story/2014/07/03/lifestyles/city-of-moose-lake-to-celebrate-125-years
/1141.html.

Koivistos: Manni, *1918 Forest Fire Stories,* 100–102, and ancestry.com:
http://search.ancestry.com/cgi-bin/sse.dll?indiv=1&db=1940usfedcen
&h=98369385&tid=&pid=&usePUB=true&usePUBJs=true&rhSource
=6224 and http://search.ancestry.com/cgi-bin/sse.dll?indiv=1&db
=1930usfedcen&h=80193211&tid=&pid=&usePUB=true&_phsrc=lot17&
_phstart=successSource&usePUBJs=true&rhSource=60525.

Sister Julitta Hoppe: "Women in Medicine," Stearns History Museum, http://
stearns-museum.org/women-in-medicine.

Coys: Sherman on ancestry.com: http://search.ancestry.com/cgi-bin/sse
.dll?indiv=1&db=FSIllinoisDeath&h=330854&tid=&pid=&usePUB=true
&_phsrc=lot18&_phstart=successSource&usePUBJs=true&rhSource
=1265; Mary Augusta (Coy) Pritchard obituary: http://www.mycourier
tribune.com/obituaries/mary-augusta-coy-pritchard/article_ae1b6166
-2894-58d1-92d9-aaa011f04239.html.

Bibliography

Books

Barry, John M. *The Great Influenza: The Epic Story of the Deadliest Plague in History*. New York: Penguin Group, 2004.

Braun, C. J. Carmichael, comp. *Marking Time: An Illustrated Guide to Brown County's Sites of Historical Interest*. New Ulm, MN: Brown County Historical Society, 2006.

Bristow, Nancy. *American Pandemic: The Lost Worlds of the 1918 Influenza Epidemic*. London: Oxford University Press, 2012.

Carroll, Francis M., and Franklin R. Raiter. *The Fires of Autumn: The Cloquet-Moose Lake Disaster of 1918*. St. Paul: Minnesota Historical Society Press, 1990.

Child, Brenda J. *My Grandfather's Knocking Sticks: Ojibwe Family Life and Labor on the Reservation*. St. Paul: Minnesota Historical Society Press, 2014.

Chrislock, Carl H. *The Progressive Era in Minnesota, 1899–1918*. St. Paul: Minnesota Historical Society, 1971.

———. *Watchdog of Loyalty: The Minnesota Commission of Public Safety During World War I*. St. Paul: Minnesota Historical Society Press, 1991.

Clapesattle, Helen. *The Doctors Mayo*. Minneapolis: University of Minnesota Press, 1941.

Crosby, Alfred. *America's Forgotten Pandemic: The Influenza of 1918*. New York: Cambridge University Press, 2003.

Esko's Corner: An Illustrated History of Esko and Thomson Township. Esko, MN: Esko Historical Society, 2013.

Friberg, Eino, trans. *The Kalevala: Epic of the Finnish People*. Helsinki: Otava Publishing Co., 1988.

Gallagher, Christopher J. *The Cellars of Marcelcave: A Yank Doctor in the BEF*. Shippensburg, PA: Burd Street Press, 1998.

Haines, Lynn, and Dora B. Haines. *The Lindberghs*. New York: Vanguard Press, 1931.

Hoisington, Daniel J. *A German Town: A History of New Ulm*. New Ulm, MN: City of New Ulm, 2004.

Illikainen, Carol. *Firebeast: The Fires of 1918*. Moose Lake, MN: Moose Lake Area Historical Society, 2016.

Jordan, Philip D. *The People's Health: A History of Public Health in Minnesota to 1948*. St. Paul: Minnesota Historical Society, 1953.

Kolata, Gina. *Flu: The Story of the Great Influenza Pandemic of 1918 and the Search for the Virus That Caused It*. New York: Farrar, Straus and Giroux, 1999.

Manni, Edwin E., comp. *Kettle River, Automba, Kalevala and Surrounding Area History: Also 1918 Forest Fire Stories*. Tamarack, MN: Tamarack Printing, 1978.

McCarthy, Mary. *Memories of a Catholic Girlhood*. New York: Harcourt Brace Jovanovich, Inc., 1946.

Moose Lake Area Historical Society, comp., *1918 Fire Stories*. Moose Lake, MN: Moose Lake Area Historical Society, 2012.

Morlan, Robert L. *Political Prairie Fire: The Nonpartisan League, 1915-1922*. Minneapolis: University of Minnesota Press, 1955.

Nelson, James Carl. *I Will Hold: The Story of USMC Legend Clifton B. Cates, From Belleau Wood to Victory in the Great War*. New York: Penguin Random House, 2016.

Olson, Olaf, and Francis M. Carroll. *The Fury of the Flames: A Pictorial History of the Great Forest Fires of Northern Minnesota, October 12-15, 1918*. Cloquet and Moose Lake, MN: Carlton County Historical Society and Moose Lake Area Historical Society, 1998.

Reed, Daniel. *Automba: A Study of a Finnish Timber Boomtown*. Kettle River, MN: Automba Publishing Co., 2004.

Shutter, Rev. Marion, ed. *History of Minneapolis, Gateway to the Northwest*. Vol. 3. Chicago and Minneapolis: S. J. Clarke Publishing Co., 1923.

Shutter, Marion D., and J. S. McLain, eds. *Progressive Men of Minnesota: Biographical Sketches and Portraits*. Minneapolis: Minneapolis Journal, 1897.

Skalko, Christine, and Marlene Wisuri. *Fire Storm: The Great Fires of 1918*. Cloquet, MN: Carlton County Historical Society, 2003.

Stuhler, Barbara, and Gretchen Kreuter. *Women of Minnesota: Selected Biographical Essays*. St. Paul: Minnesota Historical Society Press, 1998.

Ubl, Elroy E. *The Matter Lies Deeper.* New Ulm: E. E. Ubl, 2004.

Upham, Warren. *Minnesota Place Names: A Geographical Encyclopedia.* St. Paul: Minnesota Historical Society Press, 2001.

Ware, Amy Robbins. *Echoes of France: Verse From My Journal and Letters.* Minneapolis: Farnham Co., 1920, https://archive.org/stream/echoesof franceveooware#page/n5/mode/2up or http://tinyurl.com/AmyWare.

Westerman, Gwen, and Bruce White. *Mni Sota Makoce: The Land of the Dakota.* St. Paul: Minnesota Historical Society Press, 2012.

Wold, Don. *The Other West Side Story.* Moose Lake, MN: Moose Lake Area Historical Society, 1989.

Articles and Website Links

Ancestry.com provided countless details, including births, deaths, census data, and military records.

Anderson Dan. "The 1918 Fire on FDL [Fond du Lac Reservation]." *Cloquet Pine Knot*, Oct. 26, 1989. "Fire Stories," 38. Copies in Carlton County Historical Society.

Bauer, S. N. "The Influenza Epidemic of 1918." *St. Cloud Visitor*, Sept. 21, 1989, 8.

Bourbon, Philip J. "When the Flu Gets You Down, Remember 1918 and Be Thankful." *Minneapolis Star Tribune*, Dec. 29, 1991, 21A, reprinted from *Washington Post.*

Brady, Tim. "The Great Flu Epidemic." *Minnesota Alumni Magazine*, Jan.-Feb. 2005.

Carroll, Francis M., and Franklin R. Raiter. "'At the Time of Our Misfortune': Relief Efforts Following the 1918 Cloquet Fire." *Minnesota History* 48 (Fall 1983): 270–82. http://collections.mnhs.org/mnhistorymagazine /articles/48/v48i07p270-282.pdf.

Fincher, Jack. "America's Deadly Rendezvous with the 'Spanish Lady.'" *Smithsonian* 19, no. 10 (Jan. 1989): 130.

Gehrz, Chris. "Commemorating WWI in Minnesota: Overshadowed by WWII." *The Pietist Schoolman* (blog), Aug. 30, 2012. https://pietistschool man.com/2012/08/30/commemorating-wwi-in-minnesota-part-3/.

Gray, Kathryn Elfes. "Are You a 49'er? The 1918 Forest Fires in Minnesota." *Carlton County Vidette*, Oct. 11, 1967.

"The Great Pandemic of 1918: State by State." FluTrackers.com. https://flu trackers.com/forum/forum/welcome-to-the-scientific-library/-1918 -pandemic-data-stories-history/14750-the-great-pandemic-of-1918-state -by-state.

Henig, Robin Marantz. "The Flu Pandemic." *New York Times*, Nov. 29, 1992. http://www.nytimes.com/1992/11/29/magazine/the-flu-pandemic.html ?pagewanted=all.

Hvistendahl, Susan. "The Sensational and Strange Saga of Anna Dickie

Olesen." *Entertainment Guide* (Apr. 2015): 37-41. http://issuu.com/nfld
_guide/docs/eg0415/1?e=1006725/12135138.

Jenson, Carol. "Loyalty as a Political Weapon: The 1918 Campaign in Minnesota." *Minnesota History* 43 (Summer 1972): 42-57. http://collections.mnhs
.org/MNHistoryMagazine/articles/43/v43i02p042-057.pdf.

Johnson, Lois. "Fires of 1918." *Moose Lake Star Gazette*, Oct. 10, 2013. http:
//www.mlstargazette.com/story/2013/10/10/news/fires-of-1918/791
.html.

Kolehmainen, John Ilmari. "The Finnish Pioneers of Minnesota." *Minnesota
History* 25 (Dec. 1944): 317-28. http://collections.mnhs.org/mnhistory
magazine/articles/25/v25i04p317-328.pdf.

Kreiser, Christine, M. "1918 Spanish Influenza Outbreak: The Enemy Within."
HistoryNet, Oct. 27, 2006. http://www.historynet.com/1918-spanish
-influenza-outbreak-the-enemy-within.htm.

———. "Influenza 1918: The Enemy Within." *American History* (Dec. 2006):
23-29.

Krueger, Andrew. "Duluth's Worst Year: Talk to Look Back on Tragedies of
1918." *Duluth News Tribune*, Oct. 4, 2015. http://www.duluthnewstribune
.com/news/3853485-duluths-worst-year-talk-look-back-tragedies-1918.

Luukkonen, Arnold. "Brave Men in Their Motor Machines—And the 1918
Forest Fire." *Ramsey County History Magazine* 9, no. 2 (Fall 1972): 3-8.

Morlan, Robert. L. "The Nonpartisan League and the Minnesota Campaign
of 1918." *Minnesota History* 34 (Summer 1955): 221-32. http://collections
.mnhs.org/MNHistoryMagazine/articles/34/v34i06p221-232.pdf.

Nathanson, Iric. "Remembering the Other Lowry: Thomas' Son Was
Embroiled in a Bitter Labor Strike During World War I." MinnPost, Aug.
21, 2015.

———. "Remembering Nov. 11, 1918: 'A Big Siren Tore the Midnight Silence.'"
MinnPost, Nov. 11, 2014.

National Archives and Records Administration. "The Deadly Virus: The Influenza Epidemic of 1918." https://www.archives.gov/exhibits/influenza
-epidemic/.

O'Brien, Thomas. "Epidemic Proportion: With the Deadly Spanish Flu Barely
a Century in the Past, the World Is Long Overdue for Another Pandemic
Event." *American Legion Magazine* 162, no. 2 (Feb. 2007). https://archive
.legion.org/handle/123456789/2590.

Osterholm, Michael. "Preparing for the Next Pandemic." *New England Journal of Medicine* 352 (May 5, 2005): 1839-42.

Ott, Miles, et al. "Lessons Learned from the 1918-1919 Influenza Pan-
demic in Minneapolis and St. Paul." *Public Health Reports* 122, no. 6
(Nov.-Dec. 2007): 803-10. https://www.ncbi.nlm.nih.gov/pmc/articles
/PMC1997248/.

Richardson, Herbert W. "The Northeastern Minnesota Forest Fires of October 12, 1918." *Geographical Review* 7, no. 4 (1919): 220–32. https://www.jstor.org/stable/207371?seq=1#page_scan_tab_contents.

Rippley, La Vern J. "Conflict in the Classroom: Anti-Germanism in Minnesota Schools, 1917-19." *Minnesota History* 47 (Spring 1981): 170–83. http://collections.mnhs.org/mnhistorymagazine/articles/47/v47i05p170-183.pdf.

Roos, Robert. "Avian Flu May Portend a 1918-like Pandemic, Says Osterholm." Center for Infectious Disease Research and Policy, Nov. 15, 2004.

Schnirring, Lisa. "Study: 1918-like Pandemic Now Would Kill 62 Million." Center for Infectious Disease Research and Policy, Dec. 22, 2006.

Stanford University. "The Influenza Pandemic of 1918." https://virus.stanford.edu/uda/.

Steil, Mark. "Recalling the 1918 Flu Epidemic." Minnesota Public Radio News, May 8, 2009. https://www.mprnews.org/story/2009/05/07/1918flu.

Tyler, Alice Felt. "William Pfaender and the Founding of New Ulm." *Minnesota History* 30 (Mar. 1949): 24–35. http://collections.mnhs.org/mnhistorymagazine/articles/30/v30i01p024-035.pdf.

University of Michigan Center for the History of Medicine. "Minneapolis, Minnesota." Influenza Encyclopedia. http://www.influenzaarchive.org/cities/city-minneapolis.html.

University of Washington. "Researchers Link Deadliness of 1918 Flu to Severe Immune System Response." *Science Daily,* Sept. 28, 2006.

US Army Medical Department, Office of Medical History. "The Influenza and Pneumonia Pandemic of 1918." From War Department Annual Report to the Secretary of War, Fiscal Year ending June 30, 1919. http://history.amedd.army.mil/booksdocs/wwi/1918flu/ARSG1919/ARSG1919Intro.htm.

———. "The Influenza and Pneumonia Pandemic of 1918," camp-by-camp breakdown. http://history.amedd.army.mil/booksdocs/wwi/1918flu/ARSG1919/ARSG1919Extractsflu.htm#O.%20CAMP%20GRANT%20DIVISION%20SURGEON%92S%20REPORT.

Wagner, Nancy O'Brien. "Awfully Busy These Days: Red Cross Women in France During World War I." *Minnesota History* 63 (Spring 2012): 24–35. http://collections.mnhs.org/mnhistorymagazine/articles/63/v63i01p024-035.pdf.

Other Documents

Buczynski, John A. "Thank You, Mother, For Being My Hero." Unpublished manuscript. Carlton County Historical Society.

Gray, Kathryn Elfes. "This is the Way it Was!" (Sept. 5, 1968) and "My Story of the Cloquet Fire." Unpublished manuscripts. Kathryn Elfes Gray Papers, Minnesota Historical Society.

Minnesota Forest Fires Relief Commission. Final Report. Duluth, MN, Feb. 28, 1921.

Bibliography

Rhinow, Brigadier General W. F. "Report of the Adjutant General of the State of Minnesota covering the thirtieth biennial period ending December 31, 1918." Vol. 1. Minnesota Historical Society, https://archive.org/stream /reportadjutantg00rhing00g/reportadjutantg00rhing00g_djvu.txt.

Newspapers

Carlton County Vidette
Cloquet Pine Knot
Duluth Herald
Duluth News Tribune
Glasgow (MT) Courier
Grand Forks Herald
Hermantown Star
Kearney (NE) Hub
Mankato Times
Melrose Beacon
Minneapolis Journal
Minneapolis Star
Minneapolis Tribune
Moose Lake Star Gazette
New Ulm Journal
New York Times
Princeton Union
Rochester Post-Bulletin
St. Cloud Daily Times
St. Cloud Visitor
St. Paul Appeal
St. Paul Pioneer Press
Sauk Centre Herald
Spencer (IA) Daily Reporter
Stearns County Community Leader
Superior (WI) Telegram
Warren (Marshall County, MN) Sheaf
Winona Daily News

Index

Page numbers in *italic* type indicate illustrations.

Pritchard, Mary Coy, 236
Producers and Consumers
    Conference, 127

Quale, S. B., 188

Rademacher, Ruth, 122
railroads: across reservations, 63; as
    cause of fires, 36-37, 38, 90, 166,
    200-201; destroyed by fires, *39*;
    and flu, 55-56; nationalization of,
    193, 201; rescue trains, 37, 38, 141,
    145, 146-47, 166-69, 182; Rose-
    now's vaccine and, 105
Raiter, Franklin: on aid to fire refu-
    gees, 183, 184, 185-86, 200, 203;
    on Dead Man's Curve, 92; on fire
    refugees, 146; on flu, 179, 181; on
    Fond du Lac, 63; on logging indus-
    try after fire, 226
Rajala, Aina, 12
Red Cross: aid for fire survivors, 23,
    115, *115*, 147, *160*, 170, 179, 180-81,
    181, 182; nurses recruited by, 54,
    67, 121, 209
Red Cross (Sauk Centre), 23
Red Wing, 131
Reed, Dan, 6-8, 12, 226
Reed, Edna, 11
Reed, Matt, 12
Repo, Oscar, 234
Republican Party. *See* election of 1918
Rhinow, Walter F.: and disloyalty
    crackdown, 150; fire aid, 151, 154,
    155, 182; on fire survivors and flu,
    v; on Motor Reserve Corps, 150;
    saloon raids, 152. *See also* Home
    Guard
Richardson, Herbert, v; on conditions
    before fires, 36, 200-201; on con-
    nection of numerous small fires,
    37; on heroism during fires, 228,
    229; on Moose Lake mass grave, 20

Riedner, Sister Glenore, *213*
Rippe, Henry, 117
RMS *Lusitania*, 29
Robbins, Andrew Bonney, 208
Robbins, Mary Shaw, 208
Rochester, *96*, 97-100
Roosevelt, Franklin, 199, 204, 235
Rosenow, Edward Carl, 100, 102-4,
    103
Roseville, 216
Russia, 82, 130

St. Cloud, 212-14
St. Cloud Daily, 212-13, 214
St. Cloud Hospital, 236
St. Marys Hospital, *96*; fire deaths at,
    143; flu patients, 97, 98; isolation
    ward, 98, 99; opening, 100
St. Paul: black Home Guard members,
    158; farmers' convention (1918),
    125-26; *Germania* statue, 31;
    isolation strategy for flu, 51; and
    schools, 55; transit strike, 82-83
St. Paul Dispatch, 134-35
St. Paul Pioneer Press, 52, 54, 83
St. Raphael's Training School for
    Nurses, 212
Salmi, Eino, 92, 94, 95, 139, 232
Salmi, Helen, 92, 94
Salmi, Helmi, 92, 94
Salmi, Ida, 139-41, 249(note)
Salmi, John, 89, 92, 94, 95, 139
Salmi, Lydia, 89, 90, 91, 94, 95, 141
Salmi, Olga, 92, 94
Salmi, Oscar, 12
Salmi, Walter, 92, 94
Salmi family, 139, 232
Sando, Rodney, 38
Sauk Centre, *14*, 23, 25
Schierkolk, Henry, 121
Schweiger, Ernest, 119
Sedition Act (1918), 29, 31
Seifert, Benjamin J., 86, 88, *88*

Minnesota, 1918 was designed and set in type by Judy Gilats in Saint Paul, Minnesota. The text face is Cardea, designed by David Cabianca. *Minnesota, 1918* was printed by Friesens at their plant in Altona, Manitoba, Canada.